DRUNKS & MONKS

BY

JOHN H. CARMICHAEL

Laguna Canyon Press
Laguna Beach, California

First Edition

Drunks & Monks © 2015 by John H. Carmichael

Edited by Mary O'Regan

ISBN-13: 978-1515014980
ISBN-10: 1515014983

Please email any questions or comments you may have regarding this book to John H. Carmichael at *saintsofgod1@gmail.com*, including requests for additional copies. Feel free to write the author a letter or note as well!

Laguna Canyon Press
Laguna Beach, California

FOR MARY CAROL CARMICHAEL

TABLE OF CONTENTS

Part One: The City of Man
Season: Spring
Locale: In and around Los Angeles, California
Subject: Self—in perfect modern maelstrom
Age: 34
Occupation: Entertainment Lawyer
Preferred Handheld Device: Blackberry
Condition of Soul: not so hot

1

In his ferocious cinematic turn as the devil, Al Pacino declares to a young attorney that *the Law, my boy, puts us into everything. It's the ultimate backstage pass! It's the new priesthood, baby!*

After nearly ten years as an entertainment lawyer, I can relate. I spent about fourteen thousand hours in various Westside Los Angeles high rises sitting like a monk, suspended in one cube of space or another, bleeding from all my pores days nights and weekends. I pursued my legal career at a Beverly Hills law firm, a Century City law firm: mediating a sea of broken contracts, probing random skullduggery, prosecuting straight-faced fraud and forgery, raising the cudgel of righteousness at craven-hearted withholding of royalties and predatory infringements, surviving a warscape brushed with hues of Tony Pellicano, resisting a dark gravity, a perpetual sense of dread.

Litigation is blood sport in Hollywood. And I devoted a decade to it. I've seen more of what goes on backstage than I ever wanted.

Today is something of a capstone, the conclusion of my most legally significant case to date. My famous client sued an internet giant for copyright infringement about two weeks after the gentlemen heavy metalers of *Metallica* sued a strange new computer file-sharing creation called *Napster*. I got involved in my client's fight to protect his work right about the time his case and this whole subject erupted like a grease fire in boardrooms and courtrooms and newsrooms across the country.

Today we finally settle his case. The other lawyer and I write a typically bland press release full of dry stuff like: *The parties are pleased this case was able to draw the courts' and the publics' attention to the issue of online piracy and advance the resolution of the legal issues relating to copyrights in the digital world.*

Phew. That's over. My lawyerly opponent heads for the airport. My client and his wife decompress. They hug me. I collapse into the driver's seat of my car and take a full breath for the first time in four hours. I should be pleased with the end of a big case and a good result.

But all is not well with me.

My immediate problem is this: I don't know where I'm gonna sleep tonight. My wife wanted a separation so I'm wandering around out here until she comes to her senses. She said, *I feel like I've spent the whole marriage waiting for you.* So now every night I'm in a different bed, waiting for her.

A few minutes later I find myself parked in a turnout off Mulholland Drive overlooking the whole city, fighting the urge to throttle a perfectly functioning Cadillac over the embankment into the brush. I suppose I could go back to the *Sunburst Motel*—the site of my first night as a separated man—the night I left in the middle of a rainstorm, rain blowing sideways in Palos Verdes, the night I departed into the flood with one suitcase and two wrinkled button-downs.

On my way out the door my wife spoke words that hung like smoke: *I feel empty as a woman,* she said. There was a vast and hopeless cosmos of emptiness in the way she said it.

I feel empty too I wanted to tell her but I don't blame that on *you.* Why can't we figure it out together? It's a *shared* emptiness. It's what we've got in common. That's what I should have said.

But no, we divided the emptiness in half and I toted my share off into the miserable dark.

That was three weeks ago.

Today I stare out at the city.

Is that all we have? One of those sterile little yuppie six-year marriages, no children, obsessed with the climb, defending our position, connoisseurs of handbags and Cadillacs?

We're not that shallow, are we?

I guess not or I wouldn't be alone out here on this bluff.

I scan the immense view from Century City to Beverly Hills to Downtown and backwards over my shoulder into the vast expanse of the Valley.

The city I once sought to conquer looks dead to me now, like a greyscale graphic relief map. I strove to open every locked door in Los Angeles. Now I squint to make out the inert putty-colored buildings where I encountered celebrity: *Diane Keaton* in that one, backstage with *Lyle Lovett* further down Wilshire, *Morgan Freeman* in a conference room over there, *Gregory Peck* shortly after he did his *Moby Dick* remake, there's the building where I took *Majel Rodenberry's* deposition. And over yonder the icy glass tower where a coven of about thirty of us settled *The Case That Cannot Be Mentioned.* Everything down there just looks so flat and lifeless to me now.

What am I missing?

I got the girl, the right zip code, the job, the car, and the clothes. But my wife is right. The emptiness persists. What to do? I don't have a plan B. I sound so spoiled, so entitled. I know there're people whose evening meal is a cup of dirty water and they have to walk three miles to get it. I know that's bad and I'm sorry for them but it doesn't change the fact that I'm still miserable.

I slip back into the front seat and punch the dashboard in frustration. Can't live, can't die. My knuckles go white then red. Tiny rivulets of blood begin to seep out. I sob. But who am I kidding? I'm not gonna kill myself on Mulholland. I'd probably live through it and end up on the eleven o'clock news shown dangling from a stretcher beneath a helicopter.

I call up my friend Alois in Beverly Hills and tell him I'm in rough shape. He was the best man at my wedding so I figure maybe he's got some advice on how to get the marriage back on track. He doesn't. But he buys me lunch at *Crustacean* and asks what happened to my hand and I say I punched my dashboard. Alois tells me he wants me to see a shrink he knows across the street from the restaurant and he offers to stay with me if I think I'm really gonna kill myself. It seems like just a few years ago Alois and I were turning double plays in Little League. What happened?

Next thing I know I'm in a psychiatrist's office reeling off my tale of woe. The doctor gives me a promising pitch about brain chemistry and hands me a bag full of *Zoloft* samples. He tells me to ramp up on the pills and come back and see him in a few weeks. I leave the office in a daze.

Did I really just see *that-shrink-from-Beverly-Hills-you-know-the-one-Dr.-Everything's-Gonna-Be-Alright?*

2

I check into the *Lowe's* hotel at Beverly and Olympic and draw the drapes to frame out the obscenity of four o'clock sun.

The quiet dark of the room, the whir of central air, soothes. Nobody can touch me here and it's cheaper than a hospital.

I sit on the edge of the bed and stare at the mini-bar. I've not been back to my crypt of an office in a day and a half.

I check my messages.

There're twenty.

I shut the phone off and place the crinkled white bag of Zoloft samples on the bed.

I open the mini-bar and stare at the booze.

I'm thirty-four but alcohol has never passed my lips.

I had a drunk mother, a long childhood, and became a teetotaler.

People ask if I'm Mormon and I say no I'm Irish Catholic and we have our own reason not to drink, trying to sidestep the *Irish problem.* I took the pledge not to drink when I was fourteen, only to myself, but I took it: *I agree to abstain from all liquors of an intoxicating quality whether ale, porter, wine or ardent spirits, except as medicine.* I'd seen quite enough, thank you very much. Even the slightest whiff of ethyl alcohol sent me into a Pavlovian revulsion. I was never even tempted before now.

Would I become a raging naked bum if I picked up a drink at thirty-four, having never imbibed? Would I sprint down the hallway and fling myself from the fire escape?

I place a Zoloft tablet on my tongue.

I hold a sweating bottle of *Amstel Light* in my right hand and stare at little beads of condensation dribbling down the label.

Hemlock, I think, with some degree of hope.

I wash the pill down with a big swig of the beer

It tastes like cold carbonated urine.

Not much chance of getting hooked on this stuff, I think.

I place a couple of ox-stunning over-the-counter sleeping pills on my tongue and wash them down with orange juice and vodka.

Ain't so bad.

I try the vodka straight and it tastes like how rubbing alcohol smells.

Can't see getting hooked on this stuff either.

One-one-thousand, two-one-thousand—

Okay so I'm a drinker now and didn't morph into a pumpkin.

Feels kinda nice, actually.

I curl into a fetal position on the bed and notice my hand doesn't hurt anymore.

Nothing hurts anymore.

3

Twelve hours later I wake teacup-ride dizzy.

The clock says five-thirty. It looks dark and cold out.

I stagger to the front desk and check out.

I wait a long time for the valet to get my car.

My head is a fat purple plush toy.

I notice a couple fighting in a car across the street under a lamplight.

I walk a bit closer.

No fight—they're humping voraciously in the front seat of a lime green Buick.

Traumnovelle.

Is this what goes on out here all night—people pulling over and humping at the corner of Olympic and Beverly?

There's a dark alley for every perversion in your sickening city.

7

I'm behind the wheel again—driving aimlessly—staring out from my mobile cloister at garbage dumpsters and manhole covers and bag ladies and dark figures walking their dogs.

I drive to the office.

I'm the first one here.

Shirt: robin's egg blue; syrup stains on the cuff.

I sit imprisoned at my desk and look out the window at the dark clump of earth called Palos Verdes fifteen miles south. *The Hill.* I imagine I could see through the living room window of my house from here.

I wonder if my wife is there—if she slept somewhere else last night, how she's doing.

She's gotta be feeling it by now, she's just gotta.

How can she stand this?

Anyhow, I know how to fix our sad little marriage:

Today's the day I'll quit the law factory and start my own little practice—what they call a lifestyle practice.

More time for us, I'll tell her. Yeah, that's it.

Hope it's not too late.

The Chinese say the best time to plant a tree is twenty years ago; the second best time is now.

I shut my door and wait for the boss.

When he comes in at ten I resign.

4

I drive home to tell my wife what I've done for us.

I stake out my own house for a minute.

I creep down the block not sure at all what I'll find when I knock.

I hope she's not reading *The Erotic Silence of the American Wife* again.

That's never a good sign.

I ring the doorbell like an eager Jehovah's Witness.

The dogs go nuts.

It takes a while but she makes it to the door in her robe.

I have some news, I say. I quit my job and what does she think of that, an actual straight up act of love—not just words but an act?

The moment the declaration falls from my lips the pair of us are lost at sea.

She sits down at the dining room table.

I stand hat-in-handishly.

She says a bunch of things and there's that theme again, the *emptiness*.

The fact I feel empty too never enters into it. A Rumi verse comes to mind:

I want to hold you close like a lute and cry out with our loving.
You would rather throw stones at a mirror?
I am your mirror, here are the stones.

I say some stupid desperate things like, *But I wanted to feed you soup.*

But she says we're *young*—she doesn't *want* soup.

I don't mean *now*, I say.

I grab some more clothes. She tries not to watch.

I grab an armful of CDs and another armful of books.

5

I drive for hours with no idea where I'm going.

I'm a brain cell loosed in the bloodstream.

I feel suddenly vampiric, driven from the light.

I want to go someplace green/mossy/dark.

I end up in Malibu and feel a bit better.

I can breathe.

Palos Verdes is safe, wholesome, a kind of Connecticut to Los Angeles. The defense industry lives there.

Malibu is celebrity beach houses, debauchery, septic tanks, coastal amorality.

I find myself on Pacific Coast Highway and the road is a grainy filmstrip rolling off the gleaming black hood, fragmented and false like Hockney's *Pearblossom Highway*.

I feel freer in Malibu and get the urge to wear an astrological chest medallion and a flowing white robe.

Maybe I should rent a place out here and get a sense of it. The wife wants a separation? I'll give her a separation.

I make an impulsive right turn on Topanga Canyon Road and head up a steep deadly winding pass that claims many.

Hippies and horses—that's Topanga.

I check the rental board at the general store and drive around looking at places. Finally I reach a spot on the hot and dusty side way up high above town.

I pick my way down a jumbled path, avoiding uneven steps and ducking under chicken wire.

My wingtips are scuffed and dusty now. I knock on a peeling rotting door. A slight man with long gray-gold hair greets me—an aged Garth. He leads me to the vacant shack of the three. He swings open the door to my would-be retreat.

It's Walden Pond without the pond.

I get dizzy from the uneven floor, the funhouse effect of it—

Sole source of heat: wood stove.

The water pressure is gravity driven so it requires a little patience he warns me.

Cobwebs.

There's a charred wood stink like the last guy who lived here forgot to open the flue the night he asphyxiated from wood stove smoke.

Downstairs: living room, kitchen, breakfast nook for hobbits.

An oddball three hundred square feet tops.

Up the ladderish stairs is a loft—a plywood and Astroturf affair that would've been the done thing at a YMCA family camp in 1978.

It's perfect, I say.

A thousand a month, the man says, and I write him a check for two thousand. What can you do? Malibu shack prices.

It's a deal, he says, and welcomes me.

He retreats back into his hovel.

I notice my phone doesn't work up here unless I walk about a quarter mile up the hill.

The sun goes down behind the ridge and the temperature drops in a hurry. California cold.

I find a little firewood and manage to light the stove.

I set up the radio I took from my office desk earlier that day.

Zero reception.

It gets late.

I head upstairs to the spooky loft.

I spread some clothes out on the Astroturf and clump up my jacket to make a pillow.

I hear critters around the place—raccoon and possum feet skittering about.

I wonder if rats will chew my face off tonight.

A pack of coyotes corner something feral in the canyon.

They shriek as they devour it.

6

Next morning I drive into the little Topanga township to scare up some huevos rancheros.

I spot a comely and familiar face, someone I know from somewhere.

Her name is Sam and she's a mostly working actress I met at a lawyers-for-the-arts type function.

I helped her in court once.

She asks what I'm doing up here.

I tell her. She seems unfazed.

Sam says she lives on someone else's ranch in a round thatched structure called a yurt.

She says she wakes up to roosters and clopping horse hooves and meditates.

I say maybe I could come over and see her yurt sometime.

After breakfast I go to the beach.

The sea is flat today.

Color of a pigeon's wing.

7

For no reason I'm back on Lincoln Boulevard and see the sign for a coffee-house/lawyer referral service/general hangout. I met the owner of this enterprise when he came to my office years before upset about a television show he felt was based on his life story. We didn't take his case, but I became friendly with him.

I walk into his shop and my friend is right there behind the counter pulling a black death of an espresso for a hairy guy complaining about his landlord.

Hey boss, my friend says to me, big article about your case in the cover *The Daily Journal.*

He hands me a copy.

I read it and say, Hm. Just what I always wanted, to make the front page of *The Daily Journal.*

You don't seem too happy about it, he says.

Nah, the case is fine. Glad it's over. I think I'm headed for a divorce though. Kinda blots everything else out.

I tell him what's going on and he just looks at me and shakes his head.

He says, Why don't you go out and sleep with someone? You've got to break that chemical bond you have with your wife. If you get back together great but it sounds like the thing is dead.

I laugh.

No I'm serious, he says. *Pay somebody* if you have to.

I think of the girl in the yurt.

I never cheated on my wife—not once, not ever, not even close, I tell him.

He hands me a latté.

8

A few days later I get a call from the girl in the yurt.

She tells me she's doing a one-woman show in Chicago that requires extensive staging and lighting and other accoutrements. And she's asking various people she knows to invest—her agent, her manager—basically anybody she thinks has extra money.

She asks, Would you put up some dough, say, five thousand dollars?

Maybe, I say.

She asks if we can have dinner this week and I say yeah that would be great.

It isn't what I have in mind, this getting hit up for five grand, but dinner with Sam sounds better than trying to make a fire in a wood stove.

The next day I call my wife.

Before I follow through on Jeff's entreaty to commit tactical adultery I intend to convey my forceful passion for her and our marriage in a sweeping address, a declaration supported by an inescapable logic further supported by our rich history.

We were college sweethearts for crying out loud, I say. I mean, *how can you just throw all that away?!*

That was a long time ago, she says.

Boy does she sound tired.

Graveyard tired.

She informs me she's been in San Francisco the past few days and thinking quite seriously about moving up there.

This throws me. I was hoping maybe she'd had a change of heart.

But no.

I panic.

I tell her I'll move with her right now—right this minute, I exclaim.

She says it's not that simple, this is about her taking control of her own life and her own destiny, about her taking care of *herself.*

It sounds like a line from a bad TV movie.

The heat rises from my feet through my pelvis on up the thorax into the throat and comes blasting out my unlovely mouth.

I let fly with every but-what-about-me-and-my-pain that I can muster as though there could ever be a winner on the marital game show *Whose Life Sucks Worse?*

She yells back and then I yell that I'm not gonna take care of this for you, I'm not drawing up another legal document in my entire miserable life!

Then I will, she screams, and hangs up on me.

Blammo!

Whoa.

I'm in hypothermic shock.

Somebody get me one of those space blankets.

I really thought we could save it.

I don't remember driving here.

I'm sitting on a planter box in Century City in an open plaza at the start of evening rush hour, this much I know.

I place my palm on the rounded edge of concrete just to make sure, just to feel something solid.

The secretaries and hourly workers flood out of the glass buildings. The young lawyers are just gearing up for their second shift, stepping out for a dinner break, perhaps the third meal they've eaten at the office today.

Poor bastards, drifting toward divorce, every last one.

I have a heavy buzzing in my head and get that feeling like a bomb went off again.

Divorced: the shearing sound of it, like a sword slicing through the soft melon of my brain, or a butcher severing a cattle femur with an electric saw.

An agony surges through my entire being.

I mark the official moment I learn my fate:

4:47 p.m.

On *this* strip of concrete, wearing *these* clothes.

The sky is streaked with orange clouds.

No call from the governor, no patching it up—no redemption—no fiction of a mere separation any longer.

There'll be pleading paper filed in some courthouse somewhere and our names will be on opposite sides of the versus just like any other litigants in any other case.

I'm gonna be sick.

Real real real. This is my divorce—not some friend of a friend's, not a *thirtysomething* episode, not a *Lifetime* movie.

Today the grenade lands in my foxhole.

Of all the many ways a man will lose his home
there ain't none better than the girl who's moving on.

My head spins—I walk in circles—I look up at the towers.

I picture the sheets of glass in their original form as sand and the steel frames as iron ore.

How'd they all get here—what processes did they endure?

I'm peering in on an alien modern scene from sometime primitive when the villagers ate wild boar and everything was brutish and the women died in childbirth and people knew each other by their smells like dogs.

I'm an animal loosed in the streets.

I'm a brute.

I don't know my Christian name.

I don't have an address.

I've nothing but impulses: hunger/fear/run.

I find myself regarding existence as though from beyond
the tomb, from another world; all is strange to me; I am, as it
were, outside my own body...I am depersonalized,
detached, cut adrift. Is this madness?

I call Alois in a panic but can't reach him.

Can't reach anybody.

I call up Sam whom I barely know and begin to weep.

She says, Let's move our dinner plans up to tonight and we can have pot brownies in Topanga to start off. It'll be good for you.

Okay, I say, I'll come up right away. And did you say pot brownies?

My back wheels kick up a cloud of Topanga dust on the dirt road that leads to the ranch where Sam lives.

Sam meets me in front.

She shows me her yurt.

The round wall is made of a heavy ecru canvas and the roof is wooden, covered with palm fronds.

Where do you shower?

In the main house, she says.

I picture her all soapy in a rustic wooden shower box.

She asks, Have you ever done this before?

I tell her I've never eaten a pot brownie—never smoked a joint—never even had a drink until a few weeks ago and that was more of a suicide attempt than anything.

She says, It's no big deal but of the two eating a well-made pot brownie is a much longer lasting experience than smoking a joint. Meaning, do you have anything to do later because you might not be able to do it?

I say I don't and where's the brownie?

She places a large moist pot brownie on a white paper plate in front of me—a big mother of a brownie.

I ask for milk.

Milk?

Yes, milk.

She pours me a glass and I dip the brownie halfway down.

I pull it out just before it becomes oversaturated and breaks off in my hand.

It tastes good—like a normal brownie.

She consumes her pot brownie but no milk as she has become a vegan of late and, after she dabs up the last few crumbs with her index finger, asks me if I want to go for a hike.

We're on the boundary of Topanga State Park and there are some really intense trails, she tells me.

We set out a little before dusk heading up up up into the high chaparral.

She tells me there's a place called Eagle Rock that has vertiginous views of everything.

She shows me a property where they keep a captive mountain lion.

It looks at us like a sphinx.

As we walk mainly she talks about herself—what she's working on, different dudes she's been dating: one in New York and one out here.

She says some actressy things like: I wish I was fat so then I would know who really loves me.

Then she says, I think we're meant to help each other out right now.

That'd be nice, I say.

We make it to Eagle Rock and it's glorious.

The light is low—*pink rising off the Pacific.*

The sun has set.

We sit next to each other on the massive sandstone outcropping that juts out over the canyon.

Falling means death from this height.

The air is heavy, damp, still and cool but my palms sweat anyway.

Sam manages to sit quietly for a minute or two before she bursts out giggling.

What's so funny?

She says, I think the pot brownie is kicking in and I can't help but laugh.

I don't feel like laughing.

I feel like kissing her and telling her we should live together in this canyon like outlaws.

She asks, Do you feel anything?

I don't. Maybe I'm immune to the stuff, I say. After all these years living drug free like a monk.

You'll feel it, she says.

I want to put my arm around her but I can't.

Prufrock.

If you don't feel anything then you should drive us down the hill to get some fish tacos, she says. It's two-for-one night!

We stumble back down the canyon in near darkness.

Five coyotes cross our path.

11

I drive down the treacherous canyon road and start to get high.

Sam, I feel really funny, I say. My heart is racing.

You can do this, she says. Weed is a concentration drug. Your concentration will tend to stay focused on one item at a time. So if you find yourself looking at a stoplight too long you could hit the car in front of you. Don't gooseneck. Keep your eye on the road.

Relax, she says.

Yeah, I think, relax.

Suddenly the canyon doesn't seem so scary.

I start to *feel* the road, stop fighting it, lean into the curves, anticipate the shape of the road around the bend.

I'm a good driver, I say.

She bursts out laughing and can't stop until we get to Pacific Coast Highway, another well-established death zone.

We arrive at the fish taco place safely, this little locally famous barn red structure right off the highway across from the ocean.

Suddenly I notice I'm really hungry.

We order tilapia tacos and a couple of root beers and sit outside on the back patio under a heat lamp.

The food comes immediately and I chomp on the taco.

I think of the coyotes near my shack and that shrieking they do when they catch something.

I forget for a moment anyone is even with me—entirely content masticating the tilapia with green tomatillo sauce—savoring every nuance of the thing.

I vaguely hear Sam talking to me and it sounds like, Oh my god there's a skunk.

I look down near our feet and see a waddling skunk sniffing around like a terrier under the family dinner table. Sam's alarmed and stands up, backs away, and gets her leg caught on the picnic bench.

It doesn't occur to me to abandon the taco.

I continue chewing until the skunk stands up a bit on his hind legs like a chipmunk.

Somehow in the matter of fact reactions of the staff toward the skunk—and the skunk's presumption of entitlement—this is the funniest thing I've ever seen and I laugh until it hurts.

The skunk shuffles off, tail down, miffed.

Sam sits.

What a *strange night,* I say.

This is nothing in Topanga, she says. Your nights are gonna get a lot weirder if you stay out here with me.

Listen Sam, I shouldn't drive back up that hill. Can you drive?

No, she says.

I ask, How long does this last, this being high business?

A good pot brownie? Six or seven hours maybe, she says. And these ones are good. The woman I rent from's been making these since the sixties and she's perfected them.

20

Sam, I may be crossing the line here but right next door I notice there's a motel and we're pretty messed up already—

I'm not ready to go to a motel room with you stoned, she says.

But what're we going to do after we eat if neither of us can drive back up the canyon for six or seven hours?

Let's walk on the beach, she says.

We nurse our root beers and she starts talking about her big production again.

The rest of the night is a blur.

We walk on the beach, lie down, and look at a starless sky and listen to the waves.

I drive us back up the hill at four in the morning.

She doesn't want to stay in the shack with me because the *energy is bad up there,* she says, so she takes me to her yurt and asks if I'll answer a few questions on tape about destitution for some piece she's working on.

I ramble incoherently for five miserable minutes.

Dawn.

We hug goodbye and I crawl back up the hill to my shack for a three-hour nap.

12

Days pass strangely now, what with no routine. I've never been unemployed before. I hardly know what to do with myself, but fortunately money's not a problem just yet.

A few weeks later I stumble into a Tuesday night poetry reading at a coffee house in Redondo Beach that my wife and I used to attend.

Everyone asks me where she is.

They're shocked to hear of the split.

The head of the group says, Wow. I used to look at the two of you and think, that just seems *so nice.* I guess you never can tell what goes on in the inner life of a couple.

His observation sounds especially bleak.

A group of us go to *Hennessey's* after the reading is over.

It's about ten o'clock and everybody wants to drink.

I could use a meal.

I field a bunch of questions about the wife and what she's up to and they all say how terrible our separation is.

Everyone orders drinks.

I ask for water but then change my order and ask for scotch.

The waitress asks what kind and I tell her I don't know.

Just bring me whatever, I say.

One of the older poets pipes up and says no way he'd have that much faith in the well.

Bring me your best scotch whisky then, I say.

She smiles and says she assumes I want it neat and I say yes not knowing at all what *neat* means or what the *well* is.

The scotch comes and it seems small in the glass.

Now I see that *neat* means not on the rocks or with anything else.

They just pour a little bit of it into the glass. Huh!

I ask what it is and the waitress says *Laphroaig.*

She says the bartender told her to tell me it was an *Islay* scotch and not a *Highland* scotch.

She says to put a few drops of water in it.

Alright, I comply, and take a sip.

Whoa.

It tastes like smoke and sea salt.

A new heat seeps through previously unknown fissures between my cells, filling all the empty space I never knew was there.

I can't believe what I've been missing.

I don't say a word. The poets console me but the Laphroaig is all the consolation I need, the anesthetizing *heat* of it. Frankly I wish everyone would just stop talking. The group recedes and eventually breaks up for the night.

I make my exit but I'm not ready to be alone.

I'm absolutely flying on the Laphroaig.

I've no idea how much is too much, but I had three two finger pours over about a two hour period.

I think it's starting to wear off and that's no good.

I leave Hennessey's and go next door to the *Redondo Beach Brewing Company.* They have the NCAA tournament on all six of their gigantic television screens.

The bartender's a clean-shaven twenty-four, hard-working, dutiful.

I board a barstool.

It's black and cushiony with a nice footrest.

Next door I learned about the well and neat versus rocks and about fingers of scotch but I know nothing about the spirit itself.

I ask him, What's the difference between single malt and blended exactly?

He says he's not sure but that people always say they like single malt better.

I ask, What do you have?

He says, *Glenfiddich* and *Glenmorangie.*

He says they're mass market scotches but this was mostly a microbrew and if people want scotch they go elsewhere.

I tell him I just came from elsewhere and can't go back so let's try the Glenfiddich.

It's syrupy compared to the Laphroaig.

It doesn't taste like smoke or earth but more like an expectorant.

I order another one this time on the rocks.

Whoa. That's a lot of scotch.

It goes down much easier cold but I definitely don't respond to it like the Laphroaig.

When I drank Laphroaig my chest swelled; I was in the battle scenes from Braveheart and I was winning.

I say, Let's try the Glenmorangie neat, but a double.

Are you sure?

Yup, I say.

Divorce? *What* divorce?

Are you telling me that I went to all those fraternity parties in college where the guys and girls would cluster around a keg like it was a demigod and I looked down upon them when all the while they were right to booze it up?

What an idiot I've been!

Most of them didn't become drunks.

They became mothers and fathers and civil engineers.

Just because you've got the Irish problem in the family doesn't mean *you* have a problem.

Booze is necessary.

I just need some booze.

What a revelation!

But as for that something's coming over me.

The flu?

The six televisions are suddenly blaring and grotesque.

I spy the men's room in the back of the restaurant.

It recedes.

There're some couples seated at two-tops on my right, couples in all stages of undress. I try to walk by them but I pull to the right, a shopping cart with a trick wheel.

Must get to bathroom. Must get to bathroom.

Excuse me, I say, as I place my hand on the back of a man's chair for support.

Closer.

Closer to the men's room.

Closer to cool porcelain.

Closer to privacy.

I enter the bathroom.

My face is hot and my lips are numb.

Sink?

No.

Stall?

Yeah, but there're three.

I pick the handicapped stall.

It's enormous in here.

I think people avoid the handicapped stalls for some reason.

My eye is drawn to the white tile squares behind the john.

I'm one drunk sonofa—

I grab the guardrail. My hand slips.

I'm disgusting.

I'm stumbling forward toward the john.

But not the john, toward one square of tile.

I stop short about three feet from the wall.

I fall forward into space like a boxer who's knocked out but hasn't hit the canvas yet.

Can't get my hands up in time.

I see the tile approaching like a fist.

I turn to the side before I strike the wall and hit it hard with my shoulder and the side of my head like a rusher on the defensive line.

Splattle.

Ouch but not really.

There's no pain.

Like when Joe Namath thanked the single girls of New York and promised a victory in the Super Bowl. That seems entirely reasonable from the floor of this bathroom stall.

Hey, he went out and did it thank you very much.

I can't drive. I can barely see.

I clamber to a seated position the head until things are a little less turbulent around the edges of my field of vision.

I get up and splash some water on my face.

Everything tingles except the lips.

My lips are numb.

I make my way back to the bar.

People stare.

The barkeep comes over quickly like a hospital orderly about to deliver a bedpan just in the nick of time.

Are you okay?

I'm sorry, I say, I'm really embarrassed. I told you I'm new at this.

Yeah it's my fault, he says. That was too much scotch, almost half a bottle. Where do you live?

I can't tell him Malibu—that's thirty miles away.

I tell him Palos Verdes and ask him to call my wife.

The bartender makes a call then comes back over and says she wanted me to ask you to wait outside.

I head for the door and the barkeep walks me out.

He pulls a chair from an outside table and faces it toward the street.

I'm sorry about this, I say.

Don't worry about it, it's part of my job, he says.

Some kinda job, I think.

He pats me on the shoulder like an army medic sending another one off to the MASH unit.

I scoot the chair over next to a parking meter.

I wrap my left arm around the pole, lean against it, and pass out.

13

I'm startled by the glare of headlights and the buzz of the *Mini Cooper* engine.

I wake to black flack and the nightmare of fighters.

I stand up and get in. My wife just looks at me not one way or the other.

I'm sorry, I say to someone for the third time tonight.

John are you *drunk?*

I think so.

Oh my god, what's going on here?

I can't answer. Both of us grew up with mothers that drank.

Not drinking was one thing we always agreed on, maybe the last thing we still agreed on.

First our wedding vows and now this—our unofficial pledge to avoid the travails of booze—down the sinkhole.

She looks at me like I'm from Pluto.

I say I want to go home but I know that's the wrong answer.

She says she doesn't feel comfortable with me coming home especially like this and asks if she can take me to my parents' house.

My parents don't know about the divorce yet, I mumble.

They don't *know* yet?

No, I say, I was hoping we would work it out and nobody would have to know.

Always concerned about your *image,* she scoffs.

Just take me to their house, I say.

We get to my parents' street and I say, Please don't go, just wait here with me for a little while.

She sits patiently, impassively.

I ramble and slur about how sorry I am and how this is all my fault and I wish we had another chance but if not then okay but I want her to know I love her anyway.

Her reactions aren't registering that clearly but she seems kind and I reach over and hug her goodbye.

She leaves me on the sidewalk and drives away.

I stare at my childhood home.

It's brightly lit and warm looking.

I lie down face up on the sidewalk.

I listen to the shore-pounders hit the wet sand on the beach and wonder why you can hear that sound at night from this distance but not during the day.

I fall asleep.

When I open my eyes the moon is down near the horizon and throws a brilliant splash of light over the Santa Monica Bay.

I stand up.

All the houses are dark now.

What have I done?

I walk down the hill and stop at the tree where the bag lady slept at night and frightened the neighborhood children.

I used to serve Mass at six o'clock in the morning and ride my bike by her in the fog.

The bag lady slept sitting up in the hollow of the tree and she'd stir when I rode past her. All the kids laughed at her because she wore curlers in her hair.

She died young.

I look at the trunk where she used to sleep and see it's worn smooth.

I sit where she sat for a moment and get a wintry feeling.

This is still her tree.

Yup, we kids used to laugh at her in her curlers, skin burnt red from the sun.

I regret that in this moment.

I keep walking.

My car is one of two left on Catalina Avenue.

The seat is cold.

A few weeks later I get a phone call from Dad.

He says the women at the beauty parlor think Mom had a stroke.

She slumped over and went unconscious for a minute, he says.

Dad tells me Mom is at *Little Company of Mary* for some tests.

Little Company is the Catholic hospital where I was born, where my brother and grandmother died, where my Mom had a miscarriage, where I got nineteen stitches in my chin, where I went after I had my nose busted in a fight.

Little Company is a few blocks down Torrance Boulevard from Bishop Montgomery, my Catholic high school, and a few miles away from Saint Lawrence Martyr, the Catholic Church where I was baptized and the elementary school I attended for eight years.

I haven't been to Little Company in forever.

Or church for that matter.

Not since my wedding day.

I locate Dad.

Mom's upstairs having a bone scan, he says.

How is she?

I don't know, he says. She's been having these weird pains for a month or two and I've been after her to get it looked at but she keeps seeing this nurse practitioner who doesn't know anything.

Maybe they'll get to the bottom of it here, I say.

I hope. You look awfully casual for a Thursday afternoon. Day off?

All I have to do is say yes.

But then he'll ask me how the wife is.

I just don't think I can lie to him.

It was one thing to avoid him and hope we patched it up.

He's looking at me waiting for an answer.

The doctor asks, What's wrong?

I look down at his shoes before I tell him about the separation.

I'm in the middle of it when the doctor appears in the waiting room and asks us to come back.

He takes us into the little glass cubicle where Mom is struggling to put her pea green cardigan back on.

Oh hi honey, she says.

Hi Mom.

The doctor puts his hand on my mother's shoulder and says, Your bone scans are revealing some abnormalities in the skull and some other areas in your spine and ribs.

Abnormalities?

The skull appears to be calcifying in places, thicker in some spots than others. We don't have your blood work back but in the meantime I want you to go see a rheumatologist.

The doctor says they'll wheel her out to the waiting room in a few minutes.

Dad and I let her get dressed and he and I walk out front.

I tell Dad that nobody's filed for divorce yet and that I told the wife to do it but I still hope she won't.

He says if she has it in her to do this to me I should file immediately and just get it over with. She's done, he says. Don't drag it out.

That's it? What about marriage as a covenant and all that? I've been trying to save it for months now, I tell him.

A whole month you've been separated?

More.

Jeez, John. Where the hell are you living?

Malibu.

How can you afford this, two places?

We can't. I'm in a kind of a shack.

A shack? Dammit.

It's not her fault—

The hell it isn't, he says.

Mom comes out in a wheelchair.

She looks much older to me.

Dad goes off to pull the car up.

Oh honey, Mom says, I'm sorry you had to come all this way.

I ask, How long have you been feeling like this?

She says she's been very tired for months and then started to feel these shooting pains first in her back and around to the ribs then sometimes in one of her legs.

The doctors call it a traveling pain, she says.

I tell her we'll get to the bottom of it soon.

Dad pulls up with the car. Mom's unsteady as she migrates from the wheelchair to the passenger seat. I shut the car door behind her.

I head back to the Topanga shack.

Sunset.

Coyotes.

15

Weeks after Mom's trip to the emergency room she's still in pain but she's had a bunch of tests.

The rheumatologist took a long history, and blood, urine, whatever else he could take.

Mom, Dad and I are scheduled to meet him at ten this morning to find out what he thinks.

We sit in the waiting room reading all the pamphlets on disease and prescription medication.

They're unreasonably optimistic and glossy.

I decide to tell a dirty joke.

Oh heavens, John. That's disgusting, Mom says.

That's terrible, Dad says, but he kind of likes the joke.

Finally we go in. I note the doctor's diplomas, the pictures of him in a tennis outfit, the dusty shelves, the model of a resection of a human liver on the windowsill.

The doctor begins to speak:

So they sent you to me because they thought you might have an auto-immune disease like lupus or something. I checked into all that and started looking a different direction. I do have a diagnosis but it's not an auto-immune problem. You have an illness called multiple myeloma. That's what's causing your bone pain.

Dad asks whether there're treatments for it.

Oh yes, the doctor says. There've been remarkable advances in blood cancer treatments over the last few years.

I'm sorry, did you say cancer?

Yes. Multiple myeloma is a form of blood cancer. Specifically, cancer of the plasma cell. But the oncologists are starting to produce better outcomes now.

Better than what?

Traditionally the illness was associated with a thirty-six month life expectancy. It stayed that way for decades. But now you see more and more patients living five, seven or even ten or more years with it. It can be managed to some degree.

What about a—a remission?

Technically, the doctor says, there's no cure.

Part Two: The River
Date: The watery borders betwixt an eternal Summer and
Fall
Subject: Strong currents
Principle Artistic Sympathies: Surrealism
Dominant Mode of Dress: Yesterday's shirts
Preferred Handheld Device: Some cheap flip-phone

16

Dad calls to tell me he has to go up to San Francisco
on business this week.

He asks, Could you check on Mom tomorrow night,
maybe stay over?

I'm glad to have something to do.

I can't face another night alone in the shack.

The coyotes are really starting to bother me.

They hunt all night and the shrieking they do wakes
me up.

It's not the sonorous cry of a lone wolf howling at the
moon.

It's the sound of nature feeding on itself, a cacophony.

Nature is mouths.

I get to my folks' house and watch a little television
while Mom putters in the kitchen.

Her hands are swollen and red and she drops things a
lot.

She's a cancer patient now. How peculiar sounding.

Except for a traveling ache here and there she's in good form.

She's smoking heavily though, more than I remember.

I sit in my childhood bedroom that was recently feminized and painted a whisper mint green with white fluffy accents.

I look out the window.

I can still see a rectangle of ocean over the hedge.

What a sublime privilege it was to see the ocean every day.

I hear Mom in the kitchen talking on the phone to one of her friends.

She's laughing.

Suddenly I hear a crash and the sound of a chair shooting across the floor.

Blood courses through my temples.

She must've gone to sit down and missed the chair, I think, pushing it backwards, landing hard on her backside, all the force of the impact jarring those painful porous bones, the bones the myeloma is ravaging moment to moment.

The phone clatters to the tile.

I arrive on scene and she's lying flat on her back.

The phone is live.

I pick it up and tell her friend we have to call her later.

I kneel down to see if I can bring her to a sitting position.

I put my hand under her spine and apply a gentle upward pressure.

She yells uncontrollably.

It's a horrible sound, one I've never heard from animal or man.

I sit with her on the floor and slowly raise her into a sitting position.

Mom tries to get her breathing under control.

34

I breathe with her—

I'm Five.

The carpet is chartreuse and everything's bright.

I sit on the floor with a Fisher-Price dashboard.

I especially notice the rear view mirror that's not a real mirror but just a fake blurry silver sticker.

I pull at the corner to try and peel it off.

I honk the little horn.

Mom comes around the corner and she looks strange and the whole house has that sweet smell that scares me.

Her hair is stuck to the side of her face.

I say I want to eat and she says Big Deal.

She sounds funny, too.

I can barely understand her.

She looks lost again, so lost, and in our own house, wandering around like she doesn't know where to go next.

The phrase Big Deal comes up again somehow.

I say it or she says it and I can't understand why she's making fun of me.

She holds on to the wall as she walks down the short hallway to the kitchen.

I run to her.

We collide.

She falls backwards over a houseplant in a white wicker basket.

She doesn't move.

I kneel on the ground and try to pull at her shoulders.

She makes a sound and I'm scared.

She breathes that sweet smell all over me and makes me sick.

I stand up.

I watch her get into a sitting position and then I kneel down and put my hands under her shoulders.

I push with my legs and she pushes on my arms.

She stands halfway up and then falls again into the doorframe of the bathroom.

Aaaahhh, she yells.

She collapses into a sitting position, leaning up against the door frame.

I go back to the living room and try to peel the silver sticker off the dashboard again.

I look only at the dashboard and not at Mom.

Eventually she gets up and disappears into the back rooms.

Dad calls an hour later and I tell him what's happening.

He sounds disgusted.

I know what disgusted is.

Mom's in trouble.

Am I in trouble?

He asks can I put her on the phone and I say no she's sleeping.

He asks if I've eaten and I say no.

He tells me to take a t.v. dinner out of the refrigerator.

He tells me to turn the oven on to three hundred fifty degrees.

I go over to the oven.

I'm afraid of it.

I pretend I'm doing it so he'll let me off the phone.

I put the t.v. dinner back in the fridge and eat what I can find.

I walk out into the driveway and look up at nothing and think but do not ask why.

I blink away the hot kind of tears.

There's nothing and no one.

There's no answer.

There's no God.

—Flash forward to the brutal *Technicolor* present, Mom's face is wild, she cries uncontrollably; the cancer's eating her bones. Oh boy, this is really happening.

It takes an excruciating five minutes for me to get her into a chair and another painful ten minutes to get her into bed.

I sit at the foot of her bed in a darkened room and listen to her breathing relax.

I give her some pain pills and water and leave the room to call Dad.

He says he'll cut his trip short and come home tomorrow.

After I hang up I use the back bathroom to get ready for bed. There's a prayer card on the bay windowsill. *Lord, make me a channel of your peace*, it begins. Yeah right, I think. I remember the warzone this house used to become. I didn't believe in *God's peace* then and I don't believe in it now. We're alone on this rotating sphere spinning at nearly a thousand miles per hour.

In this life, you're on your own.

I wait for sleep in my childhood bedroom.

Open window.

Waves.

17

A few days later I get a call from Dad.

Mom's in agony, he says, her leg is killing her.

She can't leave it level—she wants it hanging over the side of her bed, he says.

What?

She can't feel it—it tingles—and she has a pressure sore on her heel from a lack of blood flow to the foot.

I thought everything was fine, I say.

It was, Dad says. This all started a week or so ago and we took her in and they checked her blood flow, he says. I think it has something to do with the *Thalydomide* but the oncologist keeps insisting it has nothing to do with it.

What I can I do?

Can you meet me at the hospital?

Yeah, I say.

Mom's admitted and green looking.

She's on some heavy drug, out of it, but still in pain. She keeps trying to hang her leg over the side of the bed.

I look at her lower leg and it's badly discolored.

The internist comes over to Mom's bedside.

She's not getting blood flow down there, the doctor says. It's either a thrombosis or some other kind of vascular blockage. Not sure what the surgeon has to say but he's on his way over.

Surgeon?

Yes. A vascular surgeon.

Dad and I wait outside for the surgeon and a couple of my parents' friends show up in tennis outfits.

Eventually the surgeon arrives. He looks at some films. He says it's a long shot but he might be able to save the leg.

Save the leg?

Maybe, he says. There's a very small amount of blood flowing through the pipeline down there. I'm going to try and take a vein from her upper leg and bypass the blockage, but I don't have much room to work.

If it doesn't work what are you talking about, I ask, like an amputation or something?

Perhaps, but let's not get ahead of ourselves. I think she can wait twenty-four hours but not much more. I'll do the surgery tomorrow.

My Dad and his friends and I go back to see Mom. I feel like throwing up. What's she, going to lose her leg below the knee? It's one thing to get cancer and die but to get maimed like this along the way—

She won't be able to walk. She's too unsteady as it is. She'll die for sure from the sheer horror of it.

I smile at her. She winces and tries to smile at the four of us. We tell her we just talked to the surgeon and he's going to operate tomorrow.

He's going to give you some relief from this pain, Mom, I say.

One way or the other, I think.

We wrap it up. Everyone goes their separate ways.

A few minutes later I burst into a stairwell and grab the railing for support.

Amputation.

Okay, I tell myself, these things happen. Why shouldn't they happen to us?

The next day we sit in the waiting room and wait for our own little verdict: Leg or No Leg?

The surgeon comes out and smiles.

The answer is: Leg!

Yes! Mom keeps the leg. But she loses a little toe.

In the scheme of things the toe is a gimmee.

18

The next day I come over to see Mom.

She's stoned out of her gourd.

The food here is just wonderful, she says. *Look!*

I glance at the grayish loaf of something or other in the tray.

Yeah Mom, wonderful, I say. What do they have you on?

I don't know, she says, but I'm just so happy to be out of pain!

She talks about a distant relative in the Bay Area and how much she wants to get in touch with her and again, how wonderful the food is and how happy she is to be out of pain!

I hold her hand briefly and then stop by the nurses' station on my way out.

I ask the nurse, What's the pain killer you've got her on and where can I get some?

The nurse smiles and says, *Fentanyl*. You can't have any.

That must be some good stuff, I think. It turns hospital kitchen mystery meat into Filet Mignon.

On my way down the hall toward the elevator I hear a sudden intrusion of classical music wafting over the hospital sound system. I ask a janitor on the elevator what that's about.

He says, That's the *Brahms' Lullaby*. They play it every time a baby's born here.

This charms me.

The whole hospital hears of the arrival of new life, even the sick and dying.

It's a gentle touch of Catholicity, not that I think it amounts to much but sentimentality. Yet somehow I'm lifted by this simple gesture, knowing the hospital higher-ups had to approve the heralding of new life that way. I wonder if they played the lullaby when I was born here. I would have requested *Bad to the Bone* instead.

When the elevator doors open I see the first floor chapel directly across the hall.

I don't believe God had anything to do with saving Mom's leg any more than giving her multiple myeloma but I've always liked this chapel.

There's something about a hospital chapel I find appropriately dramatic.

The hospital's got a closed-circuit television station with a camera trained on the altar around the clock so old biddies up on the fifth floor can watch Mass or just eat lime *Jell-O* and stare at the silent altar which is what I decide to do for a moment.

The chapel is empty and I sit in the domed whiteness of the space.

I stare at the tabernacle set deep into the wall like a safe deposit box.

I think about saying a prayer but know it'll pretty much end up like they all did when I was a kid:

You know what God? Never mind.

I'm Twenty-five.

Dad and I drive to Mammoth Mountain for a Father's Day trip to the family getaway.

I tell him I'm having trouble in law school getting through certain classes and working at the same time and he attacks me.

He tells me things like, Of course you're having trouble! You're trying to live beyond your means, you don't go to Mass, your parish is supposed to be the center of your life.

I don't believe Christ is God, I say.

What?

Dad, I'm really more of a scientist, I say, mimicking something I heard a law school friend of mine say a few weeks before. I don't think there's anything happening at the parish. It's just a bunch of buildings and boring people and boring rituals. I had enough of it after eight years.

41

Oh?! Oh. I see. Science! Look around, scientist, what do you think created all this? You think something came from nothing?

Yeah, I guess so—

Science, he scoffs. They just change it every decade or two when they figure out how wrong they were.

I feel sick. This isn't the father-son trip it started out to be. This is a war. I want to take it all back and go along to get along.

Dad, I say, I'm sorry. I don't mean to offend you or challenge your belief system—

Oh save it, he says. You've made your choice. You don't believe in God, that's fine.

I didn't say—

Yes you did, he says, it's on record now. We all know where everyone stands on this. We don't have to discuss it anymore.

You've made your choice, he says again.

We ride in brittle silence for another hour.

I get up and leave the hospital after a few more moments of Godless chapel-sitting and rumination. The evening coastal air is like a salty liquid and I gulp it down, glad to be free of hospital rooms and chapels and the rat trap of my own dim memory.

19

A few weeks later my wife is gone. I'm left an empty house to sell: *light and bright, recently remodeled, new kitchen, sliver view of the Santa Monica Bay.*

Let's skip the part about wandering through the rooms alone for the first time, dust particles swirling in cylinders of slanted light.

I'm sure we can all agree it just plain sucks.

I scan the empty living room.

My footfalls echo.

A bright spot of sorts: the settlement provides I get the dogs, *Wendell* and *Louise.*

Wendell is a beast.

We found him on a highway near Bakersfield.

He's a hundred twenty pounds of *Great Pyrenees,* an enormous white livestock guarding dog with origins in the mountainous Basque region between France and Spain.

A breeder dumped him out there at eight months on account of a shoulder surgery it turned out he needed.

Three grand later he was in good shape.

Wendell has a complex glistening white coat that makes him appear even larger than he is.

He's one of the giant breeds for a reason: to protect the flock. The Pyr is possessed of a huge handsome head, curling plume of tail, magnificent confirmation, agility, power, gait like a Clydesdale.

Wendell is a sauntering cloud, confused by the wolves for a lamb for a moment until they get the business end of him.

As a ninety pound puppy he destroyed couches, dining room sets, computer keyboards, drapes.

Now he digs holes the size of his giant body and lays in them smiling.

Wendell prefers a high lookout.

Can't walk him twenty feet without answering questions like: What is that thing? How much does he weigh? Is he a Newfoundland? How much does he *eat?*

I consider printing up an information card with the rundown on Wendell.

Louise is a twenty-pound ragamuffin terrier mix, a sidekick.

One ear up, one ear down.

Beige, scruffy, doe eyes, quintessential shelter dog.

Louise worships my every utterance.

Wendell is not altogether very impressed with me.

He breaks windows to drive off the *Fed Ex* guy, splintering shards of glass all over the porch. They won't deliver to the house even though all the windows are tempered now.

The Pyrenean Mountain Dog, as the Pyr is sometimes called, needs an enemy the way a retriever needs a tennis ball.

In their natural setting the Great Pyrenees divides the world into two easy to manage categories: sheep, *good*/not sheep, *bad.*

I wish things were so inescapably clear to me.

I spend half my time wandering aimlessly around Los Angeles half-heartedly looking at office space for my own law practice and the other half with Mom and Dad, watching Mom, waiting for the other shoe to drop.

The problem with finding office space is if I find an office then I will have to go to the office and if I go to the office then I'll have to work, and who wants to do that?

20

Mom gets good care.

Her pain subsides.

The oncologists give her a steroid called Dexamethazone and more Thalydomide of all things, the famously banned drug that once upon a time turned fetal arms into flippers.

It's specially controlled by the pharmacy and hard to get.

Thalydomide has a huge karmic debt to pay down.

It *does* seem to help multiple myeloma patients.

The box comes with a small picture of a deformed Thalydomide baby with a red circle and line through it.

The combination of the two drugs seems to work for Mom.

No intravenous chemo, no hair loss, nothing like that.

The cancer cells recede to imperceptibility.

It seems too good to be true.

21

Given the confluence of events I think it best to go see a counselor I used to know.

She treats a lot of lawyers and law students, a very wise marketing strategy.

I saw her for about six months my first year of practice to help me deal with the shock of 70-hour weeks.

I concluded there was no cure for that.

Haven't seen you in *years,* she says.

We talk.

She asks a few pointed questions; she empathizes.

She charges two hundred an hour, same as a call girl.

I go week after week.

I free-associate and gaze out the window.

Sometimes I say something that causes her to ask, Where did you *go* just now?

And so I explore that tangent, which leads to another tangent.

Mainly the therapist just sits there and takes an occasional note, asks an occasional question, offers the very occasional insight.

I'll say one thing—the couch is comfortable.

I really sink into it.

But about fifteen sessions in I ask, *Does this work?*

Does it *work?*

Yeah, *work,* I say.

Well, she says, *I think life is hard.*

Hmm, I say.

I feel like asking if that's *really her answer.*

I feel like telling her that when people come into a lawyer's office and they want to know if they're gonna win or at least what their chances are, we lawyers are supposed to know if what we do *works* or not.

Apparently a therapist can sit there and dodge my question as to whether this works—my sitting here once a week at four dollars a minute describing the absurd events of the last six days and how they make me feel:

House fell out of escrow (worried) Mom doing better (relieved, waiting for other shoe) ex-wife finally gone (sad, nauseous, at times oddly giddy) not sure what to do (anomie) not sure why I've never been happy (is anyone happy?) I worry about the future (near and distant) I have too many and too few choices at the same time, blah, blah, blah—

Won't somebody just tell me what's up?

I'd pay for a credible guess or even a well-meaning lie.

I ain't right, lady. HELP ME!

I've racked up a three thousand dollar bill and I may know less about myself than when I first walked in here. How much do I have to spend to feel better, to make some sense of all this?

Ten thousand?

So much for talking it out.

I don't think this works.

I think it's making me worse somehow.

After the session I leave my counselor's office and walk down Sawtelle Boulevard and catch the scent of Japanese noodles. I look over at a patch of community garden space.

I feel so alone.

I find my car in the alley.

The freeway rushes past me.

The cars sound suddenly menacing, like hissing cockroaches.

I feel the presence of evil in me and around me.

I lean out and grasp the rusty chain link fence for support.

It bends against my weight and looks insubstantial and tetanus inducing.

I ungrasp it and stumble sideways slightly toward my car.

My breathing gets shallow.

I can't believe she left me, I think.

Is this real? I'd like to wake up now.

I feel woozy.

That talk therapy isn't working.

You know what *worked?*

The scotch worked.

I mean, it *worked.*

22

The next day I get a call from Big D, an aspiring film and television producer I represented more than a few years ago. He wasn't even old enough to drink when we met in the lobby of the high-rise law firm I worked for but he swore to me I was looking at a mogul in the making. He appeared to me like a younger version of Carlos Brigante from *Carlito's Way.* Dark hair, dark eyes, closely cropped beard.

I warned him then that overnight success takes about fifteen years. He calls me today because one of his screenplays fell out of option and he wants to get something going again.

I'm not working, I tell him.

What?!

I explain.

I'm sorry to hear about it, brah. You wanna hang out?

I haven't hung out with anybody in years, I tell him.

Come on over. Let's roll out in the Cadillac. You still drive the Caddy? My M3 is in the shop.

I pick Big D up at his apartment in an area just south of Brentwood, affectionately known as Brenthood, and we *roll out* in the Cadillac.

We're in a Scorcese picture.

Big D directs us down backstreets and alleys to avoid Sepulveda.

I still feel like a truant, like a spy driving around Los Angeles in the middle of the day, no office to go to, no wife waiting for me, no *nada y nada y nada*—

But this is a normal day for Big D and so the day feels a little more normal to me.

We're committing no crime.

A redheaded model gets out of her car and prepares to jaywalk in front of us.

I accelerate past her to get out of her way.

Big D says, You should've let her cross in front, dude.

He gets us a table at *Don Antonio's,* a dark cave of a restaurant with a luminous fish tank in the entry way and a back table fit for a mob boss.

It's two-thirty so the restaurant is nearly empty.

They wait on us like we own the place.

Big D orders a pair of margaritas for us: rocks, salt, Patrón. He listens to me complain for about half an hour.

I end with the news about Mom's cancer diagnosis.

He's quiet for a minute and then asks, Did I ever tell you about my father?

Mm, not too much, I say. I know he passed.

Yeah. You remind me of him a little bit, just in certain ways. I was in high school. We lived out in Palm Desert. My Dad was the guitar player in this sixties band out of San Francisco called *Cold Blood,* but then he became this really

48

good accountant and settled down. Did a lot of work for the restaurant owners out in the desert. They loved him. So did my mom. The two of them opened a well-known supper club together.

Unfortunately, if my Dad had one drink one day he'd have twenty the next. My last memory is fighting with him the night before he died to keep him from getting in the car. I found his body the next day. We were regulars at *Betty Ford,* I did all the counseling with him, *Alateen,* all that shit. Whatever whatever.

Right before he died we were driving somewhere and he was telling me that running his accounting shop wasn't enough for him. Some part of him still needed to play guitar in *Cold Blood* or something like that. I feel like you're like that right now. You need something more than what you've got.

Before I can respond, big greasy plates arrive pooled with refried beans and cheese.

Let's go shoot guns after lunch, Big D says.

Guns?

23

We swing by Big D's pad and pick up the XD, a marksman's pistol that Big D's Marine sharpshooter cousin recommended.

We stand in the stall at the shooting range capping off rounds at paper targets.

The XD gets hotter and hotter in my hand.

I'm having a terrific time.

After over a hundred rounds between us Big D says, This shit's getting expensive. Let's go over to my boy's barber shop. Dude rolls a blunt faster than anyone this side of La Brea.

We get to an industrial façade on a scruffy stretch of Pico Boulevard. We enter a long narrow tube of a space with vaulted ceilings and a loft at one end.

Five barber stations line the right wall. One guy's *getting his fade on* in the corner, preparing a tall bong for a toke.

Big D's *boy* comes out and invites me to have a seat in one of the barber chairs.

There're about six of us in the room and I get introduced around.

One of the dudes takes a big long rip from the bong.

The column of smoke in the neck is thick and creamy looking.

He takes what another dude calls a *sick rip* from the waterpipe and drinks it down and holds it for a really really long time.

It's *epic* when he blows it out another dude says.

Big D tells the group that we've just been blasting the new XD and discussing what's important in life.

Another dude says, The important thing is to be happy. You have to start with that.

This solemn decree hangs in the air with the second-hand cannabis smoke. This notion challenges my Catholic sensibilities that emphasize the rightness of poverty and suffering.

The rumored secret-sect type Catholics are said to need to wrap their thigh in barbed wire for a few hours a day to be holy.

What's that about?

My grammar school was named in honor of Saint Lawrence the Martyr who was apparently barbequed to death and joked about it while they cooked him.

I never understood any of that.

The dudes pass me the bong.

I decline.

I know one thing: Saint Lawrence would not hit this bong.

So here's this dude with the bong telling me: The Important Thing Is To Be Happy. You Have To Start With That.

Indeed, I find fifteen years of diligent adult suffering and striving and even a little objective success have not yet produced what would be deemed *happiness* or *fulfillment* whatever that is.

Maybe I've been doing the wrong kind of suffering?

The dudes don't seem to advocate suffering at all.

The dudes are telling me to stop the upstream swim, to sit back in the inner-tube, crack open a *Bud* and float along for a while, merrily, merrily, merrily—

Is that so wrong?

Big D's Dad grew up, got responsible and still drank himself to death. There's gotta be more to the parable of Big D's father than that but—

Maybe it is time to ask myself what I really want to do, to try out this whole *happiness* idea, at least how the dudes understand it, anyway.

There's a delicate veil of cannabis smoke in here now and the room is full of dude wisdom. Clearly, I'm a mere dude-in-waiting who needs dude lessons.

Big D says, If you wanna hook up with chicks don't trust those club girls we're gonna meet, man. Make 'em prove it to you first. You just got divorced. You don't owe anybody anything. You're an unattached 34-year-old entertainment lawyer with no kids cruising around town in a handmade suit and a black-on-black CTS. Shit, your divorce gives you mystique. Hate to say it but when this kind of thing happens in a town like this it's almost a blessing. I know it's messy. But you've got what they want. Don't forget that. Take back the power. Make those bitches prove it to you! Say it out loud!

What?

Make those bitches prove it to you, he shouts.

I say, *Make those bitches prove it to you!!!*

Good!

Two of the other dudes clap.

I'm almost 35, I say.

Happy birthday. You could look 25 if you wanted.

Hey, you should bic your head dude, one dude says to me.

Bic it?

Yeah, Big D says, Lather it up and shave it off. Go to a skate shop. Get some gear. You'd look good in a pin stripe skater jacket. You'll take ten years off.

Hm.

One dude rolls a joint, lights it, takes a drag, looks up at me and says, *With chicks it's if you don't care if they like you or not—*

24

I drive to the shack and shave my head immediately.

It takes me thirty minutes because I don't know how to do it. I cut my scalp twice and it's a pair of bleeders.

I hope the coyotes can't smell it.

Amazing how much the scalp bleeds.

I would've had the dudes in the barber shop do it but I wasn't sure I wanted them to touch my head.

It feels good, maybe a little drafty.

25

A few days later I see Big D again.

We go to *Lucky Strike* in Hollywood for some bowling in DayGlo and neon.

It's a grooved out bowling alley with a dance floor and a lot of glowing cosmos and lemon drops and appletinis floating through the air apparition-like in the hands of the club girls that hold them poised at shoulder height.

No sloppy drunks here.

It's early yet.

I order *Bruichladdic* because they don't have any other Islay scotches and go sit down with Big D and his young lady friend who brought all her pretty girlfriends who work in town doing something or other, often seeming to involve the sale or application of cosmetic products, sometimes upon famous faces.

Suddenly I'm a counselor at a *Children of the Night* Hollywood safe house for teenage runaways.

I'm a fossil.

Big D introduces me around.

I can't tell what these nymphs think of me.

Eventually I'm alone with one and sit down next to her.

I start to talk and she recoils a bit.

She makes a funny face and asks, *What're you drinking?*

Scotch, I say, feeling pretty damn cool.

She looks at me like she's never heard of it.

I chat but I feel like the dude from the *Steely Dan* tune who can't talk to the nineteen year old roller skater.

She don't remember 'Retha Franklin, Queen of Soul—

Next day Big D tells me, All the chicks were *down,* man. They dug you. If you want it, it's on. Can't you see that? I'm so jealous of you. I wish I was single right now. Big D says, Dudes all over town would kill to be in your position.

I dunno, I say. The one I was talking to thought I was weird for drinking scotch. That's not gonna work for me.

She's a jealous hater. That's about her. She's bitter. She failed here. When we went down to bowl and you stayed up on the couch all of her friends wanted to know who you were, what you did, how we met, where you lived.

The tall Asian one got really drunk and looked for you but you were gone.

26

I wake the next morning on a cot in the shack and find my back is a slice of sheet metal.

When I bend it makes a crumpling sound.

Even worse there's a tight wire band that stretches from the bottom of my left bicep across my chest down to the bottom of my right bicep.

It feels like a hot copper wire most days, stronger than muscle or sinew and burning.

I need someone to touch me or I risk total ossification.

There's a little day spa in Redondo I know about a block from the beach.

I book an hour massage and drive down there.

The woman at the desk asks if I want something called a *salt blow.*

Is it legal?

She laughs.

The masseuse is a twenty-five year old olive-skinned woman with a rich smile and fawn eyes who floats down the stairs to retrieve me. She's immediately calming.

Her handshake feels cool and gentle.

We make some small talk up the stairs and she puts her arm around my shoulder.

We come to her room.

She tells me to take off my robe and get under the sheet on the massage table.

She warms some lotion in her hands and pulls the sheet up to expose my feet. She raises my right foot a half inch off the table and then drops it abruptly like it shocked her.

She asks, What's going on with you?

I uh—

Are you getting a divorce?

Yeah.

I knew it when I put my arm around you on the stairs!

Now she smiles, beams even.

She circles the table with a tone in her voice that suggests a heightened challenge, like a doctor who was told about a scratchy throat but happens upon a goiter.

I'm ashamed that my foot disturbed her so.

I'm not right, I tell her, not even on an electrical level.

Perhaps principally on an electrical level, she says.

Her hands hover three inches above my back, over the back of my neck, over the back of my legs, encircling my feet. She touches the right foot very softly and cups the heel in her palm. She runs her other thumb over the tendon that stretches from the heel to the toes, the plantar fascia.

It relaxes a bit.

The foot feels softer.

She sets it down and does the same thing to the other one.

She says, I do a lot of *energy work* and could feel it coming off you on the stairs.

Really? Are you sure all divorcing men don't have the same hangdog look?

She laughs but doesn't respond.

You're too dark, she says. Lighten up.

27

I enter a distant period, a remote viewing of Los Angeles from beneath a heavy veil.

I go days without speaking to anyone I know, only to strangers or not at all.

I forget about everything altogether.

For weeks I slink around Los Angeles talking to people at Jewish Delis and midday carwashes and coffee shop counters.

Just talk, no consequence.

I tell myself I'm looking for Raymond Chandler's Los Angeles.

I develop a smart mouth and start talking like Phillip Marlowe.

I frequent a lonely bar at noon and maybe a strip club or two.

A stripper offers me a lap dance for twenty dollars.

I ask, If I give you fifty will you try and enjoy it?

I give her the fifty but I could take or leave the dance.

I close my eyes.

She says, Aren't you at least going to look at me?

I can see you better this way, I tell her.

She sees I'm not after titillation exactly so she makes me buy us a Stoli on the rocks to loosen us up.

Strippers love drinks, she announces.

She asks me a bunch of heavy philosophical questions and then, in a weighty Ukranian accent, scolds me for my hypocrisy and intellectual dishonesty.

Regarding strip clubs: *I am a very simple man, Sayuri. I do not like things put before me that I cannot have.*

I abandon that depressing strip club scene altogether and slip into random poetry readings and sit in the back. Nobody takes their clothes off at the readings but they offer up a different brand of exhibitionism.

I guess I'm looking for some kind of connection.

Sometimes I stand up and recite *Those Winter Sundays* or something, but it all feels very half-baked to me. I'm a real mister nobody these days.

I'm becoming less conscious of the past and less aware of the future.

A numbness sets in.

The house isn't sold, divorce isn't over but all that's on its way.

In the meantime what to do?

How about not a *damn thing* for once?

I'll go to sleep when I'm tired, eat when I'm hungry, shower when I'm dirty.

In my wanderings around the city, meeting each new person is like visiting another country, Prague in Winter on Tuesday, Marquesas Islands in the heat of Summer the next day.

I assume nothing, expect nothing.

It's as though I've never spoken to anyone before in my entire life, like one of those kids raised in a basement that comes out mute and sensitive to the light.

My ignorance is total.

I want to know what everything is all about.

I have preferences, that's all, no strong opinions.

For the first time in twenty years I've not a single goal.

How strange to think of giving up all ambition!
Suddenly I see with such clear eyes
The white flake of snow
That has just fallen in the horse's mane!

Robert Bly wrote that.

I copy it on a napkin at lunch from memory and put it in my pocket. I suppose my only goal is to keep things that way as long as possible: no ambition.

What if I get stuck like that?

Oh who cares.

In the meantime I'm willing to buy someone dinner to hear their story.

It's remarkably entertaining and clearly I've nothing better to do. I find the better the dinner, the darker the restaurant the better the story.

Good booze seems to help too.

Buy a woman a trite, sugary, frivolous appletini and you might hear about a secret hazing ritual from her sorority or the tale of her dolphin tattoo. But buy a woman an *Oban 16* cut only with three small cubes of ice and if you can actually get her to drink it you hear about the child she left with her ex-husband in Portugal and hasn't seen for many years, her eyes red-rimming with the memory of the last kiss on the forehead, the small dark locks damp against pale skin but *Why,* you ask her, did you leave your child (?) and how can you stand it (?) and she even tells you that.

Over a period of a few months I encounter some more strange women in foreign rooms—or perhaps some more foreign women in strange rooms. I dunno. It's a blur. I sense that in this post-*Sex in the City* landscape falling into bed with tipsy near-strangers is not some great mountaintop but more like shooting fish in a barrel.

For many it's little better than a handshake.

Something's wrong with that, sin or no sin.

So nowadays mostly I'm alone.

How long have I been wandering around out here?

100 days? 100 years?

28

One afternoon I'm driving somewhere through Los Angeles.

The sun seems too bright for this time of day.

Traffic is oppressive.

Oh yeah, the *Dodgers* game. Damn.

Well, maybe I should just go to the game.

Just go to the game? Who does that? That's a planned thing.

You don't just pull off the freeway—

An unseen force guides me into *Dodgers Stadium*.

I find myself at the parking gate.

I give the lady in the straw-hat ten dollars.

I park.

I look at the stadium and it reminds me of an ice cream cake not so much the color but the shape and sense it could melt at any minute and I'd be looking up at a giant child peering into her train set at her tiny pet earthling, like in that creepy *Twilight Zone* episode where Barry Nelson and Nancy Malone find themselves in an abandoned train-stop town and hear nothing but distant childlike laughter.

I feel rather like an existential philosopher, like Camus:

For the first time, in that night alive with signs and stars, I opened myself to the gentle indifference of the world. Finding it so much like myself—so like a brother, really—I felt that I had been happy and that I was happy again. For everything to be consummated, for me to feel less alone, I had only to wish that there be a large crowd of spectators the day of my execution.

I buy a bleacher ticket and shuffle through the back gate with the great unwashed.

We pass through one another on our way to the hotdogs, the bathrooms, the concession stands.

I clop up the metal steps to the bleachers.

When I reach the top the smell of outfield grass wallops me with a damp rush of calm.

It's so implausibly green, the deep green of a major league outfield.

And tens of thousands of people.

I sit down and the stadium fills up like fast motion film footage.

Suddenly it's full and there's a Zeus-energy in the place.

These people came to see a visible display of excellence in their society like the Greeks.

I sit in a catatonia for the first five innings and try not to get elbow bullied by the beefy woman next to me working through her cheese fries and Bud.

The energy of the crowd picks me up and my private fog lifts a bit.

I start watching the game.

I become the pitcher for a moment like everyone always does.

Working up the tension for the next pitch—jostling the ball in my fingers behind my hip—looking in, pulling into the stretch, eyeing the runner.

The Perfect Game.

One thing is missing—the sound of hundreds of radios tuned to Vin Scully calling the game from the booth—those little black one-speakered transistor radios that people had in 1983 next to their *Mountain Dew* in the cup holder of their floaty chair in their front yard water hose pool.

They all brought them to the stadium and the bleachers became a choir of Vin Scully washing over us while we sweltered.

I know just what Vin is saying up there.

He broadcasts it to me over the field today, over the player's heads, right into the bleachers.

I hear him in my head:

Second and third, one out, Rookie settles into the batter's box.

His parents still live in Placentia where Rookie was raised.

Takes ball one low and away.

His mother says he was not a baseball star in high school, more of a Drama Club type.

Fouled off, one and one.

His favorite musical is Bye Bye Birdie.

Fastball in for a strike, one and two.

On the biggest stage of all now, after five years in the minor leagues, Rookie calls time and backs out of the batter's box.

Seems to be having trouble with his spikes.

Young players do have problems with their equipment. I've seen outfielders carried off the field for want of a good pair of sunglasses.

Rookie back in the box.

Pitcher set, delivers.

Runners go!

Rookie hits a high fly ball to left center field, and I mean high—

So-and-so is going back—it's over his head—he makes the leap but can't get there. The ball caroms off the wall and takes a Dodgers' bounce away from the left fielder, rolling along the track.

The third base coach is waving one runner home, two runners home.

And Rookie holds up at third with a stand up triple!

(six second pause; crowd noise)

Well.

It may not be a revival of Bye Bye Birdie, *but I'm pleased to give you Rookie in his very promising off-Broadway debut.*

I'm comforted by a deep sense memory of the warmth and assurance of Vin's voice—his unhurried cadence, the constancy of it, the simple lyricism, the grandfatherly charm.

On my way out to the car after the game I make an easy, gentle decision: Though I have absolutely no idea how to do it yet, *I want to live.*

Part Three: Base Camp
Season: Fall
Locale: The Greater Southern California Region
Subject: Entrer la femme
Age: Regressive
Preferred handheld device: Same dubious flip phone
Condition of soul: Yeah right

29

Yikes!

Wedding invitation.

The bride's an old friend of mine so I just can't miss it.

It's this Saturday at Saint Lawrence Martyr, my home parish wouldn't-you-know and the site of my erstwhile nuptials.

Gets even better: a reception at the Palos Verdes Estates Country Club down the street from my soon to be ex-house.

Alois will be there too, which is good. We can traverse the Boulevard of Broken Dreams together.

The day of the wedding I endure grotesque and grainy flashbacks at the church door.

I don't think I can *do* this, I tell Alois softly.

Don't worry about it, he says, maybe there's a single bridesmaid.

I shudder.

The ceremony begins.

Alois whispers, That was us up there eight years ago.

I whisper back, You were a good best man.

I still have the tie, he says.

We sit on the bride's side and watch her glide down the aisle with that expression brides tend to have.

The thing gets rolling.

Fast.

Monsignor Lenihan says the Nuptial Mass. I've been listening to him say Mass since I was twelve, back when he was merely Father Lenihan.

I served Mass for him plenty. He doesn't mess around.

But this is going to take forever anyway: After a full Catholic wedding Mass with all the trimmings—the veneration of Mary, the songs, the readings, the kneeling, the blessing of the rings, Holy Communion—you know you're married.

You never want to go through that again.

During his homily Monsignor Lenihan invokes Corinthians 1 13:8 in a heavy brogue: Put this above your bed in big block letters, he tells the couple kneeling before him, print it out on the computer: LOVE NEVER FAILS, he says. LOVE NEVER FAILS, he says again.

I feel sick.

Alois puts his arm around me and whispers:

Except fifty percent of the time.

At the reception we start with cheap tequila.

Then we graduate to Glenfiddich.

A lot of it.

I'm dizzy and my face is numb.

Everyone mills around waiting for the dinner bell.

Someone very deliberately introduces me to a clear-eyed blonde named Elle. She has sparkly cornflower blue irises.

Elle asks how I know the bride and I say high school and I ask Elle how she knows the bride and she says we work together and I say, Are you in the prosecutor's office too?

Elle says yes and asks if I came with anyone and I say, No I'm at the tail end of a divorce.

Oh, I'm at the tail end of a divorce too, Elle says.

Then they ring the dinner bell and I tell her I hope I see her on the dance floor.

The speeches drive me nuts with their naive optimism.

I drink heavily.

My high school friends who still know me as a tea-totaler are startled by my conversion to the eighty-proof club.

But they soon join in and now we have the drunkest table in the house.

I'm determined to drink them under the table.

The newly married couple looks like they belong on the cover of *Bride Magazine* and I try to look away.

Later I spot Elle on the dance floor and she smiles at me.

I move toward her and put my arms around her neck like they belong there.

I kiss her square on the lips.

She kisses me back.

We dance and I spy my parents on the periphery, along with some other good Catholic parents of friends of mine whom I've known since I was a kid.

I've never been drunk around this crowd, though they've certainly been drunk around me.

It's my turn, I think.

I dance with Elle but after about ten minutes it becomes more of a tawdry groping sway and even as a drunkard I know the dance floor is no place for heavy petting.

We go outside and sit on a bench overlooking the golf course.

We make out like slobbery twelfth graders.

I spot a caterer leering at us from the kitchen so we go back inside and smooch some more.

Alois makes an unsuccessful attempt to pry us apart.

Buddy, he says softly, you don't know how to act yet when you've been drinking. You shouldn't be making out with this woman on the dance floor in front of your parents.

I can't hear him. I'm too busy pawing at Elle.

Eventually the wedding reception spins to a vague conclusion.

I ask Elle if she'll go home with me and she says she can't.

I accept that.

In the parking lot an attractive woman accosts me and asks me who I am and what my purpose is with Elle.

I can barely speak but I tell her my intentions are strictly honorable.

She glares at me.

The rest of the night is a whorl and I end up in bed with a drunken high school mate in the soon to be ex-house.

At some point during the night he manages to rip the soon to be ex-toilet seat off the soon to be ex-john while he barfs.

In the morning I leave a note for the real estate agent: The crapper comes as is.

30

The bride whose wedding I sloshed my way through returns from her honeymoon and calls me up.

You oughta give Elle a jingle, she says.

Yeah. You guys are two peas in a pod.

Okay, I say.

I get Elle on the phone.

We're both a bit sheepish after the drunken public groping.

I'd ask you to lunch first, I say, but since I already stuck my tongue down your throat I suppose it wouldn't be too forward to suggest dinner.

I hear her blush.

I've never behaved like that before, she says.

That's what they all say, I tell her.

We arrange to meet at a restaurant. I arrive first and watch for her coming through the door but I barely remember what she looks like.

When she appears I'm pleasantly surprised.

She's very pretty but doesn't seem to realize it.

Must've had a long awkward stage in grammar school.

Those are the best kind.

Elle sits across from me and it seems her most striking feature is the clarity of her gaze, the steady blue weight of it.

So here we are, I say.

Here we are, she says.

I ask, What do you do again?

I prosecute sex crimes, she says.

Huh, I say. Do you like it?

I love it, she says.

Doesn't it make you sick?

I've always been interested in deviant behavior, she says.

We should get along just fine then, I say.

She asks if I'm a musician.

A musician?

Yeah, the woman who introduced us told me you're a musician. You're not one?

I laugh. That's hilarious, I say. I wonder why she would do that. I'm a lawyer. I mean I play music but—

What kind of lawyer?

I'm an entertainment lawyer. I guess you could say I'm into deviant behavior too.

She asks, Do you like it?

I'm kind of taking a sabbatical, I ask. Can we please talk about something else?

Later, I show her the soon to be ex-house in Palos Verdes a few days before I'm to hand over the keys to the new owners.

We spend some time there and sit on the hardwood floor and open a bottle of wine I picked up—a 1999 *Etude* Pinot Noir.

Good, huh?

Yeah, she says.

Then she says, This house needs to be cleaned out before you go don't you think?

Yeah. I gotta get rid of a bunch of stuff too. The refrigerator, the bed, bunch of crap in the closets—

I can help you clean it out, she says.

I can't ask you to do that, I say.

You're not asking. I'm offering. Besides I like to clean. It's therapeutic for me. I worked as a maid in law school.

Really?

Yeah. Until this one guy groped me.

Oh, I say.

I stand up.

I don't even know what's in some of these closets, I tell her.

I open a closet in the guest room and it's piled high with odds and ends including a *Daisy Red Rider* BB gun Dad gave me when I was twelve.

It's just like the one in *A Christmas Story,* she says.

Yep—the very same one, I say. I almost shot my eye out with it.

Does it still work?

Oh yeah. Watch, I say.

From the cluttered closet floor I pick up a little wind-up toy called *The Nunzilla*—a two-inch tall plastic habit-clad nun that walks like Frankenstein and shoots sparks out of her mouth—a gag gift someone gave me years ago.

I open the sliding glass door and walk out onto the patio and wind up the Nunzilla.

The Nunzilla makes a whirring noise as she marches across the concrete.

I take pot shots at the thing with the BB gun.

I miss once, twice—then I nail her and send her skittering sideways—the little mechanical nun feet move helplessly until the toy winds down.

I'm going straight to hell, I say. Wanna try?

Sure, Elle says.

I set the Nunzilla up on an empty milk carton and show Elle how to sight the stationary target.

She hits the Nunzilla on her third or fourth try and sends the hapless toy religious flying into the bougainvillea.

Nice shot, I say.

I think this is a pretty good date, she says. What's next?

I dunno. Let's go somewhere.

We drive down to the little coffee house in Redondo Beach where they hold the poetry readings.

They're in the middle of one when we get there. We slip in the back and sit on one of the grimy overstuffed couches.

Some of the regular folks look at me, clearly wondering about the mystery woman. We listen to some questionable open-mikers and slip out the back door and head to Hermosa Beach.

We enter a bar.

So, she says, here we are again.

Here we are, I say.

She asks, What do you plan to do on your sabbatical?

I've been trying to avoid that topic, I tell her.

We don't have to talk about it, she says.

No, no. It's okay. I haven't been able to talk to anyone about it except my shrink and that didn't go so good.

At least you've had some therapy after your divorce, Elle says.

Yeah, I say. You?

It was extremely helpful, she says.

Mine wasn't really, I say. Honestly I'm a bit lost, shattered even. I achieved more or less what I wanted by thirty-four: decent entertainment law credentials, good money with more on the way, house near the ocean, married my college sweetheart—but it seems I've burned through my great and grand early ambitions and now I'm adrift in deep space.

You weren't happy?

Not really, I say. But then happiness has never been my strong suit. As far as entertainment law goes—I mean you can become a podiatrist-to-the-stars but at the end of the day a bunion's still a bunion, you know?

Gross, Elle says.

There's a big blank spot where my career is supposed to be, I say. For the first time in my life I don't know what I'm supposed to do with myself. Before if I didn't know I'd make something up real fast so I wouldn't look idle, wouldn't fall behind. But I can't seem to do that this time. I don't want to run a hundred yards at top speed in the wrong direction.

Elle asks, You're going to turn your back on all that training?

No. I dunno. Maybe, I say.

Elle says, After my divorce I learned how to enjoy the day again.

Enjoy the day?

Yeah, you know, forget about achievement and the have-to-dos and simply enjoy whatever that particular day has to offer.

There's a thought, I say. I guess I'll call that the focus of my sabbatical then: learning how to enjoy the day. Here's to it.

We toast.

But you know, I say, I should be trying to figure out what's next. The devil makes work for idle hands. I have no concrete plans, just instincts, and some of them aren't all that healthy.

Like what?

Like drinking myself to death, I say.

Yeah, no. You should follow the healthy ones, she says.

Okay then. You wanna go to Santa Fe with me?

Are you serious?

Yeah, it'll be our next date, I say.

Why Santa Fe?

My healthier instincts have been telling me to go out to the desert, to the Georgia O'Keeffe museum out there. I keep dreaming about her and her landscape paintings. Not so much the flowers but those desert landscapes. The clouds, the cattle skulls—

Then you should definitely go, I'm a big believer in dreams, she says.

You wanna come, then?

Sure, she says.

Later that night I lay my head in her lap on the old marital bed in the Palos Verdes house.

She holds my head in her hands and begins to knead my tired melon.

She pulls her hands away gently.

Did you feel that, she says?

I was almost asleep—

This big electrical surge went through my hands, up my arms, she says.

A shock?

No, it was more of an energy stream, she says.

The next morning at breakfast I ask her how many trials she's done.

She says, About eighty-five total jury trials for my whole career.

I nearly spit out my mimosa.

I ask, Eighty-five?

Yeah, she says.

How can you even still be sitting here? That's insane. How old are you?

I've got a year and a half on you, silly. That's what we do at the D.A.'s office. We try cases. What do you civil lawyers do?

We sue people and defend people who've been sued. We send out a bunch of discovery, take a bunch of depositions, then five weeks before the trial everyone gets together in a big glass room in Century City with a mediator that charges ten thousand dollars a day and we settle. Then the partner on the side that made the better deal buys a new *Jaguar* and maybe a *Subzero* refrigerator. Sometimes we write a press release but the money is always confidential. We certainly don't go to trial. For civil lawyers an actual trial is like an exorcism. We have to dust off the old tomes and re-learn the incantations. No business person wants their fate decided by twelve retired postal workers. So you're the barrister and I'm the solicitor. Two completely different jobs really. I think they've got it right in Britain, I say.

Elle says, A lot of criminal defendants roll the dice. A lot of my defendants are looking at life say, if they've molested more than one kid. I can't offer them much. My offers are like fifty years. They go to trial.

Trial, I say. I don't want to think about anything like that for a long time.

31

Elle wants to meet my mother, so we head over to my parents' house. Mom comes out to the living room and we sit for a while. We chat about this and that and Elle tries to make a good impression, which she undoubtedly does.

Afterwards Elle leaves for Orange County.

I sit with Mom for a while after Elle leaves.

She *really* cares for you John, Mom says. It's a shame you met her so soon.

So soon?

Yeah, she says. You're not even fully divorced yet. You haven't had that much time, you know, to heal.

I don't know that just being alone is all that healing, I say.

Well, maybe, Mom says. I don't know. I've never been divorced, thank God. But I can tell Elle's intentions with you are very, very serious. So if you think you're just having a good time, look out. It wouldn't be fair to her or her little girl or really even to you.

Okay, I say.

32

The next week Elle and I find ourselves in Santa Fe to see the Georgia O'Keeffe museum.

We stay at *La Posada* and drive up into the so-called Enchanted Circle high above Taos.

We get lost somewhere in the hills and it's good to feel lost, to be traveling together in some remote snowy otherness. For some reason we rented a convertible. The top is down and it snows but we don't put the top up right away because it mostly blows over the car which is nice and toasty and dry inside from the full blast heater.

We pass a creepy sign on a wooded roadside that says, *Reintegration Center, Don't Pick Up Hitchers.*

What's that about do you think?

She says, Probably like an honor camp or something.

I ask, What's your favorite song?

Elle says, *Spirits in the Material World.* You?

Mercy Street, I say.

We have Peter Gabriel but not *The Police.*

We crank Mercy Street, and drive back through a darkening Taos, to Santa Fe.

Confessing all the secret things in a warm velvet box;
He's the priest, he's the doctor, he can handle those shocks—

We return after dark and enjoy a four star meal accompanied by a dizzying array of forks. The tripartite lobster bisque is like tasting the whole of the sea itself.

The following morning I'm disappointed in the O'Keeffe museum.

It's small and crowded.

I expected a shrine, a religious experience.

But standing there looking at a painted lily I realize that the experience belonged to O'Keeffe and her paintings were the mere residuary of it.

One of the docents tell us O'Keeffe said she hated flowers and only painted them because they were cheaper than models and didn't move.

There's no touching O'Keeffe's actual experience, whatever it was.

It can't be borrowed.

Maybe there's some other reason I was drawn out here.

It rains and snows, rains and snows, rains and snows.

The desert is lonely, isolating.

Pockets of pressing poverty and despair are evident in the surrounding area.

I feel a deep grief here in this landscape and this isn't what I expected.

Elle and I buy a couple of rings at the Native American bazaar in front of the Palace of the Governors.

She: an oval purple suginite.

Me: an inlaid Zuni rectangle comprised of spiny oyster shell, onyx, lapis, and turquoise.

Rings, I think.

We put them on in non-ceremonial fashion.

Wonder twin powers activate, Elle says, and we touch knuckles.

Later we sit in the lounge at La Posada and drink a fair quantity of scotch in front of a restless, popping fire.

That ring you got, I say, what's it called again?

Suge, suge, sugen—

Suge Knight or something, I say.

We get to talking about a bunch of stuff and then somehow from somewhere Elle tells me, *I think I'm—falling in love with you.*

You poor dear, I think.

I love you too, I say.

33

When I get back to Los Angeles I call Big D in a panic.

I told her I love her, I say, that wasn't my intention. I think I blew it. Remember what you said? I don't owe anybody anything, I just got divorced, don't make any promises, all that. I've been *taking back the power* like you told me!

Yeah, he says. But don't worry. Look at it this way: Telling her you love her isn't a promise. You're saying you want to explore every aspect of your relationship, that's all. You'd better do that before you make someone your all and everything, right?

Yeah yeah, I say. But she's got a seven year-old daughter. I haven't met her yet. I don't want to mess that up or get halfway into some kind of domestic situation and figure out I'm not ready or I'm out of my mind or something. There was all this snow and scotch and firelight—

I say, Did you mean it at all?

It wasn't drunk talk, It's just so soon. You taught me how to woo women at will through this whole—uh, not-caring method. It's like a new superpower I've never had before. I didn't think I'd have to hang up the cape already. Plus, I just really don't want to be in love right now or even worse have someone be in love with me.

Well whatever happens, Big D says, you know the deal: make her prove it to you before you take yourself out of circ-u-lay-shee-own—

I'm afraid she might be doing just that, I say.

34

I decide to get a second opinion from Alois.

He's having none of it.

It's a total rebound, he says. Textbook. I don't know about for her but for you it is. You're beyond not ready. I was there. You were wasted. She was wasted. That was just a sloppy drunken night. How long have you been alone?

About a year.

It seems shorter to me, Alois says. But either way, the divorce is just final now and you don't seem so good to me.

Very out of it. Have you thought about going back to not drinking?

What? No way! Drinking is the best thing ever. It totally helped me through this year.

Just because of your Mom and all, Alois says, and you have it elsewhere in your extended family—

Alcoholism? Oh, I'm not like my Mom. I'm just—I needed to loosen up a little.

Yeah, well, the night you met Elle you were plenty loose.

So what are you saying?

Alois says, I think you should cool it with this woman. I think you should go back to work, and I think you should go back to being a tea-totaler. You made a really good sober person.

Well, none of that's gonna happen anytime soon, but thanks.

We hang up.

Wow. What a killjoy. I think it's time to put some distance between Alois and me if he's such a square. He just doesn't *understand.* I don't think I'm doing anything *that bad.* But maybe I should break it off with Elle. I can't just date a woman with a little girl. I know she wants more.

35

A few days later I take some of the money from my share of the sale of the ex-house and rent a little yellow craftsman in Redondo Beach.

I let the owner of the dreadful Topanga shack know I won't be returning.

The yellow rent-house is a cheery cottage off Pacific Coast Highway near Redondo Union High School and across from the Redondo Beach public library.

It's a place to lick my wounds and close enough to the parents in case of their emergencies, which seem to be multiplying.

Wendell digs it, plenty of windows so he can make his presence known to the interlopers and suspicious passers-by. It's a busy neighborhood and there's plenty of foot traffic—not all of it acceptable to an edgy Great Pyrenees whose warnings cause people to cross the street.

It has a Jacuzzi in the back, a patch of lawn, two bedrooms, one bathroom and a big kitchen.

I turn the second bedroom into a law office of sorts and music room—not sure which professional activity will win out but sadly betting against music.

36

I pull my tenor and soprano sax out of deep mothballs and call up some guys I know who play music professionally. We get together at a downtown loft and jam. But they're really good. I'm not so good. It feels like the phony bohemian fantasy of a lawyer plunging through an early mid-life crisis. Is that what this is?

But the other guys encourage me and we rehearse all that week. We decide to emulate these edgy cats called *The Bad Plus* and play modern tunes upside down and backwards as a jazz quartet. It almost works, but I'm the weak link. If we're going to do this I'm going to have to woodshed for months and I don't know if I have the discipline for it.

They say we need a name. We mess around with that for an hour and they say, It's your band, dude. You decide.

So I decide on the name: *J. Alfred Prufrock Needs a Drink.*

Only one of them gets it so I explain about T.S. Eliot's *Prufrock* poem and how the guy in the poem, Prufrock, couldn't talk to this girl and there was all this handwringing and basically the guy just needed a drink.

They still don't get it but that's our name.

On my way out of the rehearsal space something strange happens to me.

I seize up.

The edges of my field of vision darken and blur.

My pulse races.

I can hardly breathe.

I'm gripped with a terror, a sense everything is going to collapse, the very ground beneath my feet.

I can't think.

I'm grasping at the wall.

The bright blue sky turns between the downtown buildings.

I may vomit.

I struggle to get to my car with my saxophone cases and drive in circles trying to get back to the freeway.

Is this a *panic attack?*

I was supposed to see Elle tonight but call her up and cancel.

She says, What's wrong, John?

I say, I can't explain. I can't breathe. I'm seeing double. I feel—

John, I care about you. I'm here for you. You're very good at describing what you're experiencing. Can we get you some help—

NO! God, no. There's no help. I, uh, I tried with the counselor. It was a big waste of time. I can't—it's just, I'll be okay—

I drive over to see Big D.

We crack open some beers and he rolls me a joint.

I smoke it.

I feel better, soothed out, but a little paranoid.

He puts some Wes Montgomery vinyl on his vintage Hi-Fi and we while away the afternoon.

37

A couple weeks later on a trip to Mammoth Mountain, Elle and I hike clear on up to some lake and back down to the car. I ask her why she would want to get married at all again after what we went through. I mean what a horror to get divorced and what does it all mean (?) and how can you trust anyone (?) and doesn't every single one of them become like gangrenous, necrotic tissue that festers, flies buz—

Marriage is sacred, she says.

Sacred?

Yeah, sacred.

You really believe that—sacred?

Yes, she says. *Sacred.*

Hmm, I say. What does that term mean to you?

It's—hard for me to describe exactly, she says. But it's like—I'd rather think about it, she says, before trying to answer that question.

I ask, You think it's time for me to meet your daughter?

Yes, Elle says.

38

Christmastide.

A member of Elle's extended family throws an annual party.

Elle's daughter, Nicole, seven, stands betwixt a gaggle of nieces and nephews and odds and ends and I'm not sure which one she is until I get closer and see her in a blood-red crushed velvet dress.

Nicole's eyes are green, magnetic.

Nicole must have her father's eyes.

I wonder what he's like.

Nicole appears totally impassive, unreadable, but not aloof.

I smile at her.

Hi Nicole, I say.

I always wonder about shaking hands with little girls. Do they freak out about that?

I extend my hand.

Nicole takes it.

She shakes it twice and lets go just as I let go, very aware of the custom.

She says hello but doesn't say anything else and reveals no resistance to my presence.

I wonder if she has a sense of humor.

Who is this girl?

What a bright beam she is.

Is this what they mean by *The Indigo Child?*

After the party I ask Elle, So now that I've met your kid does this mean we have to get married?

Ha, she says.

39

One morning I come over to Mom and Dad's house before something I have to do in a local court and things are all askew. Mom emerges from the backroom and her face is all red and puffy.

She starts to speak and her words are slurred: Ohh, hii honeiu—

—mom, i say—have you—been—*drinking?*

I can't hear her answer. I know her answer, a half denial that neither of us would believe.

The floor falls away.
All the colors are freakish and exaggerated.
Nothing feels right.
After twenty years of sobriety?
Is she crazy?
Why now?
Is multiple myeloma not enough trouble?
The whole house smells of it from the old way
I float towards the ceiling—

I'm Fourteen.

I'm in this pit orchestra for the Spring Musical.

I'm a dreadful, lowly high school freshman.

I couldn't be participating in anything more nerdy, playing clarinet in the pit orchestra in a performance of the cheesiest musical on the planet, Once Upon a Mattress.

So we've been rehearsing all week and the music director is a screamer, terrifying Italian temper, worse than an Irishman.

Lateness is not tolerated.

I'm worried because Dad's away and Mom's drinking heavy this week and I don't have my license yet and I don't know anyone well enough to ask for a ride home and it's too far away to walk.

It's 4 p.m. and Mom gets out of bed for the trip.

She pulls her Oldsmobile into heavy traffic on Pacific Coast Highway.

She weaves and other drivers try to get away from her.

This is opening night of the show so I need a flower for my lapel. It's required, I tell her.

We stop at Conroy's *and I go in and get a damn flower.*

When we come back out I notice the time and say, Mom, please hurry.

She throws it in reverse, hits the gas and backs right into a flesh colored VW Bug and pins it against a telephone poll.

She doesn't stop.

The corner of her Oldsmobile's massive rear bumper torpedoes the passenger side door of the Bug and Mom keeps going, bending the entire Bug frame into a little v shape.

The sound is cataclysmic, crumpling, shearing, like a giant trash compactor.

Gee, is there anyone in the car?!

One of the little back Bug windows pops and shatters.

Mom doesn't stop, doesn't even notice.

I see a gray haired man take our license plate number down.

Back on PCH Mom weaves like crazy in and out of lanes but stays on the right side of the road.

I'm glad she didn't notice the damage she caused the Bug and I'm glad she's going the right direction even if she's weaving because it means I'm going to get to the play on time and that's all that matters.

We play the show. It's full of archaic lines like, Yea, verily, which we make fun of in the pit orchestra. I try to cut up like everybody else but I feel peculiar, like I'm not really here.

After the play everybody piles into their parents' vans or whatever and I wait like I'm expecting Mom but I know she won't be there to pick me up.

After everybody leaves, I begin the walk home.

It's four miles along Pacific Coast Highway.

I feel stupid in my little suit with my lame-o clarinet.

I'm a full-on geek. I'm a loser. I'm nothing.

Headlights rise up behind me and the roar of passing cars and trucks grows menacing this late at night.

The next morning Mom tells me the police came by and I ask, What did they say (?!) and she says, Nothing – they just took some information down.

—Mom, promise me you won't drink again, I say. Twenty years of sobriety down the drain this morning.

Oh, I promise honey, she slurs.

Seriously. I mean it. What am I supposed to tell Dad?

He doesn't need to know.

He'll find out soon enough if you keep it up, I say. Then what?

It's just, she says, there was wine at this wake I went to and I thought it didn't seem like such a big deal so I had some—

And now you're drunk on a Tuesday morning at 9 a.m.? Is that what you want?

Of course not—

Then stop it, I say.

I leave the house after straightening up a bit.

My first impulse is to call Dad.

But what if this is a one-time thing, a phase? Maybe he doesn't have to know.

I conclude that if it's not a one-time thing Dad'll know soon enough and leave it at that.

I drive to my yellow rent house in Redondo and sit on the porch, looking up the street at Redondo Union High School—

I'm Fifteen.

I come home from school and the car's parked a little off center and the blinds are drawn.

Mom's drinking for sure, I think, and I'm right.

After a while a kid just knows.

I open the door and the house is too quiet.

No snoring, no nothing.

I look around and notice the door from the kitchen to the garage is ajar.

I open the door to a darkened carport.

I see a still, prone figure in the middle of the garage floor.

I recognize this dull heap as Mom.

A black puddle seeps out from beneath her head and I don't think it's oil.

For a moment I consider rushing up to her and trying to perform CPR like they taught us at scout camp (hey, hey are you okay?) but I get a frozen feeling and walk to the back of the house.

I stare at the ocean for nine or ten seconds and decide to call an ambulance—

I can't move. Ten-one-thousand, Eleven-one-thousand, Twelve-one-thousand, Thirteen-one-thousand...

DAMMIT JOHN, DO SOMETHING, I tell myself.

Before I can unstick my feet from the floor the front door bell rings.

It's an old family friend, Jackie, wife of my Confirmation Sponsor.

She looks at me and asks, Where's your Mom?

The best I can do is point to the garage.

Jackie disappears into the garage and I can hear her talking loudly to Mom, trying to wake her up.

I hear moaning, mumbling sounds.

Mom's alive!

The ambulance comes or Jackie takes her and I'm not sure what's happening.

Dad finds out later and says, That's it!

I hope he doesn't mean divorce, not a divorce, anything but a divorce—

A few months later Mom's trying to get sober at a place downtown they call Friendly House.

Dad and I are in this other program that meets three or four times a week to talk about all the troubles concerning life with an alcoholic.

They tell us we're sick too, the whole family is diseased.

Not a very nice thing to say but they're probably right.

Dad blows up all the time, says dark things.

My grades suck.

They tell us to let go with love and to live our own lives and to remember we can't control other people and to keep it simple and that co-alcoholics like us have a responsibility to try and raise the bottom for alcoholics through tough love and intervention.

I just want to let go already.

I'm not sure about the with-love part.

Either way, I don't expect to see Mom again.

—Maybe I shouldn't be drinking after all.

Maybe Alois was right.

Maybe I was right to swear it off before I even needed to shave.

There's no way Mom can drink but she's doing it again. Disaster.

I swore if she ever picked it up again—

But I've already taken up drinking now and it suits me just fine.

Had I known she was going to start up—

With Mom toasted right before my eyes in realtime I'm remembering all the reasons I took the pledge young and never drank a drop.

But wait a minute! I didn't start drinking at thirty-four to get drunk, I started drinking to challenge my identity, to shake up my life, to take a risk, to explore a forbidden realm—

And that's what I'm gonna do dammit to bloody hell!

I am *not* my mother.

I'm a psychonaut, bound to explore the limits of human consciousness.

I go back over to my parents' house.

I take a fifty microgram Fentanyl patch out of the medicine cabinet and slap it on my shoulder.

I grab some of Mom's Oxycontin and some Ambien while I'm at it.

I stop by the liquor store and pick up a fifth of Laphroaig.

I go back to my yellow rent house and find a leftover joint from a party two months ago.

I smoke the joint, drink a half a highball glass of the Laphroig, pop an Oxycontin and wait for nightfall.

I don't need to do this; I want to do this.

I have this idea I'm going to compose a great original saxophone quartet but then my tongue thickens and I fall asleep sitting up for two hours.

I wake up and write a poem.

Things Alcoholics say:
I don't remember anything!
Give me the keys!
I am not my mother!

Later, Dad calls for assistance at the house so I drive over there.

He doesn't seem to notice I'm on drugs.

The furniture is wavy.

He asks if I can stay over and I say yes I will and I don't even have to go back to my rent house first because I brought the dogs.

After he and Mom go to bed I take one of her Ambien.

A few minutes later I drug dial Elle.

She knows something is seriously wrong and stays on the phone with me.

I tell her I took a sleeping pill and she says I should go to bed then and I say no they told me you have to fight it—

Fight what?

Fight the power, I say, and lie down on the kitchen floor next to the whirring dishwasher. The tile feels cool on my cheek and I don't think it's such a crime to close my eyes for a minu—

JOHN, Elle yells into the phone, GET OFF THE FLOOR AND GO TO BED!

Okay, I say.

I get off the floor and go to bed.

The next day I feel pleasant, not hung over.

I drive back over to the yellow rent-house.

I look at the *Fentanyl* patch on my arm.

I look at the piles of paper in the corner of my home office.

I must admit there may be some cause for concern.

40

Elle comes up the next night to check in on me and have dinner out.

At the table I ask, Do you believe in God?

Elle says, I believe in other realities, a spiritual realm— but our mutual friend told me not to talk to you about this.

Not to talk to me about *what?*

Religion, the supernatural.

Wait a minute. She told you not to talk to me about anything religious or supernatural? That's insane, I say. I'm actually offended she would say that. She knows me better than that.

She said it might scare you off. It's well known around the office that I believe in ghosts, Elle says.

Ghosts?

Yes, ghosts or spirits, she says.

How could she tell you not to talk to me about ghosts or spirits? And you of all people listened to her?

Well—

Can't you see I'm the type of person that would absolutely *love* to hear about ghosts or spirits?

It sounds—

No, see, this is what I needed to hear, I say. You already told me once in Mammoth that marriage is sacred. Remember?

Of course, she says.

And I thought, Okay, now we're getting somewhere. I'm still not sure about the whole notion of *sacred* as a valid concept even, but I knew if I ever married again I had to marry someone who had the capacity to hold something sacred even if I didn't. And now you come out with ghosts or spirits? That's very encouraging. What else don't I know about you?

Elle says, I'm afraid I'm not very articulate about it. I believe in a universal energy and in a form of reincarnation. I believe that there are spirits, singular sources of energy, that sometimes try to communicate with us or at least inadvertently make their presence known. And for this to exist, there must be something spiritual about existence.

Not to be critical, I say, but you're saying you believe there are spirits without telling me why.

I can't—I just can't go into it all right now. I don't have the words.

I ask her what she thought of going to a Catholic high school even though she wasn't Catholic.

I loved it, she says. I loved the school Masses and the religion courses. I found it fascinating but I didn't understand it very well.

It didn't bother you to be learning about all that stuff when you believed in something else?

I don't know how to describe it, she says. I'm not Catholic but I have a soft spot for Catholicism. My father is Catholic, she says.

Ah, she takes a sip of her martini.

I was young when I first noticed spirits, Elle says.

What happened?

It's not like a bunch of crazy stories, like candelabras floating through the air or anything. Just now and then before sleep I would see something or someone.

Would they talk to you? What did they look like?

They have a *form* some of them, she says. But maybe the form is more imagined from the sensation of their presence. Particularly if it's a relative or someone you know.

So, like, have you ever lived in a haunted house?

There's an unhappy female presence that seems to have left my house in Orange County. I haven't seen anything in quite a while. I feel like that connection is leaving me. It's dormant.

I'm surprised, I say.

About what?

You're so normal for someone who believes in ghosts, I say.

Just normal?

I mean competent—

Merely competent?

No, you're amazing, I say. But most of the people I've met—especially the women—that believe in something paranormal or supernatural, they're kind of kooky. You're not kooky. Your purse matches your shoes. Your closet and car are immaculate. You balance your checkbook. You have good credit. You've listened to KROQ every morning

90

for over two decades. You've been with the same office for fourteen years—

You mean to say I'm not a total freak even though I've seen a ghost?

Yeah, I say.

41

The next day I think about that discussion a lot.

I think of Elle's sense of the sacred, her appreciation of all things related to me, her near-mystical-but-not-too-much daughter, her general stand-up galness and I decide that's it.

It's too soon I know. Everybody thinks so, even Elle. But what if this is—there are no guarantees in life—we could die tomorrow. People walk out on each other at the drop of a hat. Why can't they drop in on each other just as quick? Will my chances for happiness, for love, be greater if I break up with Elle and spend a year alone? Or *two?* Or *three?* Maybe I'll just be three years older.

Things can't stay the way they are, the two of us living sixty miles apart, seeing each other a few times a month. I might as well date someone who lives in Cleveland. And I can't just *date* a woman with a seven year old daughter. It wouldn't be right. This either has to end or go somewhere permanent. And we can't *live together* or whatever the kids are doing these days. How unseemly.

I think we have to get hitched.

Time is fleeting, we both grew up listening to Dr. Demento on late night KROQ, sometimes on Saturdays. Very few people know about stuff like that, our stuff, just one of those little cultural connections within a generation—on opposite rims of a shared childhood megalopolis, oh heck. *Why not?*

I'm gonna marry this woman right away...

The State of California says it's okay.

Girls come and kiss me, say that you'll miss me, get me to the church on time—well, maybe not the church per se—I doubt I'll ever see the inside of one of those again, but you know, get me to the hotel courtyard or something. On time.

42

I buy Elle an engagement ring, cut a hole in the central fifty pages of a Robert Frost anthology to camouflage it, and hire a helicopter to Catalina Island.

Elle comes to Redondo expecting a normal Friday night out but we fly to Catalina and wind up out to dinner at the *Buccaneer*—a pirate ship of a restaurant—drinking salty dirty gin martinis.

You drank that martini really fast, John. Are you trying to shoot it?

No, no, I just—I have to go to the bathroom.

I leave the Frost book on the table knowing the ring is in there and all she'd have to do is open the book and I'd be found out.

I splash some water on my face. My breathing is shallow. What am I doing over here? Have I lost all sense of reason?

Too late now.

When I return to the table she asks me why I brought the book and I tell her to open it to *The Road Not Taken*, the *Our Father* of American poetry, because if you know only one American poem that's probably the one.

She opens the book, sees the ring, looks all misty and surprised, and then I just ask her.

She says yes, tears up a little, and we call her Dad.

Elle and I are engaged.

Part Four: The Incline
Lyric: In the Clearing Stands a Boxer
Helpful Hint: Don't drop your hands
Movement of the Soul: About 60 miles South
Preferred Handheld Device: Jump rope

43

Our wedding is to be in late November at the Hotel Laguna.

Dad and Mom like Elle. They seem to be glad I have some direction.

Dad says, You shouldn't move into her house, though. The two of you need a new place to call your own.

We can't do that right now Dad. Partly it's money, partly we wouldn't want to uproot Nicole.

I think you're going to look and feel like a houseguest, like Kato Kaelin. It's her place, not yours. That's emasculating.

Well, it's just the way it is right now. Hopefully we can move in a year or two. Maybe closer to the beach.

How are you going to handle life behind the Orange Curtain, Dad asks?

I don't know. I've never spent much time down there. It's very beautiful in places. I feel like a stranger in a strange land, though. But I could use a change of scenery.

What about your work? There's not much showbiz law to be done down there, is there?

I'll still have access to Los Angeles, Dad. It's only sixty miles.

He doesn't mention a word about a Catholic annulment and the thought does not cross my mind. Such a disaster was my nominally Catholic marriage I wouldn't want to try it again if I had the chance. What good did that ceremonial start do me last time?

I can't wait to get married by a judge.

Let's leave the priest out of it altogether, please!

Elle and I low key it, try to keep it small, light, not too pomp and circumstance, been there done that and all.

Don't want to jinx anything here—

So let's have our little secular wedding and do this thing, seventy guests, tops. Is that even little? Maybe not, but it is secular.

Huzzah.

I select some Whitman and ask my buddy Mike to read it during the ceremony. I beg Mike to show up dressed as Whitman with a wild beard and stuff but he declines. He doesn't think I'm serious. I tell him I'm serious but he still declines.

44

Weeks pass, and the wedding's upon us.

The night before the wedding we have a rehearsal dinner across the street from the hotel at a tony brick-building bistro. I don't mean to be, but I'm over the limit on gin. I can't quite collect myself at dinner. I'm exhausted and feel like passing out in the potatoes au gratin. My eyes are heavy-lidded and I slur through a toast.

Mom limps up to me afterwards, clutching a four-pronged rubber-tipped cane and says, *I'm so sorry I passed this along to you.*

My buddies are grabbing my arm to drag me off for a last late night out and I stare at Mom in muted shock.

What is she *talking* about?

Passed *what* along to me?

I'm shuffled down the stairs while Elle and Nicole look rather serious atop them watching me ushered away. The boys throw me in the back of the car and I wake up thirty minutes later somewhere I've never been, suddenly confronted by bright lights and strange people and too much liquor.

That's the last thing I remember.

45

The next day, the day of the wedding, Mike doesn't come dressed as Whitman but nevertheless reads a few verses from *Song of the Open Road* with that robust, just-this-side-of-crazy Whitmanesque zeal:

Traveling with me, you find what never tires, Mike recites.

The earth never tires;

The earth is rude, silent, incomprehensible at first—Nature is rude and incomprehensible at first;

Be not discouraged—keep on—there are divine things, well envelop'd;

I swear to you there are divine things more beautiful than words can tell.

A judge Elle knows takes us through the vows and such.

Our civil ceremony is very nearly perfect or at least closer to perfect than anyone should dare expect upon this the most volatile of all occasions. I fight spasms of panic but that's somehow become the norm for me now. I keep

95

expecting it to pass or level off but the attacks seem to be getting closer together and more extreme.

The after-affair is like a warm chocolate chip cookie, hopefully not too gooey, the kind you leave out for Santa. The sun dips into the Pacific a little North of Catalina Island.

There's a lot of talk about how lucky Elle and I are to *find each other* after all we went through with our divorces, having been abandoned by our unappreciative former spouses. In the mythology of the second marriage we are the heroes, the survivors, the victors.

Big D gives a great toast at the reception.

He says to the assembled: When John first told me about Elle, I thought *wow,* a little blond number that listens to gangster rap, drives a black Lexus and takes down child molesters in court. What a find!

Then later Big D gives me a pair of his grandfather's gold cuff links that grandpa used to wear when he went to court as a San Francisco lawyer back in the day when men were men and had steak tartare and gin martinis for lunch and wore a lot of cuff links.

I tell him I'll wear his grandfather's cuff links to court only on the days of important arguments.

My high school mates have a tradition of forming a band for weddings and other events, a sort of fictional band that has a real persona. They call it *Rude Awakening* in remembrance of a nun that used to shark on them in grade school by threatening them that they were all in for a very rude awakening of one sort or another.

Rude Awakening is known for a thrashing atonal version of the *Lamb of God,* a Catholic Mass part we all know. This doesn't go over well in front of the parents or the priests who sometimes show up at our friends' wedding receptions where Rude Awakening adds that to their set list.

The Rude Awakening guys thank me for getting divorced and remarried so they have another opportunity to play.

They appreciate that I took one for the team.

One of them points out that I didn't ask Rude Awakening to rock my first wedding and the marriage failed; in fact, when you think about it, he tells me. Nobody who had Rude Awakening play at their wedding has gotten divorced. It's a kind of blessing, he tells me.

Three chords and the truth, I say.

They abide that well-known creed.

Today I get to be an honorary member and sing and play the sax. The five of us play *Rockin' in the Free World, Sympathy for the Devil, Seven Nation Army, Sullivan Street* and *Highway to Hell.*

They let us play but by the time *Highway to Hell* rolls around the catering manager is frothing to shut us down.

We skip the encore.

A friend of mine comes up to me after the guests leave and she says, I cried three times at your sappy wedding!

46

I find myself vaguely disoriented in my new home, sixty miles south of everything I've ever known.

I scarcely know a soul other than Elle and Nicole.

I have no professional connections here, no personal ones, just a new family.

It might as well be Omaha, not that there's anything wrong with Omaha.

It's Sunday and Elle's at the gym so little Nicole and I ride bikes together on an unpaved trail near the house and Nicole takes a spill.

The handlebars jab her hard in the sternum.

She's shocked, then the tears come.

The poor girl's short of breath.

I wheel around and pick her up and pull her to my chest.

I hold her gently for thirty seconds.

I forget my distance.

I've never held a child before.

Kneeling here with Nicole firm in my arms I so clearly remember that day I pitched over the handlebars of my *Schwinn* and tore my chin clear open, seventeen stitches wide.

I pick up Nicole's bike and walk both our bikes slowly toward the paved part of the trail.

She walks with her head down, sniffling.

That was a hard fall, I said. You're very tough.

We get to the pavement and I hand her bike back. We ride the rest of the way home in comfortable silence.

I realize I've crossed into a different landscape entirely, the land of this-kid-is-in-my-care.

When she gets back from the gym, I tell Elle that today was a big day for Nicole and me.

47

But deep down, even though I have a knack for it, I know step parenting can never be like real parenting for one important reason: When the kid calls you by your first name, you ain't Dad.

No kid says, Hey stepdad, wanna go ride bikes?

Dad is dad.

Stepdad, on the other hand, is something else entirely, a step something, an algae or a lichen or something icky.

Some men of stepfatherly ilk are reviled for wearing wife beaters and burning kids on the arm with cigarette butts.

They perpetrate something dreadful called the *Cinderella Effect* as it's known in clinical circles. I read up on it and other things I'm supposed to avoid. I want to do this right, even though I probably shouldn't be doing it at all. Isn't it plain to everyone that children need their parents, not mere proxies?

Yeah, life is messy, but still.

A stepdad has to prove his innocence as it's never presumed.

However, as between the stepdad or the divorced Dad, well, let's just say both have got it kind of rough. But the kid, the kid is all, no? We must do what we can to part the waters for the younger soul.

It's the proper way of things.

Best interests of the child and all that.

One night Elle and Nicole and I sit on Nicole's bed for a few minutes before sleep. Elle does her rendition of the eerie, imagistic *Little Bunny Foo Foo:*

Lit-tle Bun-ny Foo Foo
Hoppin' through the forest
Scoopin' up the field mice
And boppin 'em on the head!

Then the Good Fairy comes down and says:
Lit-tle Bun-ny Foo Foo
I don't wanna see you
Scoopin' up the field mice
And boppin 'em on the head!
I will give you another chance,
And if you don't behave, I will turn you into a Goon!

Lit-tle Bun-ny Foo Foo
Hoppin' through the forest
Scoopin' up the field mice

And boppin 'em on the head!
Down comes the Good Fairy again...
Lit-tle bun-ny goon goon...

They laugh.

I say, That's a major folktale right there. Do you know its origins? It's kind of creepy. It's got so much symbolism.

It's just a little children's rhyme, Elle says.

I know, I say, but it's like the folktales of old. Everything stands for something. It's archetypal, Jungian.

Pretty simple I think, Elle says.

I ask Nicole which character she most identifies with.

Nicole says: the field mouse.

I ask Elle which character she most identifies with.

Elle says: the Good Fairy.

Elle asks, How about you?

Sad to say it, I tell them, but I'm Little Bunny Foo Foo in that scenario.

48

Elle and I get along quite well at first.

She even tolerates Wendell when he destroys her plantation shutters and blows his furry white undercoat all over her house.

Her cats aren't entirely pleased with Wendell and Louise but they adapt.

We sit close at restaurants and take the same side of the table even when we're alone.

Maybe it really is better the second time around or maybe it just seems that way because it's like seeing a movie that didn't get good reviews, so it surprises you.

All I know is there's nothing I'd rather do than have dinner with my new wife in some off-track bistro.

We're good company. But also there's a shadow.

Something's incomplete, lurking beneath the surface, but I don't know what it is exactly.

I can't put it into words.

I have an ominous sensation during the day.

At night I wake up at two or three with the feeling there's a tombstone on my chest. Sometimes I sit up as if fighting through the surface of a thick liquid, gasping for breath. Sometimes I wake with a start and a pounding heart, sweating from a nightmare I can't remember. I try to creep downstairs and sit in the guest bathroom to lower my vital signs. A drink sounds good but I can't be heard rummaging around the liquor cabinet in the middle of the night.

As much as we try to pretend to normalcy, Elle is worried.

Worried that I'm not picking up much work, worried that I'm in a fog about basic things like the bills, like losing track of my keys, worried about this that and the other thing.

I think about going back to a psychologist, or maybe even a psychiatrist. The panic attacks are interfering with my work. When I sit down at my desk in the home office my heart begins to race, my mouth goes dry and I can't think at all. My powers of concentration have flown.

But I'm reluctant to see a state licensed pill pusher. The pills never helped. Oh and I took 'em just like they said, whole cocktails of 'em. Even laid off the booze and the grass while I tried 'em. Pills just didn't work. Not even remotely close. In fact, I think they made me worse.

I can't get my feet set right.

I was voted *Most Likely to Succeed* in high school, I was student body president two years running in college and gave my law school class' valediction.

I used to try to live up to the early promise.

All that means nothing now—

My challenges seem to be much greater than the push to achieve worldly success.

It's as though something sinister is following me, formidable and billowing, *wearing the Linconish coats of night*—

I can feel it behind my right ear but when I whirl to look there's nothing.

I could call it pervasive dread but the true expression of this shadowy sensation does not seem to reside in language.

All I know is a few days out of the week I wake up breathing hard.

Elle says, John, the way you wake up scares me. Your breathing—has it always been like that?

I don't know, I tell her.

The past seems very obscure to me.

50

I decide to give the pill doctors one more try. I don't like psychologists anymore so I go see a psychiatrist and he says that any adjustment he would make to my chemistry would necessarily be very slight.

In other words you don't think I'm that crazy, I say.

Ha ha, he laughs. No, I don't think so. In fact, I'm not sure you need medication at all. I haven't figured you out yet. You seem to have it made and you look good so there's something under the surface. But we can try a few things.

Good, I like this. It's all chemistry anyway, isn't it? Science!

He suggests a little *Wellbutrin* to bring me up a bit, and a little lithium to bring me down.

I say, Hey wait a minute. Don't they give lithium to manic-depressives? Is that what you think I am? Am I manic-depressive?

Those labels don't really matter, he says.

He has a warm Russian accent.

He says, ve treat *seemp-toms*. I sense you have some cycling, some manic *crea-tee-vity*, some up and down, some attentional ee-ssues, but that's not really it. I just like *lee-thium*. In Russia they did study and found towns that had *lee-thium* in water supply had lower crime rates. I want to give you trace dose, like what you'd be getting if you lived in one of those Russian towns and drank water with trace dose of *lee-thium* in it.

Alright, I say. Let me have some lee-thium then.

Just have your blood checked in a few weeks because lee-thium can be toxic in some patients, he says.

Toxic?

I wouldn't worry about it at this dosage—300 milligrams—it's lowest dose I can give you. I just want you to have very slight, very modest influence. None of these corrections should be dramatic seeming. Just take za *lee-thium* and za *Well-bootrin* and see how it is for you.

Okay, I say.

I walk out with another bag full of pills.

The psychiatrist is clever. Didn't even answer my question about the diagnosis. I look at the lithium bottle again. I realize:

This guy thinks I'm manic-depressive!

Forget that.

I take the lithium for a few weeks and stop.

I can't feel anything and I don't like the idea that it could be toxic. I'm glad it mellowed some Russians out though.

I continue taking the *Wellbutrin* and do feel a bit of a lift but to be honest not all that much.

51

One random Tuesday I wander into a local gym and think maybe I can raise my spirits that way.

I spot a friend of Elle's and her trainer doing these strange exercises with a medicine ball on the stairs outside the gym.

She introduces me to the trainer.

The trainer says, *John!* Have you ever thought about boxing?

He has a thick accent I can't quite place and a breathless cadence.

He's tall, sandy haired, lanky, charismatic.

I've never boxed, I say.

Well if you join this gym he-ah you get a free boxing lesson if you want it. I could give you the lesson now and then you could join the gym if you like.

This guy works fast.

I was just stopping by to check it out, I say.

Elle's friend says, You should really box with him. It's an experience.

Okay, I find myself saying.

Good-good, he says. Let's get some gloves for you.

He picks out a pair of boxing gloves and then says, I have to wrap your hands.

He takes the canvas wraps and places the loops over my thumbs and tells me to hold the left wrap in my palm.

He takes the right wrap and wends it around my right palm, fingers, wrist.

He does this fast, expertly, like he's done it a million times.

He fits the gloves over the wraps, tightens the *Velcro* fastener around my wrists.

Suddenly I'm all gloved up.

Okay John, he says, let's get in the ring.

Get in the ring?

I climb through the ropes.

Awkwardly.

He picks up a pair of pads and starts circling me.

He jabs at me with one of the pads. I move to the side.

Good, he says, I'm testing your reflexes.

The ring feels spongy under my feet and makes a lumbering sound as we move—a deep thumpdathumpda like an African drum.

Okay> come toward me> left foot in front> stand not quite forty-five degrees> gloves just below your eyes> curl your shoulders forward> round them> keep your arms as close to your body as possible> when you punch come straight out of that position and come straight back to it with the least amount of fuss> back to your own cheek with the glove> turn the thumb down when you strike> snap it like this.

Now, he says, left>right>uppercut>right!

What?

He says it slowly: throw a left jab, a right cross, a left uppercut, and another right cross.

I do it.

Good, he says. Snap the thumb down as you strike> You're very nearly a boxer already> Have you done this before?

No, I say, gasping.

I'm breathing like a farm animal.

LEFTRIGHTUPPERCUTRIGHT, he yells.

thwap/thwap/thwap/thwap

It feels pretty good, surprisingly natural.

You've got a feel for this, he says. Good stamina for an individual totally out of shape.

I ran pretty well in high school, I rasp.

Ah, he says. Excellent> you need strong legs and strong lungs> and aggression> you have to have bad intentions when you enter the ring.

Left>right>left hook>right hook!!!

I stumble over the combination and he stops to show me what a left hook is all about.

This was my best punch, he says. You bring the left arm up parallel with the ground and let the body carry it through the strike> Kind of like a golf swing> Let the hips pull the fist through> Good, he says.

He shouts,

LEFTHOOKRIGHTUPPERCUTLEFTJABRIGHTCROSS

thwap/thwap/thwap/thwap/thwap

Suddenly he jabs at me over the top of my gloves and nails me on the forehead with the edge of his pad.

It comes surprisingly fast and hard.

My head doesn't quite snap back.

Ouch, I say.

Sorry, I've been a little edgy lately, he says.
I accidentally knocked a guy's tooth out last week.

What?!

He's a boxer> an old friend of mine> He wanted to spar and I said put in your mouthpiece and he said> No we'll just go light> Accidentally my glove caught his front tooth and that was it> Now he'll need implants like me—

Don't break *my* teeth, I say.

No, no> You need a mouthpiece first anyway> Never box without a mouthpiece, that's the moral of that story> This is just pad work> Remember, it's not in my interest to *huut* you> Ha-ha.

After about an hour I'm drenched in sweat, breathing hard, and feel about as good as I've felt in fifteen years.

106

He stretches me out like a trainer afterwards and says, I don't say this to brag> but I want you to know I'm a former light heavyweight champion of my country> I fought for a title in another weight class here in the States> Don King was my promoter> I know what I'm talking about> You need to work out with me> the greatest sportsmen in the world do the boxing workout.

I'm in, I say.

It ain't cheap but I pony up for twenty sessions.

The next time we meet he makes me jump rope for five minutes, do a bunch of stretches, form a mouthpiece to my bite, work a single punch for seven minutes at a time, try on some headgear, go four rounds of pad work, do ten minutes on the double end bag, mangle my abs and try various old school calisthenics that I've not attempted since seventh grade phys-ed.

I can't move after.

I'm soaked in sweat.

I feel a lot better, I tell him.

Good-John-good, he says. One intense hour of exercise> at least three times a week> five is bea-tah> It's like burning rocket fuel> that's what we need> Look he> people come in and jog on treadmills and do some lazy weights and hang out at the juice bar for two hours> Who has two hours these days?

He stretches me out on the training table and asks:

So do you want to eat some leather tomorrow?

What does that mean?

You know, spaaa, he says.

What?

spa.

Oh, spar—

Some people can't understand my eak-cent, he says. I tell them I speak English, you speak American—

Isn't a little soon for me to spar?

John> Do you know why Rome wasn't built in a day?

No.

Because I was not the foreman on that job> Ha-ha.

The next day I show up to spar with my new friend.

Is this an entirely wise undertaking?

So, uh, I say, I don't know anything about sparring, we haven't been over—

John> Hiya man> good-good> Hee-ah> let's get your wraps! Remember John> Like I said, it's not in my interest to huut you. You have to still be able to write a check afterwards. Ha-ha.

He changes out of his preppy trainer uniform and puts on a ratty black tank top.

He shouts: I FEEL MEAN!

Get in the ring, he says.

He sets the timer and the bell goes off.

He shouts: LET'S GET READY TO RUMBLE!

He glides toward me and punches me in the face.

It hurts.

He punches me in the forehead.

It hurts.

The scary thing is I can't even see the blows coming and he's standing right in front of me.

He pops me in the nose.

I realize if I don't do something he's going to kill me and I start to move—

I jab.

He moves his head out of the way and punches me in the gut.

It hurts.

This is insane, I say. Why do people do this? I'm already gulping air.

I didn't realize boxers hit each other so hard when they spar.

I thought it was more like fencing or something.

He points at his chin with his glove and shouts, HIT HIM!

I hesitate, so he punches me in the face.

He points at his chin with his glove and shouts, HIT HIM—

I hit him on the chin with a soft right cross.

Good, he says.

I charge him and land a simple, rather silly combination.

He smacks me in the forehead again with a right cross but I take it and surprise him with a punch on the right side of the stomach with what he calls a Jackie McCoy, a kind of left hook-uppercut thingy to the body.

GOOD, he says, I've seen people knocked out by a Jackie McCoy to the lee-vah!

The what?

The livah, he says.

I didn't know I punched him in the liver and that's apparently a good thing, unlike a kidney punch which I've heard is a bad thing.

So, I ask, livers are in play?

Yee, he says.

Good to know, I say.

The bell rings and I move back to a corner, panting and wheezing.

The mouthpiece impedes my breathing.

BREATHE, he says. In through the nose> out through the mouth.

Every one of my cells is in flame.

The heat—

It reminds me of the first time I ran a cross-country race. I was so hot I crossed the finish line, ran straight to the locker room and jumped into the shower in my uniform, swilling *Gatorade.*

That was a good day too.

The bell rings again.

He charges me with a flurry of lefts and rights that I can't even see. He backs me into the ropes and rains down blows at twenty-five percent strength, but still—

I put him in a pretty good clinch that he can't break for a second.

But when he does break free the punishment resumes and I have no answer for it, can't even see most of it coming.

His speed is blinding.

Ten seconds is an eternity in here.

Roll with the punches, John! Ever hear that expression? You must learn to stay CALM under pressure, he orders me.

I respond instead with reckless brawling rights, not able to time the left jab to his head at all.

Wherever my left ends up, his head isn't.

Make 'em miss, make 'em pay, he says, and clocks me when I throw a wild right cross.

When I drop my guard he punches me.

When I split my guard he punches me.

Whenever he can exploit an error he punches me.

BAM, he catches me on the chin with a soft left uppercut that nearly knocks me out, buckles my knees, sends me skittering backward toward the ropes—

John, he says, are you *Christian?*

I'm leaning that direction, I manage to gasp.

He circles me like a reef shark.

Keep moving, he says. Your best attribute is your speed> You're very fast> good hand speed> You've got to move your head more though> WHOA, he says, as he smacks me hard in the face: Don't head-butt that fist. Ha-ha.

Why, I ask, do—you—wonder—if—I'm Christian?

John, God brought me to my knees about six years ago and I try to spread the good news. Boxing is like—a ministry for me.

BAM, he pops me in the nose.

I just love Jesus, he says. Knowing Jesus changed my life—

He gets a light in his eyes when he talks about Jesus so I move in quickly and hit him in the stomach again and back out while he's distracted—

GOOD, he says, drop your bombs and get out!

He jabs at me and I actually slip it.

I'm so pleased with myself I stand there while he tags me on the forehead again with a straight right.

I can hardly lift my hands.

I can't believe how tiring this is, I say.

You're tired because you're too tense> You're wasting much of your energy that way.

Relax, he says.

I tense up.

He hits me again.

Proverbs, he says, a great book to start out with if you haven't read the Bible in a while. You like philosophy?

Yes.

Jesus Christ was the greatest philosopher who ever lived, he says. I just want people to know Christ's love.

Yeah, yeah, I say.

I like it when he talks about Christ's love because he stops hitting me and I can sometimes even hit him.

We break for our corners.

I go to the white one.

No, no, he says. The white corners are neutral corners.

Two rounds and I'm dizzy. Are you kidding me?

He keeps telling me to *breathe*.

All I can think about is water.

I need water but there's no crusty corner man like in the *Rocky* movies to squirt water into my mouth. I know that when I do have water it'll be the best water I've ever tasted.

Ding, ding.

Third round.

Do we gotta?

I come out and try to sting him a little, bad intentions and all.

He moves his head like a rattler, like it's on a hidden mechanism of some kind, in box steps, square geometric shapes, trapezoids.

Now he's just showing off.

I've never seen a human head move like that.

It's frightening.

I feel like a hapless little brother whose big brother taught him how to box so he could beat the living tar out of him and call it sport.

People actually pay for this?

He says, John, I can see you put a hundred percent into everything you do> It's your nature.

I wish that were true, I think. It used to be true.

He asks, Will you come to my church with me on Sunday?

Fine, I say.

Before the last bell rings, he punches me in the face two more times and I answer with a sloppy combination, left-right-left-hook, blah—

The front desk clerk applauds when we're done, but I know she was just amazed I didn't pass out.

I go back to the house and take a steaming shower and drink a *Boddington's* while the water runs over my head.

I hold the can to my cheek which is starting to swell.

Elle comes home.

I tell her I sparred today with a man that loves Jesus Christ and punching people in the face.

What?

I tell her it's an utterly compelling combination and that I'm going to his church on Sunday but don't worry, I tell her, I'm not susceptible to religious people since I know it all already and I just let them talk and I find comfort in their faith and wish I had it but I don't.

52

I wander in to the little non-denominational worship center on Sunday.

Everyone's really friendly. The pastor wears a Hawaiian shirt as does half the congregation. They have a rockin' band up there, drum kit thumping away, keyboards, bass player. They have a slide show up above the band with a big picture of a three-masted schooner and the words to the pop-rock hymns we're singing.

The pastor gives a very dense, interesting sermon on the book of Daniel.

This fellowship started in Southern California with hippies and street urchins in the late sixties. The founder took them in off the streets and changed their lives, so the contemporary music and the Hawaiian shirts is their heritage.

But then they get to a communion-like ceremony and the former Catholic altar boy in me gets a sort of funny feeling in his stomach.

They pass out grape juice in these little plastic cups and share little bread crusts or something that are supposed to represent—

What exactly?

Catholics subscribe to the dogma of *The Real Presence,*
the understanding that during the part of the Catholic
Mass called Communion once the priest consecrates the
Host through solemn prayer and veneration and blessing, it
becomes in effect the body, blood, soul and divinity of
Christ, not a mere commemoration of the Last Supper or
something.

I suppose I never thought about it all that much, never
really looked into it, never *really* believed it.

It's a Divine Mystery, they say, the highest Sacrament.

But suddenly this unconsecrated dixie-cup wine and
bread crust business feels deeply wrong to me, whether I'm
a believer or not. I sip the juice and nibble on the bread
crust and try to get into it. But I feel suddenly ill, like I
have to get out of here. The rest of the service is a source of
great suffering.

All I can think about is the belief that the bread and
wine is not just a—well, what does it mean again anyway? I
don't necessarily *believe* in the Catholic Communion, but I
feel suddenly protective of it, like when a stranger insults
your mother-in-law.

I wonder if I could ever come here on a regular basis,
after five years serving the Catholic Mass and watching
that intense prayer surrounding the Eucharist.

I mean, these folks are really nice and all and I'm not
totally opposed to Hawaiian shirts in worship, but I don't
think I can do this. I'm struck by the strange sense of
revulsion I feel after their version of *The Lord's Supper,* and
the faint interior voice that tells me, *Don't ever do that
again.* How odd. I mean, who cares?

Afterwards everyone mills around and has coffee and
donuts.

Now that looks familiar to me, little kids running
around between their parent's legs all stoked out of their
minds on *Sunny Delight.*

Every religious ceremony in every faith seems to have this in common, this business of pastry and beverages after the service.

Nothing wrong with that.

My boxing trainer shakes my hand and says, John, man> I'm so happy you came> Try and bring your wife next time, he says.

I appreciate your sincerity in sharing this with me, I say.

53

Near midnight, Nicole comes into our room crying.

Elle says, What's wrong honey?

Nicole says something teary and incoherent.

Elle turns to me and whispers, *Nicole had another nightmare.*

Oh, I say. Does she want to stay with us?

Nicole nods her head.

She nestles in between us and we comfort her.

When she falls asleep she kicks violently and starts running what feels like a fever.

She talks in her sleep.

Elle, what's up with Nicole? She's flopping around like the kid from *The Exoricist*—

Elle says, She gets really hot when she sleeps and has super intense dreams.

This is the third night this week she's come in here, I say.

Yeah, Elle says. It comes and goes in waves. But now that you're here—I don't want her to form a habit of sleeping in our bed. She's seven already.

It's okay, I say. I don't mind. I wet the bed till I was ten.

Ten?

Yeah, ten. You got a problem with that?

Nicole wants the hall light on every night.

It's very bright and shines into the master bedroom.

I have to sleep with a black t-shirt over my eyes.

But when she wakes up in the morning, Nicole is chipper, a happy child, looking forward to the day. She can be silly, goofy, altogether charming. She's not a serious child. She has a good sense of humor. But the night, the darkness of her room and what she encounters there, scares her.

54

Nicole gets straight A's again so we take her to *Islands* for tacos and strawberry lemonade.

She colors the fish on the kid's menu with the courtesy crayons.

When the food comes I ask Nicole if she's afraid of the dark.

Yes I am, she says. I don't like it.

Why not?

When I'm under the comforter and can't see over the edge of it I feel like someone's going to get me.

Like they'll sneak up on you?

Yeah, she says.

Later Elle says, I didn't want to say this at the table but Nicole sees things at night.

Like mother like—

That's why she's afraid of the dark, Elle says.

Have you ever talked to her about this?

We've seen things together, Elle says.

What things?

It was right after her father moved out. Nicole was in bed with me and she asked, Who's the lady at the end of the bed? And I looked and I saw the same outline of the same lady.

116

This is unbelievable, I say.

Elle says, I don't want to put ideas in Nicole's head but I can't in good conscience tell her it's all in her mind either.

55

A few days later I pick Nicole up from school and we go back to Islands.

Elle is still at work and can't join us.

As Nicole and I wait for our order she colors on the placemat again.

Parrotfish, she says.

I say, Your Mom told me that you've seen things at night.

Nicole blushes.

The Cloud People, she says.

The Cloud People?

Yes.

What are they like?

They're like clouds but more clear. See-through. And they have people faces.

Do they scare you?

Yes.

Do they do anything or say anything to you?

Um, I usually run out and go into Mom's room before they can say anything.

Nicole, can you draw me a picture of the Cloud People?

Without the slightest deliberation she matter-of-factly sketches two images on the placemat and turns it around to show me.

I look at her drawing for a long time.

Nicole says, Also, there was a lady at the end of the bed and sometimes there's a man I see.

I ask her for pictures of them, too.

She does two more simple sketches.

Nicole, some people say when we're young we can see things that adults can't see. Then after a certain point they say that type of seeing goes away. It's possible you have some kind of special sensitivity that other kids have too—

I don't want to see anything at night, she tells me.

She's flat out scared of the dark.

Or rather scared of what she sees in the dark, this splendidly balanced seven-year-old girl that doesn't scare easily, that doesn't have a wild imagination, that doesn't have adjustment problems, that doesn't have a propensity for exaggeration—I can't help but believe her. She's not trying to get attention. She really sees these things. She wants it to stop.

Okay, I tell her. I think I can help with that.

I go to the mall and get the girl a bunch of soft lights: an incandescent amber turtle, a glowing crescent moon, a backlit aquamarine panorama featuring translucent dolphins and bright orange Garibaldi.

When it's time for bed, Elle and I tuck her in.

Nicole's walls are now illumined with soft tinted light.

She looks happy.

I ask her, Do you still need the hall light on?

Yes, please. Until I'm older—

Over the next few weeks Nicole doesn't come into our room as much and starts sleeping through the night.

I wish Nicole did want to see things at night so I could ask her to draw me pictures of them in the morning.

But that's just selfish.

56

A few weeks later Elle and I meet over some red wine at a rustic seaside haunt. It's foggy. There's candles and everything. I say to her, *I'm changing.*

She asks, Into *what?*

I don't know. A werewolf maybe. Lately I think about different forms of energy all day. I want to stay on that frequency, plugged in. It feels—

Supernatural?

I don't know. I'm sorry, I feel very strange most of the time, I say.

Yeah, I can tell, she says.

This thing with Nicole, the things she sees. I believe her, I say.

You can try to stay *plugged in* like that, Elle says, but it might be the reason I don't see anything at night anymore. It's hard to live in that realm and do all the other mundane things we have to do.

I have this new sense that nothing is merely mundane, I say, and there's no other realm, only one realm that we've arbitrarily divided into natural and supernatural. Yet circumstances keep prevailing upon me that we live in both all the time. Also, everything is starting to feel as if it were a kind of *prayer.*

Elle asks, Do you pray?

No, I say. I never really have. I don't think I know how. I said little petition prayers when I was a kid like, *Dear God please let me find my baseball in the ivy.*

I never overcame this sense that prayer is just an empty act rendered to nothing.

There's too much evil and randomness it seemed to me to believe in a loving or even responsive God.

What's changed?

A lot of little things, I say. Weird stuff. Strange sensations, heightened awareness. Like when I left the law library today I handed the parking attendant my ticket at the gate. There was this split second when I held the ticket and he held the ticket. It was as though someone called a time out and I could see for the first time how the other

119

guy's hand and my hand and the ticket were all made of the same—a kind of charge went through me.

Made of the same what?

I don't know. My quark your quark, red quark blue quark—

Particles?

Maybe, I say, but what animates the particles? Everything's moving. That can't be a casual question for me anymore.

Whatever it is, she says, I don't think it's just another particle.

57

A few days later Elle comes home and says she met someone at work who knows a psychic.

This one's supposed to be the real thing, Elle says.

Elle is curious and asks if I'd like to go see the psychic too.

Why not?

Next Saturday we drive to Seal Beach to meet the psychic.

Elle told me last night this woman flies in from Hawaii every so often to meet her Los Angeles clientele.

I ask, What does this woman know about us?

She knows our names, Elle says.

We meet the psychic in the lobby of her hotel.

She's jet haired, fair skinned and attractive, high cheekbones, deep aqua eyes, dark pantsuit, lipstick a little on the bright side, there's a heat about her, she's somewhat ageless, perhaps fifty-something. Or maybe older but looks younger; or maybe younger but looks older.

She takes us up to her suite and says, As you were driving here I wrote some of my general impressions.

120

She shows us her notepad and it's full of large, looping script.

I ask, Is that automatic writing?

She asks, What do you know about automatic writing?

I've just heard the term, I say. It interests me.

I don't tend to be spooky about things, she says. As people are driving toward me I get general impressions and put them down on paper. Whether that's automatic writing or not, I don't know.

How did you come to be a psychic?

She says, The ability seems to flow through my mother's side. She's from Ireland. I've always had it. I've developed it. I'm also a Ph.D. in Psychology and have a Masters in Public Administration.

I'm half-Irish, I say.

Have you ever been to Ireland?

Nope. Not yet, I say.

When you go you're going to step off the plane and burst into tears, she says. That's what I do. By the way, I prefer the term intuitive because psychic gets such a bad rap and there're so many charlatans out there.

Okay, she says, let's begin.

I expect her to ask me a few tricky, seemingly innocuous questions to find out just enough information to extrapolate into a plausible reading.

But instead she just starts reading her notes out loud.

So, she says, I'm thrilled to meet the two of you. You're a very unusual couple. John, you're in a major transition. Your energies are powerful but you don't want to be here. You're confused. You have a lot of interference. You're unusually interested in the way the brain works. You need to be in the saltwater, not just water, but saltwater. Did you grow up near an ocean?

I tell her growing up I could look at the Pacific Ocean from my bedroom window.

Get in that saltwater as much as you can, she says. Your mother and father are still alive. I sense you have a sibling, but something's wrong there. You're definitely the dominant one. Do you have a younger sibling, maybe with an impairment of some kind?

I say, Whoa. Now you're freaking me out. My mother had me and then two years later she had another boy named Christopher. He was a premature live-birth baby that died after a few hours. He's buried in a Catholic cemetery in Los Angeles. My mother's never even seen the grave.

She nods her head. She says, Your mother is an artist, or lives close to art. She's a seer. But she's never wanted to be here either. She's pure Irish?

Yes.

I feel that you and your mother have been here before together many times. You're the stronger of the two. She's an alcoholic?

Yes.

Your father is strong, powerful, a bull. He can be harsh. He cares for you but he doesn't understand what you really are. He's in turmoil. He can be angry. Really angry.

I'm not entirely sure what you do for a living, she says. I'm feeling law or medicine around you. I wouldn't want to cross you in the courtroom or the operating room, she says. You were a war general. But you have an artist's brain. This causes you innumerable sufferings that you've not reconciled. You're an intuitive, but undeveloped, she says. The two of you are druids. John, you're a shaman.

Elle, you're a medium, whether you want to be or not. You have one child, a daughter.

Is she your daughter too, John?

Step-daughter, I say.

You're supposed to be a spiritual father to her. She is Georgia O'Keeffe, she says.

Elle and I turn and look at each other.

She continues this way for another fifteen minutes, with a cascade of peculiar insights and observations coupled with suggestions.

So this is a *reading?*

Toward the end of the session I tell her a few months ago I had this experience in court where I started to sense everything and feel this, this—

It's been said that the thing about enlightenment, John, is that when you first encounter it you shout, It's a tree! Then later, when you understand more, you say simply, It's a tree.

58

Elle and I drive home in silence for a few minutes.

That was crazy, I say.

I told you, she says.

She must have known something about me—

No, nothing, not even your birthday, Elle says.

Some people would say we just met the devil, I say, that a psychic reading is not of God.

Elle asks, What do you think?

I dunno. She knew us, who we were, and generally where we were going, what our challenges were, and offered a little advice. What's wrong with that? Is that the dreaded spiritualism they warned us about?

I never got those warnings, Elle says.

She so nailed it. I mean if that was some kind of trick it was an awesome trick, I say.

I can't explain it, Elle says.

Why not, you're apparently a medium—do you see dead people right now?

Yeah right, she says. I've no control over that. I can't do it on command.

One thing charlatans employ a lot is flattery, I say. I was on the lookout for it. When someone flatters us, we tend to accept it. Some of what she said was flattering, but some of it wasn't.

Elle asks, That part about your Mom being an artist, she's not an artist is she?

Mom has some postgraduate credits from Stanford in art history, I say. She taught art appreciation to schoolchildren. She knows a lot about art and literature. So I'm giving that to the psychic as a *hit*. To my knowledge Mom's never painted but it seems to be alive in her, unexpressed.

Maybe that's partly why she drinks, Elle says.

She's an alcoholic, period. But yeah, unexpressed artistic longing—that and the death of my brother. I never met the little dude so I don't feel the lack. But that's pretty bad, isn't it, losing an infant?

Uh, yeah, she says. How old were you again when it happened?

Two, I say. I don't remember anything about it.

59

Later that night, I wake with a start.

The panic attacks are worse than ever.

Part Five: Ascent
Theme Song: Where or When
Fellow Travelers: Opium addicts who sleep under bridges
Preferred Handheld Device: A walking staff
On Speed Dial: Doctors and pharmacies
Condition of Soul: Stirring like a drowsy subterranean vole, perturbed by surface vibrations

60

A few days later Dad calls and says he and Mom just got back from Italy. They went on a Catholic pilgrimage to walk the path of Saint Francis of Assisi.

Assisi was amazing, he says. I feel so close to Saint Francis. You should really go sometime. It might change your view of the Church.

Yeah maybe, I say.

One thing though, he says. Mom drank wine. I know I shouldn't have let her do it but she just took some and when you're in Italy you feel like you're on another planet—

Dad, she's been drinking at home too.

What?

I caught her months ago—

Why didn't you tell me?

Clearly it hasn't been a problem—

No, there is a problem, Dad says. I can't believe I missed her drinking. I wonder where she's getting it, where she's hiding it. She's been acting strangely, she's becoming incontinent and papers are all strewn about, she's not organizing the bills like she used to—

Dad, she's a cancer patient.

No, this is different. There's something else the matter with her.

I ask, How did she get around over there in Italy?

There was one nice young priest that stayed behind and walked with her, Dad says.

It's a strange thought, the two of you drinking wine, I say. I mean, you don't drink at all since Mom quit.

That was a mistake, he says. You feel excused from normal behavior over there. It's like another world.

When she's on steroids she goes through the roof, I say. The steroids take her so far up she wants to come back down somehow. Not somehow—with wine. She has bad judgment on steroids. I know if I took steroids I'd probably throw a chair through a window—

Dad asks, What are we gonna do with her?

I don't know, I say. Just watch her for now I guess.

61

Next week Dad calls me up and says Mom took a taxi to the store at midnight, bought four bottles of wine, came home, broke them against the wall because she can't open them with her hands the way they are, poured Styrofoam cup after cup for herself and finished three bottles, spilling a neck's worth of wine in each shattering, but still—

Three bottles of wine in a row?

Then she fell down the hill and broke her hip.

Great, I say. Where is she now?

Little Company of Mary, he says.

When I get to the hospital I see Mom's a bloody mess. She looks like a full-on alcoholic again.

Red, splotchy, puffy.

But much worse, since the entire right side of her face is purple and bruised from the tumble down the hill. The paramedics scraped her up out of the neighbor's flower garden.

Mom, I tell her, I swore if you ever started drinking again I'd turn my back on you. What the hell are you trying to pull? We might as well let you die of the cancer.

I'm sorry, she says.

Forget sorry, I say. STOP DRINKING NOW! There's a lot we can do for you if you don't drink, but otherwise—

I'm sorry honey, she says.

After a successful surgery on her hip she spends a month in physical therapy then comes home and starts drinking every chance she gets. Wine seems to appear out of nowhere. She drinks it like grape soda.

I come over once or twice a week. When I get near the house my stomach flips around like a halibut on a boat deck. Dad and I poke around and find shards of green wine bottle glass all over the side yard, the back yard, the front yard, in the ivy.

Every four or five days, or every eight or ten days, or every fifteen days, or every twenty days there's an *incident* of some sort or another and it usually involves Mom taking a cab in the middle of the night, writing bad checks, tricking a friend into taking her to a restaurant for lunch so she can drink, or swiping Dad's Cadillac, a one ton bomb parked in the driveway. I get nervous when the phone rings if it's one of Dad's numbers.

As the saying goes, Mom doesn't admit to a problem. She drinks, she gets drunk, she falls down. No problem.

Then she loses consciousness for hours just like the old way.

Long forgotten questions burble up from murky fathoms:

Where does she go when she drinks to oblivion?

What's down that long dark spiraling tube?

Dad calls me every other day with an edge in his voice that makes me green about the gills.

I don't know what to do with her, Dad says. I can't watch her every second of the day and night. I sleep with the car keys and phones and credit cards and checkbooks under my pillow in the TV room. Sometimes I forget something or fall asleep early and she finds a way to get wine. I can't take this.

I say, When she went to Friendly House twenty years ago I never thought I'd see her again. But somehow they sent her home to us sober—let's send her back there.

That was a long time ago, John. She's different now. Tough love doesn't seem as appropriate for a seventy-two year old cancer patient. Plus it's sixteen hundred dollars a month. I checked, he says.

After another fall and another illicit midnight trip in Dad's rig to *Ralph's* for five bottles of white wine, two packs of *Marlboro's* and a *Hershey's Bar*—all purchased on a credit card she opened without Dad's knowledge—Mom agrees to go to Friendly House.

A month or two later I go visit her.

62

Friendly House is a worn old craftsman on Normandie big enough to shelter a baker's dozen or so women trying to recover from substance related horrors of one sort or another.

The well-known head of the house, Peggy Albrecht, greets me.

Carol Burnette played her predecessor in a film about Friendly House.

Peggy herself has saved more lives in this town than penicillin.

Nice to finally meet you, Peggy says.

Likewise. When Mom was here twenty years ago I couldn't bring myself to make the trip.

You were just a boy, Peggy says.

I look around and notice that all the residents seem to be women in their twenties, thirties and forties.

I ask Peggy, Is it alright having a seventy-two year old cancer patient here?

I'm even older than your Mom, she laughs. I'm not here at the House as much now. But your Mom's getting along alright. The women seem to take her under their wing. She seems to be having a fine time, maybe too fine. She goes to *AA* meetings during the day, cooks with the women at night. Whether it'll stop her drinking or not I don't know yet. She seems rather jolly.

So, I ask Peggy, anything in this field change much over the last twenty years?

The drugs are different. Cocaine and crack were bad twenty years ago, now it's a lot of pills. The pills are hard to deal with.

Alcohol hasn't gone out of style, I say.

The old reliable, she says.

I talk to Mom.

Mom keeps calling out to people to introduce me to them like we're at a party or something, like she thinks she's in a sorority house.

Mom asks, Guess who I met at the AA meeting we went to yesterday?

I ask, Aren't you supposed to preserve anonymity?

Mom mentions the name of a famous boxer anyway.

I held his hand when we said the *Serenity Prayer*, she says. He has a huge hand. He was very nice. There's a lot of celebrities at the AA meetings we go to.

Great, I say. Alcoholism's an equal opportunity destroyer, right? Remember that one from twenty years ago?

It is, she says.

She smokes like a chimney.

Most of them do, she says.

I wish her well and then, as I'm leaving, Mom says, We went by a bookstore the other day. I bought you this.

Like a little girl giving a parent a ceramic ashtray she made in school, Mom thrusts me a copy of *The Hound of Heaven*, a 182-line poem published in 1888 by an opium addict turned Catholic poet, Francis Thompson. She takes a final puff of her cigarette.

It's about being pursued by God, Mom says. The best part is the introduction by Chesterton.

I hug her goodbye.

I flip through the little book at a long downtown stoplight.

The poem begins:

I fled Him, down the nights and down the days;
I fled Him, down the arches of the years;
I fled Him, down the labyrinthine ways
Of my own mind; and in the mist of tears
I hid from Him, and under running laughter.
Up vistaed hopes I sped;
And shot, precipitated
And down Titanic glooms of chasmèd fears,
From those strong Feet that followed, followed after.

The poem's a little formalistic for my taste but it has a nice ring to it.

I give it a seven.

Mom highlighted sections of the intro in green. The uneven lines reveal her loss of motor control. She seems to like what this Chesterton guy had to say almost more than the poem itself, which isn't marked up at all. She highlighted one passage from Chesterton's intro:

In The Hound of Heaven, Chesterton wrote by way of introduction, *Francis Thompson was not running away from a mere Life Force. He was not swiftly escaping from a slow adaptive process called evolution, like a man pursued by a snail. He was dealing with the direct individual relations of God and Man. Francis Thompson was a Catholic, and a very Catholic Catholic. All Christians have their part in him.*

And then she underlined this next one three times:

But the mere Humanist, the mere Humanitarian, the universal aesthete, the patroniser of all religions, **he** *will never know what it was about;* **for he has never been near enough to God to run away from Him.**

Wow, she likes this Chesterton fellow whoever he is. He's a pretty good writer. There're some real zingers in that intro.

Suddenly horns blare behind me.

The light is green.

I throw the book in the back seat and peel forward.

I can't believe Mom still has the wherewithal to buy a book out on the daytrip with the house women, or that she was reading so deeply, underlining and gifting the book to me. How can this be the case when she steals wine and falls down the hill every other week? How can these two capacities co-exist in the same person?

And perhaps more importantly, of all the hundreds of books she could have bought me from the bookstore today, why *The Hound of Heaven?* It's so overtly religious. And she just has never seemed so, or engaged me that way.

Oh well, I'll ponder this over a few martinis momentarily. I'm so glad I'm not a drunk like those Friendly House girls.

If anybody needs a drink they look like they do.

But they can't have one.

Poor things.

63

Dad calls me a few days later and tells me he's got some trouble at the company.

He says his longtime employee and right hand man, Dick, resigned and started a competing business.

Basically, Dad says, the guy's been stealing from me. He's been taking the customers one after the other. Here we'd been talking about a buyout of the business but instead he quits and goes and just steals the customers anyway. He's using our school food service systems—

Theft of trade secrets, I interrupt.

What?

I might be able to stop him in court. A California Supreme Court case came down recently called Reeves v. Hanlon. It says that customer lists can be trade secrets if they're kept confidential. We can get an injunction if the judge follows the law. That's a big if.

Good, he says. But then there's this other guy I hired who said he knew how to run a thermoforming operation and completely lied about his qualifications. I'm into it for hundreds of thousands. On top of that, I think he's trying to take kickbacks from our suppliers. This could shutter our whole operation if I don't do something.

Anything else?

Yeah, we're being sued by three different companies, he says. One says we sold a machine that doesn't do what Dick said it would do, another says we owe them sixty thousand dollars for material that we couldn't use, and the last one says we're infringing on their trade dress with a container we make. Some other people are holding a fifty thousand dollar machine hostage that they never paid for and tell me I have to get a court order to get it back, he says.

Wow, I say, somewhat dazed.

There's more where that came from, he says.

What else could there be?

I have prostate cancer, he says.

The contents of my head begin to liquefy again—

I'm Fifteen.

Mom's at this place called Friendly House supposedly trying to get sober.

That's a laugh.

Doesn't matter anyway.

She's gone.

I don't expect to see her again.

Turns out I know how to let go.

With love?

For now there's just the letting go.

Got my letter jacket for cross-country and track this week.

Turns out I've got some speed.

Whew. Not just a band geek anymore.

One Tuesday Dad says, Hey, wanna go up to Frasier Park and deliver a heat sealer to Safeway with me?

Sure, I say.

He picks me up after practice and we drive on up into the local mountains. We're bachelors now. We do everything together. Even cook our lonely little dinners together.

We deliver the machine to the bakery, do a simple install, make sure it works and head home. No fuss no muss.

A pink and purple sunset sweeps over the Grapevine. The sun disappears and a great wash of fading light remains, periwinkle and lavender.

We listen to Sinatra, Dad's favorite. This time it's Only the Lonely, *a record Frank Sinatra Jr. says should be sold by prescription only:*

So drink up all you people
Order anything you see
Have fun you happy people
The laughs and the joke's on me
Pardon me but I got to run
The fact's uncommonly clear
Got to find who's now her number one
And why my angel eyes ain't here
Excuse me while I disappear

Dad's thinking about Mom I suppose.

I'm thinking about this one dark eyed girl on the drill team I want to ask out.

I'm discovering how to pine away for a woman.

I'm a man now, out with Dad doing manly things, delivering a heat-sealer to a grocery store for money, real money.

Dad uses this money to pay for this car, for my track shoes, for everything we eat.

Is this what awaits me in the world?

Commerce?

I suppose.

For now I'll run.

—Dad, um, what're you going to do about the prostate?

I'm thinking *City of Hope,* he says.

Whatever it takes, I say. Let me know when you want to go out there. It's like eighty miles from the house. You want me to start on those legal problems?

Yes. Please.

So I sue the guy that left the company and tried to take the customers. We get an injunction on theft of trade secret grounds and end up settling for a hundred thousand dollars and an agreement he won't poach Dad's customers for two years.

I file a suit against an alleged creditor and negotiate the alleged sixty thousand dollar debt down to thirty thousand dollars.

I sue the people who hold the machine hostage and eventually get them to give it back after an exchange of the nastiest correspondence I've ever read or written. It just keeps coming. It seems the world has turned against us.

64

A few weeks later Dad's in Las Vegas for a school food service convention.

I get a phone call from a man he's traveling with.

He says, Your father's in the hospital. He may have had a heart attack. I think you'd better come up here. He can't drive back and he might need to have open-heart surgery.

I fly to Las Vegas and meet Dad at the hospital.

He's all hooked up.

I can't get a straight answer from the cardiologist about what he thinks is wrong but he says he wants to transfer him from one hospital to the other and do some kind of exploratory procedure. He says the other option is we could take our chances and drive home to our local hospital in Los Angeles.

I don't like the vagueness of the non-diagnosis.

So we opt to make a run for it.

I get behind the wheel of my Dad's Caddy and squeal out of Vegas headed for a hospital in Long Beach.

Dad keeps popping nitroglycerin and praying.

We listen to Sinatra, *nice 'n' easy.*

I top out at a hundred five miles per hour.

We make it to the hospital.

Dad doesn't need a stent. Turns out it's related to the prostate cancer treatment he'd been receiving.

That's it, he says. I'm taking the damn thing out.

He has the prostate surgery, they take the damn thing out, and he has a few painful complications.

One week I end up at City of Hope twice with Dad and Cedars Sinai once with Mom.

I'm increasingly thrashed.

I've never wanted a sibling so bad, I tell Mom.

You had one, she says.

Christopher, I say.

He would have helped out this week, she says.

Maybe he did, I say.

65

These days I'm broke a lot.

I can't concentrate.

I'm tempestuous, unpredictable.

It gets worse.

Elle and I go with a group to a club in Laguna Beach and everyone drinks way too much.

I'm wasted and dancing with a strange woman. Elle comes out on the dance floor to inquire just what it is I think I'm doing. I'm so drunk I barely remember where I am and inexcusably storm out and begin trudging six miles home up Laguna Canyon Road.

Halfway up the hill, Elle passes me in her car and we have another spat.

I throw my cell phone in the general direction of her car.

It shatters on the pavement.

When I get home I find out Elle fell down the stairs and ended up in the emergency room.

Another weekend we go to Las Vegas with a group and, again, everybody drinks way too much.

One couple gets into a nasty fight.

I end up stuck in a stairwell at *Treasure Island* for hours.

When I come back to the club Elle is dancing with some random guy.

She's drunk, I'm drunk, and we fight all the way back to the *Bellagio* until I leave her in the lobby and head back to our room.

This is not working.

My grandmother dies in Chicago and I go pay my respects. After the funeral, I attend the wake and attempt to match my much tougher and more experienced Midwestern kin gin-gimlet for gin-gimlet in a tribute to grandma and her favorite cocktail.

I wind up lost in the downtown snowdrifts for hours and eventually call Elle weeping about my grandmother, nothing in particular and everything in general.

I fall asleep in the window seat of a Rush Street bar and wake up disoriented.

I call Dad who comes down from the hotel at midnight to get me.

He says, You're lucky the cops didn't pick you up and throw you in the drunk tank for the night. This is Chicago.

They don't coddle you here. You're drinking too much and hard grain alcohol to boot.

He says that like it's a bad thing.

On the same trip I manage to lose my wedding ring.

When I get home, Elle is less than pleased.

66

A few days later Elle and I have *a talk*.

John, she says, I want you to get some professional help.

Gladly, I say. What should I do?

I want you to come see my counselor with me and then get a referral for one of your own, she says.

I'm sorry, I say. This has been bothering me my whole life.

Elle looks at me quizzically.

What has been bothering you your whole life?

I—I don't know.

First the white coats think I have ADD, so they give me a bunch of *Adderall* (legalized speed) and I end up on the roof of the house raking off the leaves for hours and weeping uncontrollably.

Then I go to get some neuro-feedback done, where they wire my head up and tell me to play a specially designed *Ms. Pacman* or other type of videogame with my brainwaves.

I do this three times a week to start.

They sit me in front of a monitor and I look at the game.

I touch nothing.

I try to alter my brainwaves and thereby control the game.

If I think the *right* way—that is, produce the appropriate type of brainwaves, faster or slower—then the little *Ms. Pacman* eats more dots.

But if I think the *wrong* way, *Ms. Pacman* stops or gets eaten by goblins because I was too dumb to produce the right kind of brainwaves.

After a few sessions they inform me they don't think I have traditional ADD because instead of slow cycling brainwaves that cause people to act out or get antsy to wake themselves up, I'm showing overall increased electrical activity in all areas of the brain.

Major anxiety, they say.

They tell me I just need to relax.

No offense doctor, I say, but they've been telling me that my whole life.

Who has?

Coaches, teachers, my boxing trainer, clients—

You have an efficient brain, John, he tells me, but you just need to learn how to shut it off.

They focus on breathing techniques.

You came in here knowing how to breathe, the doctor says. Do that. In through the nose, out through the mouth, maybe six breaths a minute. Not too deep.

They show me my vital signs and my brainwaves with and without the focused breathing.

One day Elle comes with me.

My vital signs are much more soothed out when she's in the room with the brainwave lady and me.

The lady says, Ah—you see what she does for you?

Thanks Elle, you lower my vital signs, I say.

You *raise* mine, she says.

After the next session I take a printout of my brainwave activity to a bar and grill for lunch.

I'm exhausted from the session.

Exhausted from working so hard to relax.

Nothing a crisp lager won't help.

I stare at all those columns of numbers, page after page of figures, all that Hertz from the different lobes, all that electricity coming from where exactly?

Look at all that *energy* recorded on the printout of my brainwaves. It reads like sheet music.

It's like there's a generator up there somewhere.

Is Saint Thomas Aquinas' Uncaused Cause underlying the electrical storm between my ears?

Am I looking at some kind of electro-numeric dispatch from Rumi's *Secret One?*

Who *knows?* Does anybody know?

As it turns out, I don't have time for this sweet-mystery-of-life crap after all. I just want my equilibrium back. A steady income wouldn't hurt either. But whatever's going on in the world it's hard to believe all that electrical energy emanates solely from inside my cranium.

They want me to come back three times a week to play Ms. Pacman with my brainwaves but it's just too weird and too expensive and even though I think there's something to it and after about 20 sessions I end up not going. I felt a little bit different after each session but not much and the effect seemed very short lived.

67

The brainwave games prove inconclusive so other doctors ply me with *Zoloft* and *Lamictal* and Lithium and *Bupropion* and *Adderall* and *Wellbutrin* and *Strattera* and *Buspar* and lions and tigers and bears, oh my!

I'm on a carousel of pills chasing symptoms with drugs that produce more symptoms, and chasing *those* symptoms with more pills, all the while riding a play horse in a maddening circle accompanied by clownish carnival tunes that become increasingly mocking.

I don't like where this is going and I suspect it's going nowhere.

68

One night Elle and I are reading *Nancy Drew* with Nicole, amazed that this strange dated prose regarding a certain Titian haired sleuth is still so captivating.

We read one out loud together called *The Sign of the Twisted Candles* that's so complicated and contains so many references to intellectual property theft and contested estates I wonder if we're accidentally preparing Nicole for the Bar Exam:

At the front porch Nancy came upon another dramatic scene and stepped back a couple of feet into the hall so as not to intrude. Her father was talking to Frank Jemitt, whose back was against an open window in the dining room.

"What was your income from the pastureland last year?" Mr. Drew was saying.

"Only about two hundred dollars."

"Did you give Mr. Sidney an accounting of it?"

"I spent the money fixing up the place."

"In general repairs to the building, or in the restaurant equipment?" Mr. Drew asked.

"I—I forget," Jemitt said, wiping his brow.

"General repairs, of course. Sure, that's right."

Nicole reads leaps and bounds further each time we do it, the amazing plasticity of the child-brain on display, enjoying the wonderment of those tantalizing illustrations that come rarely enough to make them delectable.

I consider Nancy's father for a moment: the ever appropriate and natty Carson Drew. He's a totally flat character, completely virtuous, treating Nancy like a person, not making any moves on his frumpy housekeeper, Hannah Gruen, so named perhaps because no reader would ever picture Mr. Drew in florid passion grabbing a thusly named woman from behind while she does the dishes.

This guy Carson Drew has no problems whatsoever except I suppose for a dead wife—Nancy's conveniently excised mother—whom Mr. Drew is apparently content to mourn in solitude, living for nothing other than the wearing of tweed, community esteem, the steady, dutiful, remunerative practice of law, and to offer Nancy his uniformly sage mentoring as follows:

"What's happened to your appetite?" Hannah Gruen asked Nancy.

Mr. Drew regarded Nancy thoughtfully. "Now then, partner!" he said, rising from the table and putting an arm about his daughter's shoulders.

"Out with it! Something's bothering you."

"Oh dear! You always know, don't you?" Nancy said with a pensive smile.

My man Carson Drew supplies his coltish sleuthing daughter with a stockpile of flashlights for all those caves he allows her to explore—

—in the dead of night—

—with Russians chasing her and her wholesome girlfriends and that handsome Chiclet-toothed footballer Ned, of whom Mr. Drew wholly approves, not the slightest indication he'd like to bury a hatchet squarely between Ned's randy bright blue eyes.

Everything's normal here people.

Carson Drew's nothing more than Nancy's lawyerly father and Nancy's just a Titian-haired sleuth, okay?

Nancy's Mom is dead.

When will you accept it?

Carson Drew has!

We don't see any of Carson Drew's inner struggle.

That's because he doesn't have one.

As a flat character Carson Drew always knows exactly what to do. And if he doesn't Nancy or Hannah will tell him.

Most comfortingly, there's no evidence of any creepy transference between Mr. Drew and Nancy, no hint of Nancy taking the place of her dead mother in Carson Drew's perverse and troubled mind as it inches ever toward madness, prostate swelling like a basketball—

No, no, no. Carson Drew is just fine, man, just fine all the time like a fine red wine—

Great Scott, that's it!!!

I'm gonna try to be like Carson Drew!

What would Carson Drew do?

After all, I'm already a lawyer like him.

I hereby resolve to be practiced, politic and polite.

I could develop a country law practice here in the Greater Los Angeles Area—

I've got some tweed.

Somewhere.

Actually, no. I've still got the showbiz lawyer wardrobe.

Showbiz lawyers don't wear tweed.

But maybe I've got some herringbone or houndstooth in the back of the closet that would prove Carson Drew-like enough.

We'll see.

I commence the next morning to be as steady and boring in all my ways as Carson Drew.

I'll do it for Nicole.

I proceed to rustle a bunch of legal work up from nothing.

My phone keeps ringing and I keep signing up clients.

Client after client after client.

Big, little, civil, criminal, wills, trusts, complex business litigation, two sixth grade girls fighting over a playground injunction in open court, a guy in Georgia who's been awaiting a trial for four years on home arrest, another guy in Federal Prison for slanging some MDMA, a $2,000,000 business loan workout across from Comerica Bank.

I become One Part Carson Drew/One Part Encyclopedia Brown—

No case too big or too small! Or too weird or hopeless!

I wake up one morning and notice my opposing counsel consists of *Jones Day Reavis and Pogue, Lewis Brisbois Bisgaard, & Smith, Katten Muchin Zavis, The District Attorney of Gwinnett County Georgia,* and the *United States Attorney in the Central District of California.*

Suddenly I'm in deep waters with no backup.

One night I go over to the nearby Senior Community and finalize a trust amendment for an elderly woman.

Young Nicole is with me.

She sits in the living room while the family and I pore over the documents on the dining room table.

I wear earth tones tonight.

The notary is here.

My client signs her trust amendment.

It all looks very official and boring.

This is how Carson Drew would do it, I think.

Orthodoxy.

Nicole and I head for home.

I wish I had a mystery to ask her to solve.

She'd solve it, too, I bet.

I bill about $120,000 worth of legal fees in eight months, taking my total earnings for the marriage above $200,000 for the three years.

A wife can't complain about that, can she?

Well perhaps, if none of it sticks.

Well perhaps, if it comes in fits and starts.

Well perhaps, if you still manage to pay the bills late.

Well perhaps, if you're still waking up with a racing heartbeat and shallow breathing and don't know why.

Well perhaps, if you're practicing out of the den and filling the house with the acrid smell of panicked motion practice.

Well perhaps, if you're still having monthly tantrums of one sort or another and smashing the odd inanimate object.

Well perhaps, if you're drinking beer and smoking grass on the sly in the middle of the day just to bring yourself to open the mail.

So even after my earnest Carson Drew Experiment and a six figure earnings demonstration I'm still not right, still in some kind of flat spin over the Azores, spiraling out, out, out and down?

Survey says: yeah, pretty much.

I'm doomed.

There appears to be no origin for my distress, no answer.

I just suffer.

All the time, for no good reason.

I loathe myself. I need a drink.

70

Elle and I agree the new plan is marriage counseling for us and cognitive-behavioral therapy for me.

Well why not?

I've already wired my head and played Ms. Pacman with my brainwaves.

I've taken *Lamictal* and Lithium and Wellbutrin and Adderall and Strattera and Buspar and Zoloft. *Cymbalta, Lexapro* and *Prozac* can wait.

I dumped money on a talk therapist who did no talking.

But marriage counseling four years in?

No good.

Last time it took seven.

And it didn't even work.

Does it ever?

71

This particular marriage counselor seems to get us, to like us even.

That's nice.

We're reasonably clean.

She tells us she's been sitting here since 1977 in this same room counseling people.

I'm confident in her.

After taking our history she first addresses me:

John, she says compassionately, you know our research has shown that the brain scans for people who have post trauma-induced anxiety don't look all that different than the people who have some forms of attention deficit disorder or even aspects of bipolar disorder. There's a therapist down the hall that does good work in this area. I think you should see her on your own.

Elle unloads her frustration about all of the above.

Tearfully.

It kills me to hear it.

I try to take it like a man, respond gently.

I care for her, she's trying her best, but I'm in some kind of a—a vortex.

I don't know what's wrong.

I try to absorb Elle's pain and stay positive about the session but I have this sinking feeling about marriage counseling.

If a couple can't solve their own problems in the quiet of their own bedroom they're probably doomed.

I know I'll come through it, I want to tell her, I just know it!

After all, I made the *Law Review.*

I was voted *Most Likely to Succeed!*

I can't fail. We can't fail. Right?

72

A few days later I go to my first individual counseling session.

I'm told we're going to do some kind of therapy that involves cognitive restructuring.

It's called Eye Movement Desensitization Reprocessing, or EMDR.

My therapist, Jane, says, There's nothing occult or space age about EMDR.

She says, It just has to do with the bilateral engagement of your brain. We're simply going to overwrite or bypass the traumatic memories and resulting impulses and create something new in their place.

Jane tells me that a woman named Francine Shapiro, herself a psychologist, developed this method. In 1987 Dr. Shapiro observed, during a walk in the park, that moving her eyes side-to-side seemed to reduce the stress of disturbing memories. Based on these initial observations she developed standardized procedures to maximize these effects, she conducted further research, and published a study in 1989 describing good results.

It's a bit like pulling a red thread out of a blue quilt, my therapist says, or like recording over a tape.

She continues, The eye movement isn't all that complicated: When you do something like eye movement left to right, or patting your thighs with your palms, left-right, left-right, etcetera, it engages your whole brain and allows the overwriting of the new, good memory and associations to take root, or to be fully received and absorbed by the whole brain. It also helps you keep from being re-traumatized because you sort of switch back and forth between the memory and the safety of the present moment. We believe you create new neural pathways that bypass or overwrite the old neural pathways developed in trauma.

Okay, she says, let's begin: Do you feel discomfort somewhere in your body?

Yes.

Can you describe it?

It's like a tightness in the upper chest, like a hot copper wire stretching from wrist to wrist over the biceps and across the sternum. I can't breathe too good.

How would you prefer to feel?

Calmer, I say, like I can take a full breath.

My eyes spill those hot held-back tears.

I can't stop it, dammit.

It's alright, she says, you're going to cry a lot here. Look at all the tissue on the end table. It's my biggest expense. The tears are a kind of evaporation of the trauma—you'll see, just let them come when they come.

She takes a history. I tell her what I can about my life, about what seems to be ailing me.

In these first few sessions, she says, I'm going to help you to feel safe. Take this box of scented beads; choose a scent that makes you feel calmer if only slightly.

I sniff about ten different scented beads and choose peppermint.

Good choice, she says. Peppermint has been shown to cause a cognitive shift, usually toward confidence, positive stimulation. Keep it with you during the session, in your car, at your desk.

She says, Now I want you to think of a mastered experience, a time where you felt a sense of mastery in the doing of something. But as you do that, watch my right index finger as I move it slowly left to right, right to left. Just keep talking as you do that.

Alright, I say. Uh—

It's okay, she says, take your time.

I pause.

Here's one, I offer. It was my first big race on the high school track team. It was my sophomore year. We were at league finals. I ran varsity all year but the coach thought we should try to pick up points in the frosh-soph division so he dropped me down to that level for the metric mile. But a rival school of ours had the same idea and dropped this sophomore red headed Irish looking kid down to pick up points too. He had flashy spikes.

Jane continues to move her hand and index finger very gracefully. I follow it. Left to right, right to left. Slowly, steadily.

That's okay, she says, just let it come forward as it does—

—When we got to the starting line it was extremely tense, I say. Everyone knew it was a two man race, me against him flat out for four laps.

The gun went off and I almost didn't hear it I was so nervous.

The points were close so everyone was watching this race.

I exploded off the line like a sprinter, like a rabbit.

I was blind. Everything was bright.

I stabilized into a comfortable lead.

The redhead decided to draft off me.

He stayed on my right shoulder until the third lap when I put some distance between us.

But in the second to last turn in the fourth lap, the final lap, he made a strong move.

He surged up on my right shoulder.

I could hear him gasping, I say.

Then I caught his profile out of the furthest reaches of my peripheral vision.

Red hair, red spikes.

I found another gear.

He pulled up, I pulled ahead, he pulled up again, I pulled ahead, he pulled up one more time but fell back.

We were both in a dead sprint.

Everyone was really loud.

I heard someone yelling, *Swing your arms!*

I kicked hard and won by ten feet.

Dad was there, some of my teachers too.

The boys' and girls' teams were all there watching.

It was my first league finals and I went up against a good runner and won the race.

My time was good also, a personal best.

I felt like I was burning from the lungs outward after. I shook hands with everybody, ran into the boys' locker room and blasted a cold shower with my uniform still on.

Jane closes her hand and rests it in her lap.

She asks, And what does that tell you about yourself?

Sometimes—I can rise to the occasion.

How does your chest feel now?

Better, I say. My breathing is deeper. I still feel the wire across my chest but it's not as tight.

Good, she says. When you come back see if you can bring some of your school records. And we'll see if we can't disappear your copper wire altogether. It's hard now because you've got redheads all over you.

73

At our next session we get into the grade school years.

I break out my grade school report cards and standardized tests.

I only have them because Mom catalogued them in a little book with an illustration of happy schoolchildren frolicking toward a little country schoolhouse.

Jane, I've never opened this book, never wanted to review the carnage that was my elementary school academic career.

She says, But you did it. How was it for you?

I expected to see a disaster from the get-go, I say. But when I look at these report cards I see they're solid through fourth grade. The yearly standardized test scores are really high. Even after I fell behind in math class my standardized testing in math stayed strong. I have this memory of always falling behind, getting in trouble, shame, fear of the report card. But that really didn't start until—

Until when exactly?

At the end of second grade little notes start to appear from the teachers. *John seems distracted this quarter,* that kind of thing. Then in third grade I start to act up in class.

The notes say things like, *John is inattentive and disruptive.*
But the grades are still good.

How old were you in the second grade?

Seven or eight, I think. Funny, you know, when I was
in third grade they took me to a doctor because I suddenly
started biting my fingernails. They gave me this sour nail
polish I was supposed to put on but I just chewed right
through it. I still bite my nails. Then in fourth grade I wrote
the word *Help* on a spelling test which I crumpled up and
threw away.

The Sister pulled it out of the trash, read it, called Mom
and a few weeks later I was at a child psychologist's office.

What happened there?

Nothing. I didn't tell him anything. I didn't know what
to say. I didn't want to rat my parents out plus, I don't
think I even connected my problems to the drinking and
the craziness. He had no idea what to ask. It was useless.

Any other physical issues, along the lines of the nail
biting?

I was a bed-wetter pretty late, like ten or something
crazy like that—

Oh boy, she says.

What?

Nail biting, bed wetting, these are hallmark symptoms
of trauma in children.

I ask, Was it really *that bad?* It seems like other kids
went through much worse in their childhoods.

Think of Nicole, she says. What if she were left alone
for two or three days at a time twice a month with your
mother in that state? And then went through the
aftermath? I think what you experienced was at least a
seven out of ten. And, you know, *it just went on for so long*
in your case cutting right through your formative years,
unrelenting until you were fifteen. Your *entire childhood*
was spent in uncertainty: Is there going to be a divorce or

not, is Mom gonna die, what will happen to me? Am I going to get yelled at, shamed, hit?

I stare out the window in some way that concerns her.

Hey, look at me, she says. Enough of the shame-sorrow here. Nail biting, bed wetting, you're lucky you came out as well as you did—what you went through was—there are men your age now in prison, in domestic violence clinics, sleeping on heating grates, even dead—

Stop, please, I say.

Okay. That's enough for today, she says.

I sit in the parking lot in a daze, wiped out.

I don't think my childhood was that bad.

I drive over to *Houston's* and chug two Manhattans and a *Fat Tire.*

I can't do anything for the rest of the day.

I can't even walk the dogs.

Wendell sulks.

74

At the third session I play her a tape I found in a box of old memorabilia, odds and ends and other records.

My parents sent me three or four places over the years to try and help me with math. Ha! There was this interesting operation called the *SOI Institute.*

What was that?

It's based on the work of J.P. Guilford who developed a theory of the intellect stating there are many types of intelligence that are not tested in school and that some people learn differently and that by studying aptitude in these different areas using special testing, you can identify people's strengths and weaknesses. It's been born out, but it's hard to administer and I'm not sure if anyone really uses it anymore. This tape is an evaluation of my test results.

I press play.

The woman going over my results said I aced their test in every area but one and suggested I must have some kind of emotional problem with math because there was no cognitive problem.

She also said my aptitude test says my ideal career would be in the clergy.

I press pause.

What are you thinking of, John?

A couple of things. First, how shocked I was that the test said my ideal career was in the clergy. Ha! What a laugh.

Mm-hm, she says. What else are you thinking about?

I'm Ten.

Nana died a few months ago, right before Thanksgiving.

She made breakfast for us, then said she needed to go to Little Company, and died there by noon.

I learned what Code Blue meant that day.

Mom's been bad again.

Drank three days straight, unconscious for most it.

Couldn't get her cleaned up in time.

Dad yelled at her last night, said something about how he CAN'T BE MARRIED TO A WOMAN THAT—

I put the pillow over my head.

It's like that now.

I've got to keep them from fighting.

It's too dangerous.

They didn't fight as much in front of Nana.

The next day Dad comes into my room and asks me if my math is done.

I say no.

He says, Sit down right now and do your math!

SIT!

But I—

Get it out, he says. NOW what is it?
Long division, I say.
Alright, show me what problems are due today, he says.
I show him.
Do the first one, he says.
He's standing there watching me.
I don't know what to do—
DO IT, he says.
He says, GODDAMMIT JOHN DIVIDE THE FIRST NUMBER—
I write something down.
Dad asks, Does that even make sense?
I—I
SHUT UP. DO IT AGAIN!
I can't.
My eyes burn.
BULLSHIT. DO IT!
I write something in the wrong place.
Dad says, IF YOU PUT THAT REMAINDER IN THE WRONG PLACE AGAIN I'M GONNA BREAK YOUR FINGERS—
What did he say?
Things are getting blurry—
The page goes white.

—A few days later I discover I've missed a deadline to file an important legal brief and I have to beg the court in writing to undo the damage.

I never missed court deadlines before.

I pushed them, maybe blew one or two in ten years, but it was always no harm no foul.

This is different.

If not for the mercy of the court which I must now seek, I will incur millions of dollars in malpractice liability. Because of my lapse, the client stands to lose that much and so I have to pay the client if the court doesn't revive the action.

The clients like me, but if they come after me I'll have no defense. I'll have to declare bankruptcy or leave the country or worse.

I hope the judge is in a good mood when she gets my motion to reinstate the case.

I punch the wall in Elle's living room.

The knuckle above my right ring finger breaks through the drywall, cutting the top of my hand clean open.

Blood drips onto the gleaming wood floor.

Elle's gonna love this.

She'll ask, Why'd you punch a hole in the wall?

I'll say, Because I just incurred a two million dollar debt today.

That'll do wonders for us.

I bet Carson Drew never punched a hole in the wall.

Hannah Gruen would've slapped him stupid.

75

Mom finishes her stint at Friendly House.

She comes home and starts drinking again immediately.

Dad tells me the business is on the brink.

He says he may have to close the doors on a moment's notice.

After thirty-seven years of continuous operation, I say.

I should be helping more.

The drinking, the pressure, the anger, the body's comic fall.

What to do about it?

I don't know but the water is rising around me.

I need a diversion of some sort.

Good thing my twenty year high school reunion starts in five minutes.

I've been hanging banners all afternoon with the other member of the reunion committee who saved my hide when I procrastinated on this thing.

But it came together last minute and we've got two hundred fifty people coming.

It's like planning a wedding.

I'm getting good at that.

The crowd gathers, streaming through the front doors, stopping for their nametags.

It's a pretty, uh, spirited group.

Five hours in the event is totally without restraint.

The music is good but the caterer sucks and everybody gets drunk because there's no food.

We've got *Pretty in Pink* projected on the wall.

People are making out in the photo booth.

Oh Lord, they're bringing in kegs now.

The management threatens me.

I tell them they'll rue the day if they shut us down.

We do a raffle which quiets things down for about a half hour.

Toast to us, one guy yells.

I raise my glass and say, We're the best class that ever was or ever will be. We totally dominate all other classes. We're rad.

Sláinte!

A classmate of mine named Rose places a cross in my hand, a very special cross, one of the ones that they passed out on our class retreats back in high school.

Our class retreats had a *Breakfast Club* quality, except with Catholic overtones—like prayer and no doobage—and took place up in the local mountains.

It's hard for teenagers to really talk to each other but up there it seemed possible.

I never got one of the little retreat crosses for some reason.

I haven't seen one in years.

They have an unusual byzantine design and hang on a maroon string.

My classmate places it in my hand and says, It seems to me you need this right now.

Thank you, I say.

I place it around my neck.

Eventually the Torrance Police shut us down and dozens of us migrate over to the besieged Torrance *Marriot* bar.

I get to talking with some old Latin classmates of mine.

Hey man, you were hi-larious in Latin, they say.

A legend, another guy says.

One says, Yeah, do you remember the time Carmichael didn't have his homework done—

Which time?

They laugh and slap me on the shoulder.

I'm Fourteen
Latin.
Second period.
I love the green-eyed girl in front of me.
So I make funny noises and bug her.
She hates me.
But she likes me too.
How does courtship work in high school?
There's got to be more to it than funny noises.
The Principal is our Latin teacher.
Father Murphy.
He has a heavy Irish brogue—
John, he commands, conjugate this verb: Amo.

Amo, Amas, Amant...
The third word is Amat, he bellows.
I—
Did you do your homework last night, John?
Yes, I say.
Where is it?
I—I left it in my locker.
A big, obvious lie.
Why didn't I just say no?
Go get it then, Father says.
I stare at him dumbly.
We'll wait, he says.
I burst into the hallway in a panic.
Can I manage to do the homework on the way back to class, maybe on the back of the book as I walk?
No, I couldn't even do it sitting still.
I can't think.
Plus, I know nothing about Latin.
Mom's drinking; Dad's away.
I'm staying at a neighbor's house and they have two girls.
How embarrassing.
Finals are only a week away.
Dad's gonna be out of town then, too.
I get to my locker and spin the combination with a fumbling hand.
Oh, I don't know what to do.
I told Father the homework was in my locker.
It's not in my locker.
Are they all sitting there in silence waiting for me?
I hate being a Freshman.
I want to die.
I wish I could die. Can I just die now?

I burst back into class empty handed and shout, SOMEONE BROKE INTO MY LOCKER AND STOLE MY LATIN BOOK! MY HOMEWORK WAS IN IT—

Father Murphy looks at me for a minute.

His face turns crimson.

Everybody stifles laughter.

Father says quietly, Sit down.

He says nothing further on the subject until after class.

When everybody's gone from the room he asks, John, why did you take Latin?

I say, I don't know. I just like the sound of it, I guess. It's like music.

Huh, he says. That's one of the better reasons I've heard. It's still the official language of the Catholic Church, you know. One might say it is a language eternally unchanging and specially reserved for prayer.

Oh, I say.

He says, You're very clever and I don't understand why you're failing. Can you tell me why?

No.

I still think we can make a diplomat out of you, he says. I'll get you a tutor, he offers.

Tomorrow's Friday, Father says, so I'm gonna recite the whole of Elegy Written in a Country Churchyard. No Latin for an hour. I think you'll like it. It's a grand poem. So no homework tonight, okay?

Thanks, I say.

I'm about to cry. I throw my backpack over my shoulder and head for the door.

Father Murphy says, John—

Yes Father, I say.

I'm going to tell you the most important thing I can think of to help you. It's a famous Latin saying with which every young Latin scholar should be familiar: Age quod agis, he says. Ah-jay quod ay-yees, he says more slowly.

I don't know what that means, I say.

Of course not, he says. Translate it. It's worth knowing.

—At the reunion the now grown up green-eyed girl from Latin class whom I loved taps me on the shoulder.

She says, I've always wanted to tell you something.

I'm married now, I say.

She laughs.

I'm serious, my wife's at the bar, I say. That was then this is now—

You didn't even shave then, she says. I was taller than you. And I was only five-two.

The testosterone finally kicked in when I was thirty and I took a growth spurt—

I liked you, she says, but you were a little boy. And plus all you did was bug me!

Yeah, all you did was sit there—

While you made those strange noises, she says.

Depriving you of your education, I say.

Father Murphy actually called me into his office and said I had to ignore you. I got in trouble for it, she says. For *your* rotten behavior!

I didn't know I had the Principal working against me, I say. I feel better now. There's no way I could've overcome that. Not even with Dad's *Old Spice*.

There you have it, John. The Principal shut you down.

Sounds like he shut *you* down, I say.

She laughs.

I could be upset with Father Murphy for salting my game, I say, but that guy was looking out for me for some reason.

Here's to Father Murphy, she says, and clinks the rim of her wine glass against my tumbler of scotch.

161

I ask, Did he ever tell you any secret little phrases in Latin?

Ha, like I would remember, she laughs.

He said something to me once—it was a saying, *Age quod agis*—He told me it was the most important thing he could teach me.

Did you ever look it up?

Yeah, I say.

It means, *Do What You're Doing.*

He really liked you, she says. So do I.

She kisses me on the cheek and disappears into the throng of *Bishop Montgomery Knights,* God bless every one.

I stand alone for a minute and then the wife of a friend of mine walks up to me.

She's an impressive sort. Tall, gorgeous, whip smart. You can't dismiss her even if she has some cosmic-type ideas.

She says she's starting a dating website that uses playing cards to determine love matches.

She says the so-called Birth Card is the most important one and can tell you a lot about a person.

Playing cards are mysterious, I say.

She asks, What's your birthday?

June third, I say.

She says, Oh, you're an Ace of Spades. Your wife's one too. I just asked her about her birthday.

I ask, What happens when one Ace of Spades marries another Ace of Spades?

She says, You can go on our website and find out.

The class reunion finally ends.

Later, Elle and I are alone on the balcony of our hotel room.

She kisses me hard.

She saw that girls used to like me.

Elle says, There were these women in line that said, Oh look there's John Carmichael!

Ha. Old class presidents never die, I say. They just run for their homeowner association boards.

It was good for me to see that, she says.

There was like, a desperation in it, though, I say, the way I tried to be memorable to people back then.

High school's a desperate time, she says.

Now's a desperate time, I say.

I love you, she says.

The next day I go on my friend's Love Cards Dating website and check it out. I look up my, uh, birth card. The copy reads:

The Ace of Spades is the Birth Card for people who were born January 13, February 11, March 9, April 7, May 5, June 3 and July 1. The Ace of Spades is the ancient symbol of the secret mysteries, the most spiritual card in the deck, and yet, also the most material. The Ace of Spades person usually has a life-long conflict between their material, worldly urges and their deep spiritual heritage. Their displacement and Karma Card, the Seven of Hearts, suggests trials in the realm of relationships. Their mission is to find the inner peace that comes through a life of service and dedication to higher principles. They come to realize this and learn to follow the unwritten law of spiritual truth. In many ways they have put themselves upon the cross. Whenever they deviate from the law, or disregard their spiritual nature, they seem to be unjustly punished. Those Ace of Spades who are mostly materially minded seem to have one problem after another. However, whenever they do follow the law, they are protected, finding the inner peace they seek through awareness of their wealth of spirit.

Hmm. Interesting, but—
Doesn't that apply to everybody?

Part Six: The Mountain Lake
Quote of the Day: Anima Christi, sanctifica me
Preferred Handheld Device: iPhone
Condition of Soul: Like a newborn infant, slapped awake

77

It was deep in Aliso Canyon, which spills out onto the southernmost spot in Laguna Beach, when the questions first seriously, well—no, *urgently,* occurred to me:

Are all my problems purely *psychological?*

Or could I perhaps be in the midst of a genuine spiritual awakening?

I'm not talking woo here, or subtle musings about *energy* with Elle over a bottle of wine.

My catastrophic breakdown seems to have a shape somehow, a *form* of some kind, a purpose.

Can both things be occurring at the same time—a psychological breakdown and a spiritual awakening—or does one masquerade as the other? This is no longer an academic question. I'm in serious trouble here.

Is that what my grave disturbance is?

A *spiritual* thing?

People throw that word around like it's nothing.

And yet great volumes have been written.

I don't know where to begin.

There's a discipline to real inquiry.

I'm not a dilettante.

The spiritual longing—if that's what it really is, and not just psychological pain—aches deep in me now.

All this psychology I've been doing to try and feel better, to function better—am I rearranging the deck chairs on the *Titanic?* That's how it feels, like I'm missing the point somehow.

78

I spend another three-hundred miles on foot traversing peaks and canyons with Wendell and Louise, the three of us drinking down more than our share of salty air. Then on a Spring afternoon in a stand of fifty thousand yellow blooms, I decide the answer is *yes*—absolutely. There seems to be a truly *spiritual* component to my anguish!

I seem to know suddenly and with great clarity, standing here in this rush of green sprigs and young flowers, that it's my spirit that aches and groans. I know this as plain as I know my unseen lungs gasp within my thorax. And all this time I've been trying to treat the psyche alone. It seems the spirit is distinct from the psyche. Perhaps I know this from process of elimination, having tried everything else, or perhaps I'm receiving a special inspiration of some sort. In any case the awareness presents itself as knowledge, not as a mere hunch.

The implications of this assessment are huge. I'll probably have to accept the validity of the word *spiritual* once and for all—accept it as a description of a *reality*—accept it as more than just a mere placeholder for ineffable human yearning, more than a mere metaphor for yet another dimension of the psyche.

So it's body, mind, and *spirit* after all. That's not just something *they* say to sell granola bars and yoga videos.

I'll have to satisfy myself of what the word *spiritual* actually means, not only what *they say* it means because *they say* a lot of different things.

It sounds like an awful lot of work.

What if it comes to nothing?

Everyone's already lost patience with me.

I'll surely lose everything now if I set out to do something this impractical.

I look down at Wendell panting.

I glance around at the grassy hillside.

The surging two o'clock gusts press the grass flat against the earth then release—

Light green, dark green, light green, dark green—

I hold on to my hat.

Wendell and Louise beam looking into the sun.

A hawk makes a reverberating sound near *Robber's Cave.*

the temple bell stops
but the sound keeps coming
out of the flowers

After the walk I head to a library and commence a vaguely directed scientific, metaphysical, religious, philosophical, and artistic quest—I suppose I'm to start looking for a rationally satisfying intersection between all five.

Where to start—online or in the stacks?

We'll go to the stacks first.

Among many other writers who troubled themselves with such God-bothering inquiries, I find myself drawn to C.S. Lewis and George Santayana. They were spiritual fence-sitters and wrote reams and reams about their doubt and, in Lewis' case, his eventual conversion to Anglicanism.

Santayana, by his own admission, remained forever standing at the Church door, calling himself a mere *aesthetic Catholic,* but content to end his life at the Convent of the Blue Nuns of the Little Company of Mary on the Celian Hill in Rome, where he was happily cared for by the Irish sisters until his death.

Lewis, like Santayana, was an intellectual.

Perhaps that's why Lewis consumed so many pages to explain his conversion first to Theism, and then to Anglicanism.

It would be important for an intellectual like Lewis to show he'd really *thought it through,* since his self-conception at that time was rooted in his smarts, his Oxford professorship, his academic acuity. Of course, as with most literary geniuses, Lewis was not without a gift for brevity:

I was at this time of living,
like so many Atheists or Anti-theists,
in a whirl of contradictions.
I maintained that God did not exist.
I was also very angry with God for not existing.
I was equally angry with God for creating a world.

79

Wendell forces me out for miles into the rises and gullies of Saddleback Valley. Sometimes we go up to the foot of the mountains, or down into the dramatic wilderness above Laguna Beach.

My walks with Wendell and Louise begin to mirror the monastic prayer cycle of lauds and vespers.

One morning early I go away from the ocean toward Saddleback Mountain and find myself completely lost for the first time ever while walking the dogs.

I'm in a steep valley surrounded by long grassy rises and see upon a distant ridge what looks like a monastery or a church.

I head for those remote structures in search of directions back to the main road.

I find a Buddhist monastery nestled into the foothills below the mountain.

There's a giant bull sitting in the middle of the road at the entrance gate.

It glares at the dogs as we pass by.

I think it must be a really calm Buddhist bull that they've taught to meditate.

I enter further into the grounds and this one guy who was there on a retreat says, Did you walk by the bull?

Yes, I said. It's amazing he's so calm. Is he a pet?

No. He's from a neighboring stud ranch. We don't know what he's gonna do. They're coming to pick him up. I'd go back the other way if I were you.

Oh, I say.

I head West and stop at a Catholic Abbey for semi-monastic priests.

I'm fairly well stunned to find the two religious centers up in these remote hills. Who knew?

The habit-clad priests look striking as they process from an outer building toward their chapel for what must be some kind of noon prayer.

I stop one of the priests. He smiles looking down at Wendell and Louise.

What a beautiful creature, he says in reference to Wendell.

I tell him I'm lost and ask for directions. He points the way down the hill back to my car. It's still quite a ways off he tells me but I'm heading the right direction at least.

I ask what kind of priestly order they are.

He says, We're a religious order of Catholic priests that believe in a balance between contemplative prayer life and active involvement in and service to the community. Our order was founded about eight hundred years ago in Europe.

That sounds pretty good to me, I say, stunned that a Catholic priest in full habit stands before me amidst the glib modernity of the surrounding housing developments that dot the hillside.

80

Later that same week a strange story hits the international news. The Pope has announced that the Latin Mass would be made more widely available again. It was a complicated announcement, but it seemed everywhere all at once.

First I bump into the priests up in the hills and now this.

I feel like I should go to one of them Latin Masses.

I wonder if those priests up there do anything like that.

They seem like they would.

I get online and find out they have a Latin Mass at the Mission in San Juan Capistrano.

I made a little Styrofoam model of one of the Missions just like every California kid who endured the fourth grade.

But I don't know Mission San Juan Capistrano except for something about the swallows.

The Latin Mass, otherwise known as the Tridentine Mass, was always described to me as a sort of superstitious affair where the priest turned his back to the congregation and mumbled in Latin.

It always sounded really obscure to me.

Yet I'm suddenly and inexplicably driven see what this thing is all about.

81

I arrive at the Mission grounds on a Sunday morning and wander into the main Basilica—a grand and cavernous domed structure far larger than the original church at the South end of the property that crumbled during the great quake of 1812.

There's no Latin Mass in here, a man tells me.

No?

You gotta go over to the Junipero Serra Chapel, he says, you'll love it. It's the oldest building still in continuous use in the State of California. It's a very special place, built in 1771. Junipero Serra himself said Mass there you know.

Thanks, I say.

On the way over to the Junipero Serra Chapel I happen upon an attractive silver haired woman clutching a *Saint Gregory's Hymnal* and a bunch of sheet music.

Pardon me, I ask her, but do you know the way to the Junipero Serra Chapel?

I do so, young man. I'm going there right now, she says. Would you like to walk with me?

Sure. This is my first time going to a Latin Mass, I say.

Really? That's so wonderful for you, she says. I was lucky enough to grow up with it.

She drops the sheaf of papers she's holding and the music flutters to the ground, revealing page after page of Gregorian chant, Latin incantations, and other compositions I've never seen with names like *Adoramus Te* and *Panis Angelicus.*

I'm a bit of a musician, I tell her.

Oh really? Would you like to join our little choir?

Oh, uh, here—

I hand her the music.

We need a man, she says. *Any man will do!!!*

That's a pretty low standard, I say, but I can't sing.

You can sing, she says. What instrument do you play?

I play the saxophones and other reeds—

Perfect, she says, just perfect. I used to teach music in grammar school in Los Angeles Unified. If you can play a horn of any kind, you can sing. Did you play in college?

Yes, I say. I was in the jazz ensemble at the University of—

In a conservatory?

The jazz band was in the conservatory, yeah—

And you claim you can't sing, she says. You can sing! Don't try to get out of this.

I took Latin in high school, I say, but I wasn't a very good student.

If you play music and took Latin then God surely sent you here, she said.

Ha, I say.

We need you, she says. Think about it. We're singing the High Mass today.

She smiles and walks ahead of me to catch up with a few other veiled and intriguing women who must be her choir mates.

I clop down the red-tiled ninety-foot entrance to the Junipero Serra Chapel.

A trellis bearing an ancient looking grape vine shelters the walkway.

I notice a courtyard cemetery off to my right and feel a quavering along the base of my skull.

The ruins of the original stone church are on the other side of the covered walkway.

I see some swallow nests clustered in one of the remaining arches.

Unlike the big stone church in ruins right next to it, Father Serra's little chapel with the thick adobe walls fared well in the quake of 1812.

82

When I enter the doorway in the back of the chapel I'm spellbound by a gilded retablo covering the wall behind the altar—a regal blast of gold leaf baroque wood carving.

The apse above and across from the altar features an unseen window that invites morning sun to strike the golden backdrop.

The walls are four feet thick.

The steps to the choir loft are composed of rough-hewn masonry, heavy on the mortar, uneven but artful.

Whoa. I thought there was nothing to Orange County architecture but strip malls and tract homes—

What is *this* doing here?

What am *I* doing here?

The chapel is long and narrow, framed by a series of cross-hatching beams painted an intricate pattern of flawless maroon, maze and Spanish green.

To the right the rear of the chapel is a small anteroom housing a statue of Saint Peregrine—the patron saint of cancer and serious illnesses—his sculptural likeness tucked in a bank of flickering candles in red holders.

People are praying intensely in and around that room, some of them in wheelchairs.

Many of the women in the chapel wear veils—white, black, navy, grey. Most people are kneeling, praying the Rosary.

Where *am* I?

I'm dizzy with the time machine lurch of it all.

There's only here.

I sit next to the most devout looking woman I can find.

She looks like Celia, my grandmother, and prays the Rosary like her, with a deep fervency—like there's actually something to it.

I look around.

To think I showed up here in jeans and a flannel shirt.

What a bum.

At this Mass people dress like they're dressed to meet God for the first time. I sit for a minute and try to get quiet but all I want to do is look at everything, to merge more fully into this living European painting inexplicably lodged in Orange County, California.

The congregation is composed of dark oils.

Their movements are heavy brushstrokes.

The sun rises further and the altar becomes a conflagration of golden light.

He sees angels in the architecture,
spinning in infinity.
He says, Hey! Hallelujah!

Dank incense pervades the chapel and the air itself seems to have been sealed since 1777.

The organist plays a mysterium tremendum of a chord progression that invigorates the sturdy, thick-walled structure with slow-wave vibration.

The priest and four altar servers process from the sanctuary behind the altar.

The choir begins to sing.

The first delicate note emerges from the lead soprano's throat, caroms off the high earth wall and strikes me clean in the left ear.

The small bones of my ear are electrified by the sound of it.

I spin around to see who or what is making that sound.

The choir is backlit, and the women are veiled silhouettes, outlined in luminosity.

They sound like angels.

Plain and simple.

Angels.

No other way to say it.

Singing directly to God.

The lady in the parking lot was right though.

They could use a man.

Some male voices would really balance the sound. I mean, how can they even do the four part harmony—

They can't really.

Mass lasts for an hour and twenty minutes.

There are moments where I fight back tears.

What's that about?

It is without a doubt the most beautiful, most mystical, most deeply fulfilling religious ceremony I've ever witnessed.

Even within the hour I felt something shift in me.

Mainly I leave with a hot stone in my throat and a ringing in my ears.

Is it *possible*—I'm—*Catholic?*

83

Two weeks later I join the choir.

Our first rehearsal is at the choir director's home which I find to be comfortingly Catholic.

It just smells Catholic.

I can't explain it.

Most Orange County houses I've been in smell like cleaning agents and newness. This one, well, I just sense something a little homier, a little more familiar, a little *safer* somehow.

There's a statue of Saint Cecilia, the patron saint of musicians, atop the organ in the corner of the living room.

A grand piano sits in the other corner.

There're only eight of us: six women, one of whom also leads the group and plays the organ, and two men, consisting of a local certified public accountant and my stunned-to-be-here self.

They found two men, it turns out, him and me.

Two men, six women, one pipe organ.

I'm informed the choir must now get ready for Easter, and thus we're to learn and rehearse the Mass of the Shepherds composed by Pietro Yon.

They pass it out.

It's thirty pages long.

It's in Latin.

And I can't sing.

The first rehearsal is painful.

We men are bad.

Really bad.

The women try to be encouraging, but I can sense in at least one of them a deep concern, bordering on horror, that the two male neophytes are going to destroy more than a millennium of mostly consonant liturgical tradition by singing the *Mass of the Shepherds* as though it were something that emerged from Stravinsky's round file.

Our pitch is off, flat or sharp, our tone is thin and reedy, our rhythm is questionable, our reading of the Latin not so bad but choppy and *Hooked on Phonics*-like.

And yet the choir director has Saint Cecilia on her side, the patron saint of musicians. She works with the two of us after hours and makes some progress.

That's good since Easter is only six weeks away.

84

One day I call my accountant choir mate and tell him we need to have a sectional like I used to have in school bands. You know, all the saxes get together and do their part—

That sounds good, he says. I just bought a keyboard at *Target* for a hundred fifty bucks. He asks, Can you come to my office say Friday at one?

Sure.

When I get to his accounting office I see the poor man is drowning in the chaos of tax season, with his hundred fifty dollar keyboard on an outer-office desk, plucking out bass notes and trying to match them with his naturally deep voice.

Surrexit Christus! he sings, and goes plunk, plunk/plunk, on the keyboard.

That sounds pretty good, I fib, hoping that after an hour together we'll cause something resembling choral music to emerge from our dry, crackly throats.

We sit for forty-five minutes picking our way through the Kyrie and the Gloria, trying to get the emphasis in the right places, never mind the pitch:

Glória in excélsis Deo: et in terra pax homínibus bonae voluntátis. Laudámus te, benedícimus te, adorámus te...

Pretty scary sounding the way we do it.

Then the mailman walks in.

He stares at the two of us in coat-and-tie hunched over the tinny sounding keyboard singing in Latin and asks, *So I guess the accounting thing isn't working out, huh?*

85

Easter Sunday arrives.

We two men know seventy percent of the *Mass of the Shepherds* to sixty percent proficiency.

We'll see what happens.

This is to be my first time in the choir loft.

The men have been under wraps for six weeks, woodshedding in Latin.

This is our big debut.

I climb the asymmetrical brick staircase.

I have a hopeful sense about the ascension into the loft.

This is the Mission San Juan Capistrano.

We're in the oldest usable building in California.

Father Serra offered Mass here.

I can't wait to see the view of the chapel from the loft.

It's going to be magnificent!

I enter the loft and get an attack of vertigo and claustrophobia—

It's only six by twelve with two risers and an organ.

It's a stunningly small space, disorienting in its dimensions and angles.

Hundreds of organ pipes stand behind primitive wooden slats that open and close for volume control.

The loft is under construction; the organ is in a million pieces.

We stand on a plywood floor among buckets of bolts and organ parts. There're strange and dangerous work tools leaning up against the walls offering a dozen ways to trip.

We take our places, two men on the back riser, five inches in front of the disassembled pipes of the pipe organ, and the five sopranos and altos in front.

Then the choir director arrives with her own *Target*-bought keyboard to compensate for the disassembled organ.

She sets the keyboard atop the organ and prepares to play it at chest height.

This looks physically impossible.

She balances the music precariously atop the keyboard and begins to play. She's out of breath, we're out of breath, but suddenly the Mass begins.

Everything starts to move real fast like in the boxing ring—

In the middle of the *Kyrie* the choir director's little keyboard starts to slide off the top of the large inert organ beneath it and into my ribcage.

I grab the keyboard—right it, hold it—hold her music with my left hand—hold my music with my right hand, and sing—

And sing and sing and sing and sing and sing.

They warned me the High Mass is mostly singing but this is like wall-to-wall stem-to-stern singing that goes the length of the Mass for an hour and fifteen minutes.

The whole thing is sung!

We sing the entrance, the Mass parts, an offertory hymn, Communion hymns, the propers, a recessional.

The priest chants Scripture.

We engage in call and response with the priest.

Whatever else can be sung we sing it.

We're on our feet practically the whole time—

The Mission bells ring at nine and light breaks through the window wholly illuminating the altar and the gilded retablo.

The robust clanging of Mission bells punctuates Communion.

86

When I get home Elle asks, How was it?

I tell her that either I'm high on incense or that was the best thing I've ever done in my entire life.

The best thing?

Yes, I say. Better than my first kiss, winning, chocolate mousse, a massage, catching a wave, throwing a football in the surf—in fact the only thing that ever came close was playing in a big band in college.

Nice. Was the chapel totally packed?

Yeah, but I didn't really notice that too much. It went so fast. I was looking at the music most of the time. Or upwards through the rafters. We're so close to the ceiling in that crazy little loft. I read somewhere that in the Latin Mass the choir is supposed to be singing to God. Just like the priest and the congregation face God together, all souls facing the same direction—the symbolism is just, well—it reminds me of court somehow, but spiritual. I kept thinking of the last star at the edge of the universe, or before the universe curls in on itself, back to itself, back to its origins. Our voices were directed beyond there—to the Most High.

She eyes me warily, as I'm sounding a bit too specifically and suddenly *religious* for her taste, she of the *I-believe-in-ghosts-and-marriage-is-spiritual* persuasion.

87

This *spiritual* versus *religious* thing: I can feel the debate approaching. I'm not sure with whom it will be, but it's coming. The phrase *spiritual-but-not-religious* rolls off the tongues of so very many Californians it's damn near becoming a state motto, an irreligious creed. It sounds so good and tumbles from the lips so easily.

But suddenly now, it falls hard on my ear.

It sounds rather like a slur, implying of course that religious people are *not* spiritual, just mindless automatons pantomiming prayers and rituals they were brainwashed into mimicking. But I think of the priests in the hills, I think of the choir, I think of the Mass itself. These people and these rituals embody a level and form of spirituality I have never before encountered. Frankly it puts the *spiritual-but-not-religious* people to shame.

Most of the people I know who espouse the *spiritual-but-not-religious* creed don't have much to say about their spiritual life, don't seem to have much discipline, don't really seem to *do* much of anything except go about their daily business seeking whatever it is they'd otherwise seek if they weren't *spiritual-but-not-religious*.

If *spirit* exists in truth, then declaring oneself spiritual is of the same character as declaring oneself corporeal. So *what* you're spiritual? You've got a spirit as sure as you've got a body and a mind so *of course* you're *spiritual*. And corporeal. And intellectual. Now what about it? It would seem that's where religion just begins to speak—at the acknowledgment of spirit—just as medicine and nutrition and fitness begin to speak about the body as a necessity merely of its welfare. One doesn't end the discussion of the body by declaring that they have one. So what? And neither should someone declare themselves *spiritual* without considering the implications of just what it is the spirit may need.

What a fool I've been.

A few weeks later I start taking pictures in the various Laguna canyons with my phone.

When I'm out in nature now I'm less and less startled by the enormous surges of energy coursing through my being.

I don't know what to call it.

Is this *ecstatic love?*

I find myself both viewing the landscape and seeing Majesty in it, but now also experiencing a somewhat unsettling sense that something is looking back at me.

This last sensation I'm not so sure about. It recalls the experience described in *The Hound of Heaven* Mom gave me, a sense of being pursued. It's not entirely pleasant:

I FLED Him, down the nights and down the days;
I fled Him, down the arches of the years;
I fled Him, down the labyrinthine ways
Of my own mind; and in the mist of tears
I hid from Him, and under running laughter.
Up vistaed hopes I sped;
And shot, precipitated,
Adown Titanic glooms of chasmèd fears,
From those strong Feet that followed, followed after.
But with unhurrying chase,
And unperturbèd pace,
Deliberate speed, majestic instancy,
They beat—and a Voice beat
More instant than the Feet—
'All things betray thee, who betrayest Me.'

I have to go back and read all that stuff Mom underlined from the introduction by Chesterton:

What we mean, Chesterton wrote, *when we say that 'The Hound of Heaven' is a real religious poem, is simply that it would make no sense...if we supposed it to refer to anything but a personal Creator in relation to a personal creature. ...The poet was dealing with the direct individual relations of God and Man, and the story would be senseless to anybody who thought the service of Man is a substitute for the service of God. But the mere Humanist, the mere Humanitarian, the universal aesthete, the patroniser of all religions, he will never know what it was about, for he has never been near enough to God to run away from him.*

Mom couldn't speak of these concepts to me, but she could pluck a book out of the tens of thousands at the bookstore and underline a few key passages from the introduction. Again, I ask, how was that even possible in her terribly diminished state?

I go back to the stacks to learn more of this Chesterton fellow and find out what a major figure he was as an English writer, apologist, and eventual Catholic convert. Chesterton's own conversion to Catholicism took place over a decade or more. I find an essay by Dale Ahlquist, President of the American Chesteron Society on the subject of Chesterton's analysis of conversion to the Catholic Faith, wherein he describes three stages. As a cradle Catholic coming to a strange new understanding of the Faith, I can relate to this:

Five years after he finally entered the Church, Chesterton wrote The Catholic Church and Conversion. *He says that although all roads lead to Rome, each pilgrim is tempted to talk as if all roads had been like his own road. The Church is a house with a hundred gates; and no two men enter at exactly the same angle. But he needn't have worried about making too personal a statement. Almost every convert will recognize the three stages of conversion that Chesterton describes: The first stage is, Patronizing the Church. The second, Discovering the Church. And the third is...Running away from the Church.*

The convert takes his first step rather unwittingly when he decides he's going to be fair to the Catholic Church. He does not think the Roman religion is true, but for the first time, he also doesn't think that the accusations against the Church are true. This important first step leads to a long and enjoyable second step, which is the utter fascination of learning what the Catholic Church really does teach. Chesterton says this is the most pleasant part of the business, easier than joining the Catholic Church and much easier than trying to live the Catholic life. It is like discovering a new continent full of strange flowers and fantastic animals, which is at once wild and hospitable. But then the convert suddenly realizes with a shock that he can no longer be detached and impartial about the Catholic Church.

Chesterton wrote: It is impossible to be [merely] just to the Catholic Church. The moment a man ceases to pull against it he feels a tug towards it. The moment he ceases to shout it down he begins to listen to it with pleasure. The moment he tries to be fair to it he begins to be fond of it.

But then comes the final stage: fear. It's one thing, says Chesterton, to conclude that Catholicism is good and another to conclude that it is right. It is one thing to conclude that is right and another to conclude that it is always right. At that delicate last stage, Chesterton observes that it is no longer the Church's enemies who are holding the convert back, but only the word of a Catholic can keep him from Catholicism. One foolish word from inside does more harm than a hundred thousand foolish words from outside. He points out a problem that plagues the Church still: Catholics who not only do a very poor job of presenting their faith, but actually manage to repel converts who are pounding on the door trying to get in. Every Catholic would do well to read this book. Besides being better equipped to deal with converts, they would have a deeper appreciation of the faith in which they were formed. Especially the realization that the Church, as Chesterton says, is larger on the inside than it is on the outside.

Every era tries to create a new religion, something more befitting the age, but new religions are only suited to what is new. And what is new is soon old. Chesterton argues that the Catholic Church has all the freshness of a new religion, but it also has the richness of an old religion. It does not change with people's tastes. It is a religion that binds men to their morality even when they are not in the mood to be moral. The Church often has to go against the grain of the world. It has preached social reconciliation to fierce and raging factions who would much rather destroy each other. It preached Charity to the old pagans who did not believe in it, just as it now preaches chastity to the new pagans who do not believe in it.

Chesterton wrote, We do not really need a religion that is right where we are right. What we need is a religion that is right where we are wrong.

Chesterton had already proved himself a champion of tradition against faddism, but he made it clear to his doubters and detractors that one of the main reasons for becoming Catholic was that Catholic Church is the only thing that saves a man from the degrading slavery of being a child of his age. He found everything else narrower and more restrictive. In the Church he found freedom. Dizzying freedom, he claimed. If that is not surprising enough, it should be sobering if not stunning to any honest reader of Chesterton to consider that this intellectual giant found a home for his mind in the Catholic Church. Not a home as a *place merely to rest, but as a place of great activity and excitement. This is revealed in one of the most challenging statements Chesterton ever made: To become a Catholic is not to leave off thinking, but to learn how to think.*

89

On my twice daily treks with the dogs above Laguna Beach and along the foot of Saddleback Mountain, I find myself hungry to try and photograph the experience of being *hounded* by Majesty—not the experience of staring at pretty flowers—but the sense of the flowers staring back.

Surely I've gone mad.

The dogs have to wait on the trail or in the brush while I set up the shots.

I step on the leash with my foot and try to hold the camera steady as Wendell attempts to take me off my feet.

It's really a kind of contact sport; can I get a shot off with Wendell having none of it?

I've never been a shutterbug but some of the things I'm feeling out here demand to be photographed.

Or is it the way I'm suddenly seeing things out here?

It's like, uh, energy sources, energy changing form, fog evaporating over the rim of the hill, shafts of light, the sun, emerging annual grasses, translucent leaves, *God?*

Does one really presume to try and photograph God?

Is everything God?

Or is this merely His creation?

90

God/God/God

How can I even begin with this God business?

For real, I mean.

186

I have to overcome the spiritual impediments of a lifetime: a hundred cheesy figurines, a thousand inspirational refrigerator magnets, Charles Burns as God, the seeming silence from the throne, the idea that central to the Grand System consists of living things eating other living things, the horrors methodically devised by people to torture, control and humiliate other people, the conflicting religious views—

It's these and a cavalcade of other images that make it barely possible for me to even formulate the word God without immediately dismissing the idea as I always have.

We're just meat puppets, right?

Just primitive biological machines, as my psychiatrist put it.

Well—

I need to think about that a little bit.

I've seen some things lately—the electrical energy from my brain in the neuro-feedback sessions, the subatomic swirl becoming more apparent with every passing experiment in particle physics, the strangely heightened awareness that began some months ago and continues, flourishes, even in the face of my seeming inability to function, Nicole's Cloud People, the searing sense of otherworldly power in that Mass—how long will I listen to *them* tell me I'm just a meat puppet?

But that leap from a general sense of a spiritual reality to *Catholicism,* I mean, how would I ever make it? Funny how some Protestants say Catholics aren't Christian. How silly. The Mass is jam packed with Jesus alpha to omega. It's a Jesus fest. We listen to His teaching. Then we eat Him and drink Him like He said to. You can't get more Jesus-y than that. But I've got a bit of a Jesus problem. I think I'd like Catholicism a whole lot more if they'd ease up on the Jesus stuff.

I gotta look into it. I mean, I'm in the choir loft every Sunday now. *What's happening to me?* I'm almost afraid to look into it because I'm sure I'll see rather quickly that it's just a cultural thing, just the old religion of Europe, and I'll conclude that if I'd been born in Yemen I'd be a Muslim, and blah blah blah. Oh how I wish any of it could be true.

You know what? I'm doing it. I'm going to hold this Catholic religion up to the rigorous standard of truth. If Catholicism doesn't hold up against everything else, then so be it. I'll have to drop out of the choir. That's one of the reasons I stopped going to the Mass I grew up with. I just couldn't say the *Apostle's Creed*. The Apostles may have believed it but I didn't. The Apostle's Creed is so declarative, so clear, and so full of things I just didn't get at the time. How can you stand there and say something like that if you don't really believe it?

Anyway, why *wouldn't* a person who becomes suddenly alert to this unbridled sense of the divine look at every articulation of spiritual reality?

We comparison shop before we buy a car but why won't we read the central texts of the world's religions and their critiques before we make a huge purchase like that? Ultimately however, after all the investigation we are urged to participate. Rumi says:

These spiritual window-shoppers
who idly ask:
'How much is that?'
'Oh, I'm just looking.'
They handle a hundred items and put them down,
shadows with no capital.
Even if you don't know what you want,
buy something!
Be part of the exchanging flow.

Elle and I go to USC for a Sufi poetry and dance performance. We are conspicuous. A few people look at us like we must be with the FBI.

I'm affected by the Sufi poets, the fervency, the dance, the proclamations of devotion.

It bothers me that people claim exclusive truth in the traditions they were born into.

How can you ever be sure you aren't just following your herd?

The cynical say if I were Indian I would just become a Hindu and that would be that.

Could I be a Sufi?

And if a Catholic, why?

Well, start with this: Of late I've been inexplicably called to the most traditional, orthodox, reverent and strict expression of the Catholic Faith.

Two years ago I no more expected to be singing the Latin Mass than to become a jet airplane pilot. The chances of me finding this, of doing this, were small.

But here I am, suddenly and tentatively participating in something dogmatic and doctrinal.

The dogma and doctrine are narrow, highly specific.

They include concepts like the exclusivity of Christ as a path to salvation (John 14:6), and that the Church is the pillar and ground of the truth (1 Timothy 3:15), instituted by Christ through the Apostles with special primacy afforded to Peter, the one to whom the Keys to the Kingdom and the responsibility of feeding Christ's flock were entrusted (Matthew 16:18, John 21:17). By the sweeping decree of Jesus, whatever Peter and the Apostles bound on earth would be bound in heaven; whatever Peter and the

Apostles loosed on earth would be loosed in heaven (Matthew 16:18-19, 18:18). And further, Christ instituted certain sacramental practices which he indicated were *necessary* for salvation, like baptism (John 3:3), and the Eucharist (John 6:53-54), and certain charitable practices that he said would separate the sheep from the goats (Matthew 25:39).

Jesus Christ founded a religion with a capital R. This is not a mere philosophy or collection of motivational aphorisms. It's comprehensive, setting forth not just our necessary moral conduct toward others but the necessary means of corresponding with God. We're called not just to a *personal relationship* with God through prayer, but also quite clearly an *ecclesial relationship* with Him in His one *Church,* and a *sacramental relationship* with Him in and through the sacraments He instituted that flow through the operation of His Church.

At least I see it now, the enormity of the Catholic claim.

There's a fierce logic to it.

But the premises have to be true, the first principles, otherwise it's no good, it would be just some kind of very impressive fraud. I don't think I can follow a religion I don't believe to its essential premises.

. *Christ has died, Christ has risen, Christ will come again.*

That's quite a premise.

I don't think I now participate in the Catholic Mass out of a desire to be part of a mere *faith community.*

If it's fake it's bad.

If I thought I belonged at my boxing trainer's little Sunday meeting I'd be there.

But that's not *Church,* as it were.

If I thought I should be a Sufi, I'd be a Sufi.

If I thought I should be a Buddhist, I'd be a Buddhist.

One of my law firms voted me an honorary Jew.

But my recent call, quite specifically, is to aspects of Catholicism I never knew existed.

I was led past the Buddhist monastery to a Catholic abbey, and now I'm being led through the Sufi poets to the Catholic mystics.

Why?

There could only be one *valid* reason for me to continue down this ancient path and that would be if Jesus Christ was and is divine and the Church he founded is the Catholic Church. If those things are not true, who needs it? If those things are not true the whole enterprise should be publicly condemned, like any other lie.

Rather ironic that in making a plunge of this magnitude into a highly structured and devout practice of Catholicism, I'm taking the advice of Rumi, Sufism's greatest poet, who urges me to *buy something, to be part of the exchanging flow.*

Rumi is right: As it stands now, I'm *a shadow with no capital.*

No doubt he would cast such aspersions at Santayana, standing forever at the Church door, a weak-eyed *aesthetic Catholic.*

I will not do that.

But if I go all the way as a Catholic, I'll never be able to say I didn't have Rumi to thank.

What am I to do? Never read the spiritual writings of anyone outside the Church? Well, I have to look to Saint Augustine:

The truth is God's truth wherever it's found, he says. But he would be among the first to discard the ideas that conflict with the dogmas and doctrines of the Catholic Faith and he'd tell us why.

But I'm not ready to leave the ecstatic love poets behind. They've given me so much over the years, but in truth not anything comprehensive, resembling a cohesive plan of life I could really follow. However, for their good faith expressions about the attributes of God, of the nature of existence, I feel I owe them a debt. Perhaps merely an artistic one.

Thank you for this, Basho:

Inside this pitiful body which has one hundred bones and nine holes, there is something called Spirit, which is like a flowing curtain easily blown around by wind. It was Spirit that got me to writing poetry, at first for amusement, later as a way of life. At times, my Spirit has been brought down so low that I almost quit writing, and at other times the Spirit became proud and powerful.

Thank you for this, Mirabai:

The colors of the Dark One have penetrated Mira's body; all the other colors washed out.

Making love with the Dark One and eating little, those are my pearls and my carnelians.

Meditation beads and the forehead streak, those are my scarves and my rings.

That's enough feminine wiles for me. My teacher taught me this.

Approve me or disapprove me: I praise the Mountain Energy night and day.

I take the path that ecstatic human beings have taken for centuries.

I don't steal money, I don't hit anyone. What will you charge me with?

I have felt the swaying of the elephant's shoulders;

And now you want me to climb on a jackass? Try to be serious.

The Energy that holds up mountains is the Energy Mirabai bows down to.

He lives century after century, and the test I set for him he has passed.

Thank you for this, Kabir:

We sense that there is some sort of Spirit that loves birds and animals
and the ants—
perhaps the same one who gave a radiance to you in your mother's womb.
Is it logical you would be walking around entirely orphaned now?
The truth is you turned away yourself,
and decided to go into the darkness alone.
Now you are tangled up in others, and have forgotten what you once knew, and that's why everything you do has some weird failure in it.
Friend, hope for the Guest while you are alive.
Jump into experience while you are alive!
Think...and think...while you are alive.
What you call salvation belongs to the time before death.
If you don't break your ropes while you're alive,
do you think
ghosts will do it after?
The idea that the soul will join with the ecstatic
just because the body's rotten—
that is all fantasy.
What is found now is found then.
If you find nothing now,
you will simply end up with an apartment
in the City of Death.
If you make love with the Divine now, in the next life you will have the face of satisfied desire.
So plunge into the truth, find out who the Teacher is,
believe in the Great Sound!

Kabir says this: When the Guest is being searched for, it is the intensity of the longing for the Guest that does all the work.

Look at me, and you will see a slave of that intensity.

Who is it we spend our entire life loving?

Thank you for this, Rumi:

Ecstatic love is an ocean, and the Milky Way is a flake of foam floating on that ocean.

The stars wheel around the North Pole, and ecstatic love, turning in a wheel, turns the stars.

If there were no ecstatic love, the whole world would stop.

Do you think that a piece of flint would change into a plant otherwise?

Grass agrees to die so that it can rise up and receive a little of the animal's enthusiasm.

And the animal soul, in turn, sacrifices itself. For what?

To help that wind, through one light waft of which Mary became with child. Without that wind, all creatures on Earth would be stiff as a glacier, instead of being as they are, locustlike, searching night and day for green things, flying.

Every bit of dust climbs toward the Secret One like a sapling.

It climbs and says nothing; and that silence is a wild praise of the Secret One.

Thank you, thank you, thank you all.

Amazing stuff.

But not Christian.

These poets evince a sincere *reaching up to God*. But I have a serious decision to make: Can I really accept the Incarnation of Christ or not? Because the Incarnation of Christ as a person of the Godhead is vastly more than man reaching up to God. Instead, it is said that to recognize the

194

Incarnation is to see that at a singular point in history, *God reached down to man.*

And in that reaching down Christians recognize that God offered us an *exclusive* means of relating to God, a *necessary* means. If I accept the Incarnation of God in the person of Jesus Christ, I would surely accept the authority of those God chose to lead His Church and accept all the graces, sacramental and otherwise, that flow through Her.

What other choice would I have?

If the Catholic Faith is true—a prospect I never seriously considered possible before—then I must have it, no matter how much I admire Rumi.

For Jesus famously proclaimed that He is *the* way, *the* truth, *the* life. If that's reality, then pretty poetry from the wisdom tradition won't cut it, erudite philosophy won't cut it, modern secular self-help books definitely won't cut it.

But truly now, just *who* is this Christ at the center of the Christian religion? The ecstatic love poets from other times and traditions cry out to God but leave Christ almost completely out of the picture, except for Rumi and some of the other Sufis who bring Jesus and Mary into it from time to time.

Am I really thirsting for Christ?

Sanguis Christi, inebria me.

Blood of Christ, inebriate me.

I can hear the chorus of jeers. Puh-lease, the intelligentsia seems to say to me. The religion of Christ has been discredited six ways to Sunday, from Galileo to the priests' sex scandal, you've got to be kidding me they say.

No question there's a rasping dryness in me, and it burns for something cool and drenching.

It has to be God. I've had everything else.

But the *Christ* as God?

I'd dismissed it out of hand so many years ago.

I can't avoid the question anymore and still continue to attend the Catholic Mass which places Christ so profoundly at its golden center, like something shining at the bottom of a stream.

I've sought the modern cures for my ailing psyche but I now see that's like trying to hold the tide back with a push broom.

Who was it that said practicing psychiatry without reference to God is like giving a hungry man a toothpick?

But I can't sort all this out in one day.

Saint Augustine's notion of the *God shaped void in our heart* makes more sense to me by the hour.

Regarding Jesus the Christ, Yeshua, I will have to seek further. Maybe something will come to me. If it's true, it will have to be made more known to me. I can't chase it down. *Lord, help my unbelief.* I'm not going to be able to get there on my intellect alone. That's what *The Hound of Heaven* was all about, being *pursued* as it were by the Christian God, the Father, Son and the Holy Ghost, the only God Francis Thompson would have confessed.

92

During college I drove out in the middle of the night to meet a Catholic priest to talk to him about a possible vocation, an impulse that seemed without context at the time. He told me to go back to my dormitory and ask myself what kind of relationship I had with Jesus Christ because, after all, he told me, to become a Catholic priest is to become a foot soldier for Christ's ministry on Earth. It's an apostolic mission.

So I went back to my room and sat there for hours and realized I felt no particular relationship with Jesus Christ. It was a mystery to me.

And that was that.

I was twenty and I never looked back.

But this is different.

If ever I've felt pursued, beaten about the head and neck by some invisible force, that time is *now*. I've read enough of conversion to think that's what this is. It feels like a tumble from a horse and a hard knock on the head.

People used to speak to me of a *calling* they had to do something or other *for Jesus* and I would be polite, scoffing internally at what I presumed to be a hearty dose of delusion and self-suggestion.

I can scoff no more.

It feels as though someone is calling me collect and I dare not refuse the charges. I *do* feel something like *swift feet following after* and I nearly cry tears of gratitude to Francis Thompson for capturing the strange phenomenon in the Hound of Heaven, lest I think I've gone totally wigged.

The psychiatrists and psychologists and bartenders seem suddenly small to me, like a royal court viewed from the window of a jumbo jet. Dwarfed, doling out their little apothecary-ground *pills and powders to get us through this passion play,* setting up that astringent brown liquor so I can knock it down in rustic seaside haunts. Ha!

I need to seek God for God's sake. Forget the substitutes and alibis.

Oh, this is an old story but how new it feels to me after a lifetime of sneering and worldliness and idolatry.

So *this* is what they were talking about, *this* is conversion?

I need a plan.

First of all, I cannot lose my connection to that Mass no matter what else might happen.

That liturgy is life to me, lifeblood for this conversion.

I have to have it.

I've been growing weak and crooked my whole life, eating processed food, *asking questions of those who know very little.*

I also need to go talk to those priests up on the hill. They seem to be plenty bright. I'm intimidated by them, however. I wouldn't know where to begin. Perhaps I should read some more first. I feel like an outsider, like a convert.

The Mass in which I now participate is not a waypoint on some mystical journey. Instead, it feels like a kind of destination. And the circumstances of my finding it were so peculiar, so tailor-made for my circumstance, so specific. It had the feel of a kind of personal invitation, despite all my protestations to the contrary. There's got to be something to it.

Beyond the Mass I'll try and do everything I can to understand this Christian idea of God. I'll try to understand this phenomenon of conversion by reading the experience of those who came before me, and to understand something of what they call the *moral law* or the *natural law.* If such a thing truly exists I'm certain to be found operating outside its contours. And I'll not confine my search to purely religious material, purely Christian material, I'll leave everything in the mix but read it with a mind that holds open the door for Christ, that holds open finally the possibility that, well, there's no other way to say it—that Jesus Christ is divine and He founded the true religion.

I can't do this all day every day. I'm not a monk. I have to work. I have to pay attention to Elle and Nicole. I have to take care of my parents. I have other interests. I don't know how I'm going to handle this.

Now that I'm reading Chesterton and coming to understand what a major figure he was, I look to him for some help in what appears to be a hard conversion to the Catholic Faith.

One day, when I'm beset with frustration over the seemingly insurmountable burden of theology, and my fear I'm going to lose every earthly thing I ever loved just like the speaker in *The Hound of Heaven,* I come across this Chesterton quote and the fog lifts a bit: *Let your religion be less of a theory and more of a love affair.*

Yes, I think I might be able to do that.

93

I'm not ready to say goodbye to all my worldly interests just yet. Or perhaps that's exactly what I'm doing. There are a few people I want to meet, literary figures mainly. I used to feel they had some answers for me, or at least they were asking the same questions I was. Robert Bly, David Foster Wallace, people like that.

It's just that now I've been catapulted into another dimension so I'm not as concerned with finding *truth* through secular poetry, literature or any other art. For the first time I'm considering that *truth* may have inspired the greatest art the world has ever known and it's Catholic.

But nevertheless, the day I meet Robert Bly is a grand day and I've had it on my calendar for some time. He comes to California periodically. I decided I should meet him in person, after reading him all these years. Derided by some, I always appreciated his spiritual seeking, his attempt to educate himself in public.

He's around eighty now, the poet and author responsible for poetry collections such as *Silence in the Snowy Fields, Loving a Woman in Two Worlds, The Light Around the Body,* as well as non-fiction including *The Sibling Society* and *Iron John.*

As a certain band of people seem to know, Bly became nationally famous via a Bill Moyers' interview introducing him both as a poet and unofficial leader of the strangely controversial Men's Movement of the 1990's—later to be dubbed by Bly and others as the Mythopoetic Men's Movement to distinguish it from *Promise Keepers* and other prominent social phenomena of the time.

He was working with mythology then, and that's not my primary interest. Instead I noticed he was a strong performer of his own poetry and that helped me in to the form. I enjoy *Silence in the Snowy Fields* and *Loving a Woman in Two Worlds*—I think they're just beautiful.

The group that I'm with gathers every year in San Jose and then in Monterey to hear Bly read and attend a literary workshop of sorts, a conference. I had to really work to get in; it's a collection of professors, psychologists, earnest housewives, real estate agents, some wonderful and acerbic eccentrics, one or two wingnuts, and me.

Bly is a famously broad shouldered and imposing Nordic type with piercing blue eyes and a shock of white hair. *The best part of me,* I overhear him tell a woman who dared to touch his hair. Not immodesty, he simply knows that his hair is where it's at.

At breakfast in Asilomar I sit at Bly's table, dare to introduce myself, and ask him a few questions.

I try to be succinct and not look at him like he's the Delphic Oracle.

Robert, I say, they talk about your poetic style as being deep image subjectivism—

He stops me with the wave of a large Nordic hand.

Yeah that's all pretty much nonsense, he says. What I look for in a poem is something I like to call the vertical line—the line that cuts through the psyche coming down from the heavens and straight through to the core of the Earth. Most poetry is horizontal. If it doesn't have the vertical line in it I'm not interested.

At the conference he gives a reading and stuns the crowd.

Then he leads a workshop and people soak it up, rapt.

That night the group reads some of their own poems and Bly is gracious.

Afterwards I meet him outside by chance and I'm holding a copy of his *Selected Poems.*

Bly looks at me and says, I thought your poem in there was pretty good. Want me to read one of those to you?

Sure, I say. How about a prose poem?

I flip to the one I want. It resonates with me these days. He sees which one it is and looks at me. You're a good reader, he says. Not one in a hundred people would pick out this one.

He takes the book from my hand and reads this aloud in the half-light:

WARNING TO THE READER

Sometimes farm granaries become especially beautiful when all the oats or wheat are gone, and wind has swept the rough floor clean. Standing inside, we see around us, coming in through the cracks between shrunken wall boards, bands or strips of sunlight. So in a poem about imprisonment, one sees a little light.

But how many birds have died trapped in these granaries. The bird, seeing freedom in the light, flutters up the walls and falls back again and again. The way out is where the rats enter and leave; but the rat's hole is low to the floor. Writers, be careful then by showing the sunlight on the walls not to promise the anxious and panicky blackbirds a way out!

I say to the reader, beware. Readers who love poems of light may sit hunched in the corner with nothing in their gizzards for four days, light failing, the eyes glazed...

They may end as a mound of feathers and a skull on the open boardwood floor...

Enough with the theologians and poets for a while!

I've got to get some money in the door.

Fortunately I get a call from an actor on the original *Star Trek* series who played a character called *Captain Pike,* a very nice man named Sean Kenney.

He tells me he's heard of my work for long suffering science fiction writers and others like them and asks perhaps whether I might be able to get him some royalty payments for the use of his likeness over the years.

I ask, Like what?

Well, he says, there's a wedding cake ornament of Captain Pike with full radiation burns like I had in the show. He tells me of many other uses.

I marvel at any bride who adorned her wedding cake with a tiny sculpture of an irradiated Captain Pike.

I take his case and we file suit.

One day he calls me up to his house in the Valley.

He tells me, apropos of nothing, that he's had a strange experience of late, wherein he was inspired to write screenplays about figures of the New Testament, including John the Baptist and Thomas of Didymus, so-called *doubting Thomas.*

He wonders if I might be able to help him get the screenplays made into films.

I stare at him, mouth agape, wondering if I'm being set up.

He says that in order to write about Saint Thomas, he lucked into the help of an Indian priest who knew the history of Saint Thomas in India.

Sean tells me they sat around the pool and wrote it up.

I'm dumbfounded.

Here I am just trying to ply my trade, do a little entertainment law, bring in some money, and now Captain Pike gets apostolic on me?

I can't get away from this, can I?

Sean says he's Catholic and undergoing a strong reversion. His story's not mine to tell, but it's nothing short of inspired. I tell him I'll read the script, *Thomas the Believer,* and get back to him.

As I sit reading about Saint Thomas, I'm struck by the historical ground for believing in the existence of Christ's Apostles. I don't hear much from skeptics calling the Apostles into question. There were enough of them that the volume of evidence for their existence and ministry seems quite well established. Strange that so many would doubt the existence of Jesus or His reality but accept the being and doing of his closest followers.

95

A few days later opposing counsel calls on the Captain Pike matter.

He's really smart.

We have a good talk about the case.

He says he understands the issue and he's looking forward to sussing it out. He knows more about studio accounting practices than I do. I learn something from him and there's no phony toughness on the phone, we're just breaking down the case the way two morning sports talk guys break down games.

The trade talk is comforting.

I feel like a lawyer.

Something in me begins to thaw.

Things are looking up.

I'm back in the saddle.

Yeah, this is my field—trying to get artists credit and compensation for their work, keeping the media giants I used to work for honest because deep down they really want to be, don't they?

I'm doing my old job again with a shift in perspective.

That's good, right?

Maybe I can combine the spiritual and the worldly into one spectacular life.

I don't know though—

I'm deeply reluctant to leave the purity of spiritual questing.

It's as though I must now become a double agent:

Entertainment Lawyer by Day/Catholic Hermit by Night

That won't fit on a business card.

What I'd really like to do is to remain out in the canyons forever among the manzanita with Saint John of the Cross, to flourish in rapture *beyond all towns and all systems,* to live inside a sacred chord up in the choir loft at the Mission.

And yet I sense something ominous in the very longing.

I can't forget Bly's *Warning to the Reader: The bird, seeing freedom in the light, flutters up the wall and falls back again and again. The way out is where the rats enter and leave; but the rat's hole is low to the floor.*

I've seen God's majesty in the hills and through my camera lens. I've had something profound occur in my spirit up in the choir loft at that Holy Mass. It's all so beautiful, and yet I know, I *know,* more is still yet required and it has something to do with the rat's hole.

I wish I knew what it was.

The thing about happening upon a mountain lake is that while it may be a beautiful surprise, we're not necessarily meant to stay there.

The mountain lake is a place of stunning beauty, but one in which we are greatly vulnerable to the ravages of earthly elements.

There is always terror near the quiet garden.

In the high passes, heavy weather strikes with a quickness.

Part Seven: Descent

Grim awareness: Mountain climbers are more often killed on the descent

Preferred Handheld Device: None

General Idea: *The mark of Descent, whether undertaken consciously or unconsciously, is a newly arrived-at lowliness, associated with water and soul. The lowliness happens particularly to men who are initially high, lucky, elevated. When a man enters this stage he regards Descent as a holy thing, he increases his tolerance for ashes, eats dust as snakes do, increases his stomach for terrifying insights, deepens his ability to accept the evil facts of history, accepts the job of working seven years under the ground, leaves the granary at will through the rat's hole, bites on cinders, learns to shudder, and follows the voice of the old mole below the ground. – Robert Bly*

96

A dark turn of events occurs. A close friend of the family, Dean, was diagnosed with multiple myeloma a couple of years after Mom. He was one of the healthiest people we knew.

But his course with this vicious cancer was faster and harsher than Mom's.

This February the myeloma overtakes him.

He loses consciousness.

Mom and Dad go to visit him one last time before he dies.

I'm informed it wasn't a peaceful final few hours.

Dad says that when he and Mom entered Dean's hospital room Dean was gasping and lying sideways on the bed, gone from sight and hearing.

When Mom got back to the house from the hospital visit—having glimpsed her own future—she apparently escaped the live-in caregiver and Dad, made it down to the store with Dad's car, then came back home with five bottles of wine and drank herself unconscious. Again.

She took a terrible fall. Again.

Dad tells me she's in Little Company's locked down psychiatric unit over in San Pedro and asks if I'd like to come visit her.

Yeah, I say. I have court this afternoon, but I can come over in the early evening.

After court I drive West on Wilshire to see Big D's new pad over near UCLA.

I get there and it's all high ceilings and good light.

Nice place, I say.

Big D is spinning vinyl, Wes Montgomery.

He gives me the tour, we talk about music for a while, and then we break out a Cold Blood record. Big D shows me his Dad on the back cover dressed in brown suede boots, red pants, a Nordic warrior jersey of some sort and a giant perm.

Cold Blood knew how to play, Big D says.

I tell Big D I have to go down to the hospital and see my Mom in the psych ward and I really don't want to go. I'm afraid, I tell him.

He lights a blunt, takes a drag, and passes it over to me.

I cough until my left eyeball pops out of my head.

Big D found his father dead the night after he drank himself to death. He understands.

Nobody else I know really understands.

Big D reminds me he'll drive out anytime anywhere if I need him, that I'm doing everything right, that I have to remember to be *temperate* with aging parents, that he's met my mother and she has a lot of *life energy* left in her, that these are the times when we have to *man up.*

I take another look at the album cover.

Do you think it literally killed your father to go from being a rock star to a CPA?

Nah, he just didn't heal right.

I want to ask him, *Heal* from what? But there's no time.

Big D gives me a man hug.

He says, Hey—this is the toughest stuff in life you're dealing with right now. You're doing good. Don't be afraid.

I call Dad from Big D's place to let him know I'll meet him at the hospital and he sounds discouraged.

Dad says the doctors told him that they can't hold Mom much longer, she's not crazy, she can make her own decisions, and what was the matter with *him,* anyway?

She's smoking again, Dad says. They let them do that there. They call them fresh air breaks. Ha! She told me she still thinks she can have wine with dinner, he says.

There's that edge in his voice that scares me—

97

When I get to the Harbor Freeway my palms begin to sweat.

I glance out the driver's side window at the Vincent Thomas Bridge and get the overwhelming urge to say a prayer.

I've not progressed much beyond this:

In nomine Patris, et Filii, et Spiritus Sancti.

But I need my own language this time.
Fact is, I need a child's prayer.

Dear Lord, please protect me.

That's all that comes.

98

San Pedro, dusk.

I run from my car to the hospital, to the lockdown ward, there's no other way to say it, the psychiatric ward, *alright?*

So Mom's been up here a week now and I haven't been over to see her. I've been unusually busy—*yeah*—that's it. Busy.

It has absolutely nothing to do with the way my guts churn every time I think about it.

And now I manage to get here with ten minutes left to visit.

How convenient.

I speak briefly to the head psychiatric nurse who acknowledges that we're in a tough position. Mom's a case of high functioning and low functioning all mixed together, he says. Mom's not necessarily fit for assisted living in the lockdown wards with people who are total pudding heads. But left to her own devices at home she can do terrible damage, he acknowledges.

What to do?

She can't be alone, that much is for sure, he says.

The nurse also prepares me that Mom's psych ward roommate is taken with running down the hall naked and laying her hands on Mom in prayer.

They let me in through the security doors and the ward is clean, bright, uncrowded.

209

It's a Friday night and so there's a low energy in the place.

I pass through a common visiting area and see odd couplings on the plastic chairs, a sane person sitting next to a psychiatric detainee. In at least one case it's hard to tell the visitor apart from the visited.

I take a hard breath and enter Mom's room.

She's in bed.

Hey Mom, I say, how're you doing?

Oh Hi honey, you just missed your father.

Where's your roommate?

I don't know. Maybe getting a fresh air break, she says.

Is she naked?

Oh, I don't think so honey. But earlier today well— she's really very intelligent but she just—who knows?

I glance around.

The room is stark, painted two shades of green—a deep sage and lighter institutional green.

Out the window: a spire and cross.

There's still enough light to make them out.

I ask, Do you mind if I open the curtains?

Go ahead, she says.

That's actually a beautiful view don't you think?

Yes, she says. There's just so much glare during the day.

I ask, Do you know what that spire and cross are all about?

No, she says. Well, isn't it *Mary Star by the Sea?* You used to play them—

Don't think so, I say. I passed it on the way. This is a different church out your window, *Holy Family,* I say. You look good, Mom.

Thanks honey. I'm not sure how long they're going to keep me.

Have they talked about moving you to the alcohol rehab portion of this facility?

No, Mom says.

As between the alcohol and drug rehab and this ward maybe you should be there, I say.

There's an outpatient program that they've told me about where we come for group twice a day, she says.

Hmm, I say.

All these groups we're in, the focus is on self-esteem. And that's never been my problem. No. Or even depression. I don't feel I've ever fought depression, she says.

So there's nothing wrong then?

I wouldn't say that, she says.

One thing you do have is anxiety, I say.

Oh heavens yes! I don't know what got me in here this time, but walking in on Dean's death—it was like watching my own death. I know how I'm going to die.

So Mom, just because you don't have problems with self-esteem or depression doesn't mean that you're not contending with some psychological difficulty, I say.

Right, she says.

What do you think anxiety is all about?

Fears I guess, she says.

When your father died did you experience fear?

Oh yes. I didn't know how we were going to make it, who was going to take care of us, I worried constantly. I was only fifteen. I didn't know what was going to happen.

Did you ever discuss that with Nana?

No. And she didn't seem to have those fears, or at least she never showed them. Her faith was very strong.

Funny you mention that, I say. I've been thinking of Nana recently and the years she lived with us. My memory is watching her pray the Rosary in the morning. She knelt at the side of the bed, closed her eyes and fingered those beads and said prayers like I've never seen anyone say prayers—

Oh yes, Mom says. *Her* faith was very strong.

And then when you lost Christopher—

That was terrible too, she cuts me off quickly.

Note to self: dead brother is a no-go zone.

She says, But I was very stressed by the business. When your father made me the bookkeeper that was horrible. I thought I was going to die. I was much better at helping the customers.

You felt super-high anxiety at the office?

Terribly, Mom says.

Me too, I say. You know I've been reading a little about *Alcoholics Anonymous.* Not the *Big Book,* but more about how it started, I add. There was a strong spiritual component—

AA is very spiritual, Mom says.

A doctor who gives an opinion in the book says alcoholism is an allergy, like a peanut allergy. You may love peanuts but if you eat them you know you could die. It's different than the disease concept, but I think perhaps more useful, more specific—

But whatever it is you've got it, I say. And that's why you can't have wine with dinner any more than some school kid with a peanut allergy could have a peanut butter and jelly sandwich. That's what *don't take the first drink* is all about, right, like they say in AA?

Yes, yes, she says. Thank you, honey.

So when you come home, don't eat the first peanut, I say. But you know, that doesn't do anything about the underlying anxiety, what I feel most alcoholics struggle with.

Why do you think some people respond that way?

I don't know, I say. I think about it every day. In these recent years I've begun to feel like some kind of prey animal. There's a sense of threat all the time no matter what. It's not a good feeling.

No, she says.

I hold her hand for a bit. One of the nurses stops by the door and points at her watch. I've stayed over at least twenty minutes past visiting hours.

I stand to leave and squeeze Mom's hand. It's splotchy, red and bruised from long-term steroid use.

I tell her I love her and she tells me the same but that's only partly the point.

What I came to say to her feels daring for some strange reason, perhaps because it's the first time I'm willing to say it out loud to anyone.

Bill W. was right about one thing, I tell her: *We're not alone.*

Since going to that Mass at the Mission, I believe in God now Mom. I don't understand very much, but I think it's real somehow.

99

Two days later I'm back in the choir loft, the only place I truly feel safe. After Mass the choir goes to breakfast and then rehearses. I learn much from these breakfast table discussions. I had no idea the enormity of the changes the Catholic Church experienced just prior to my arrival here on planet Earth.

There are many shocking opinions about why the changes, what they mean, and what we are to do now. None of these people advocate any sort of separation from the Holy See, but they have volumes to say about the state of the Church and the state of the world.

I find it strange I could have gone through twelve years of Catholic school from 1975 to 1988 and have heard none of this. Not to mention a doctoral level degree from a

Catholic law school in 1997! But that's part of the drama I'm told, the Great Amnesia, they call it, resulting in a whole generation of Catholics who know next to nothing about the Catholic Faith and thus can't hold it either.

100

After breakfast one of the men pulls me aside and says, John, you know you really need to make a general confession before you go to Communion again. It's very dangerous for you to go to Communion in the state you're in.

Dangerous?

Yes, dangerous and sacrilegious as well. You also need to get your first marriage annulled if you have the grounds to do it and get this civil marriage you're in now blessed, or end it.

What?

I hate to be the one to tell you this but you're in a state of mortal sin. If you died the way you are right now you'd probably go to hell.

Hell?

He looks at me calmly and so objectively I find myself very nearly in agreement with him.

Okay, I say, what exactly is a general confession?

Well, you know, he says, you tell a priest all the sins of your entire life and receive absolution. And then afterward you keep it up by going to confession once a week or so. It becomes easy after that. You have to be in a state of grace to receive Communion, *don't you know?*

He tells me of his general confession and how he wrote all his sins down in a notebook and then drove through the rain up to the Abbey hoping he wouldn't get in a car wreck and be found with the details of his life of sin on the seat next to him.

He told me of his annulment.

He did not, however, tell me the theological reasoning behind any of this. He just said it to me like a man might tell another man he needs a new carburetor.

101

A few days later after choir practice one of the sopranos accompanies me to dinner at a candlelit eatery in San Juan Capistrano. I find her voice inspiring. I have to tell her it was her reading of the *Asperges Me* that turned my brain inside out the first day at Mass. She says she's not the owner of her gift, but thanks me for the compliment.

I tell her I'm absolutely overwhelmed by the prospect that the Catholic Faith might be true. I tell her I'm going to read everything I can and travel to Jerusalem and—

John, she says, *John!* Please, would you put your general confession at the top of that list and get that done before you do anything else?

The look on her face startles me. She holds a beautiful cabernet in her hand but she looks stricken.

Okay, I say to her, but *why* the confession first? Why is that so important?

She says, Because the way you are right now, that *scares* me.

Before we end the meal she pulls a rosary and a booklet out of her purse. The booklet is entitled *The 54 Day Novena.* She hands me both the rosary and booklet.

It's pretty self-explanatory, she says. I think it would help you if you prayed the Rosary this way for fifty-four days. Ask for healing. Ask for an illumination of conscience. Ask for the capacity to make a good confession.

I'm touched to stunned by the gift. I find it so odd to be holding these items. It seems absurd to me that I might pray the Rosary even once, let alone for fifty-four days. I think of Celia. It never really occurred to me that anyone but old Irish ladies prayed the Rosary.

I open the booklet. She's written something to me on the inside cover. It says, *Dear John, All for Jesus, through Mary.*

This is a bit much for me.

Mortal sin, hell, general confessions, the Rosary, Mary.

This is like, *way* Catholic. There's no confusing it with anything else.

I'm continually surprised by the understated matter-of-factness with which these people really seem to believe this stuff.

In their calm objectivity they seem credible.

In the context of that extraordinary Mass, it almost seems possible.

Holy God.

After dinner, alone in my car, I make the sign of the cross then stash the rosary and novena booklet in the center console of my Cadillac. I'd better not breathe a word of any of this to Elle. She'll have me committed.

102

A few days later there's a party for a work friend of Elle's.

It's a bunch of cops and high octane attorneys and other law enforcement types and again everybody drinks way too much.

I'm on a new round of *Buspar* and probably shouldn't drink at all.

But since the Buspar doesn't work worth a damn, I feel entitled to try the *Patrōn.*

Yikes!

I have an out of body experience.

Sometime later that night I end up asleep on someone's lawn in some fancy neighborhood and the cops pick me up.

They cuff me and throw me in the back of the patrol car.

Next morning Elle tells me it took two lawyers and a cop or two from the party to convince the patrol to let me go.

Remembering none of it except a hazy dreamlike memory of staring at cop boots for twenty blacklit minutes, I'm shocked and horrified and say some miserably nasty things to Elle she doesn't deserve like:

Shut up, I tell her, *don't say anything—*

Lovely.

Elle withdraws for weeks.

So finally I write her a sharply worded note asking her if she's with me or against me. In this missive I demand her support, tell her that whatever mysterious all-consuming distress is ailing me I will overcome it and does she really think I'm going to fail us for God's sake?

Good letter, strong letter, I think to myself as I finish it and place it in an envelope for her to find later.

103

That night, Elle asks me to move out.

I ask, Do you mean a divorce, like you don't want to see me again?

I think so, she says. I'm not doing well.

I start to say, What about Nicole—

Elle's eyes glisten with a tearful resolve.

The room spins.

With me or against me I said and she's against me.

Oooph. I'm beginning to rethink that letter.

Nicole—

Hell, it's not my choice. I'm just the stepdad. All that investment, all those school lunches, all the band-aids and the listening I did—

Ah well, the stepdad's a throwaway item just like I always thought.

Life's a bitch.

Sorry kid—

I can't even imagine Nicole's reaction.

I'm glad I won't be around to see it.

Elle's decision, let her explain it.

I'm not even afforded the opportunity.

What a joke.

She'll probably have to paint me out to be a monster to justify this.

I'm not a *monster.* Am I?

Nicole won't see it coming.

Nicole and I just saw another damn Miley Cirus movie together, the one where Miley and her Dad sing that syrupy duet to each other.

Now two weeks later I'm gone? The dogs, gone?

Elle's called both our fathers in preparation for this split.

Her father's here, my father's here and I just about want to puke.

It's an ambush, a sneaky prosecutor's trick.

For our safety she says—

Whose safety?

Dad insists I come home with him.

Where else, after all? If I'd even had a week to find a place, borrow some money—

I'm at loose ends, reeling.

I pack up my stuff and leave.

Don't look back you can never look back

I blow a tire on the way to my parents' house.

Thought I knew what love was

I unpack the trunk to reach the spare.

What did I know?

I kneel in the dark on the shoulder of the Seal Beach offramp.

Those days are gone forever; I should just let 'em go but—

I make a decision not to let another woman take me to the floor.

I know I'm difficult, this is difficult, but I deserve better.

I've given as much as I've taken.

Can't anybody stay married anymore?

I mean, I know it's bad but this is—

Both my parents have cancer! I'm working on it!!!

I know that's no excuse, that's what parents do eventually, they get cancer. What the hell is wrong with me???

104

At three in the morning I limp through my parents' front door thoroughly defeated.

Mom's still in the psych ward.

The house, which was always reasonably orderly, is now in chaos: one toilet ripped out, bills and newspapers piled high, dishes in the sink.

A live-in caretaker occupies my childhood bedroom.

I'm shocked by the condition of the place.

Dad, I say, Mom's gonna be home in five days. We've got to get the bathroom put back together.

I know, he says.

I don't want to talk about the separation, I say.

From the looks of things there's no time anyway.

DAY ONE

Dad, the caretaker and I sit around the kitchen table under a bright light. We talk about what Mom did to make it into the psych ward.

We gotta stop her from drinking, I say. We're way past *let them lay where they fall*—her judgment's impaired somehow. She can't work a program—

We've tried, the caretaker says.

Dad says: I fall asleep with the car keys and the phones under my pillow most nights but sometimes I forget. Then she either takes the keys and drives the car to the store or she calls a cab.

We need to get a safe, I say.

DAY TWO

Dad and I re-seat the john and do up the linoleum in the bathroom. We try to work on the bills, but it's just too much.

He goes to the office.

I sit there and stare at the ocean.

DAY THREE

Dad calls me from the office and says, Elle called. She wants to talk to you. She said she wants to reach you but you don't have a phone.

Yeah, I threw it out the window on the freeway.

You did what?

I don't want one. A phone, that is.

How can she reach you?

I guess she can't reach me, I say.

Don't you want to talk to her? She said if you would just do a few certain things she'd take you back in a heartbeat. She was crying, he says.

She *should cry,* I say.

DAY FOUR

Dad and I head to the hospital to collect Mom.

On the way over Dad says, You really should give Elle a call. She phones me every day asking—

She kicked me out, Dad. That's the kind of thing that happens once. I swore I'd never let a woman—

She loves your ass. Don't you think she had good reason?

No! Not to hand down a summary execution. She didn't ask for a separation. She said it was over. I had to come to terms with that on the ride up here.

Oh, people say things, Dad says.

Yeah, like marriage vows. In sickness and in health, remember? I made over two hundred grand in the first few years of our marriage. I've had a miserable year this past year. I wake up with a tombstone on my chest in the middle of the night. Is that my fault? I'm trying to figure it out. I wake up in the morning with a pounding heart. I've been back and back and back to the fucking doctor and I can't get it right but I started a new type of therapy that seems to be working a bit. Do you know how many drugs I've taken? Nothing works! We were in marriage counseling. She should've stuck with me.

John, just give Elle a call, okay?

I'll think about it, I say.

I call Big D instead.

I tell him Elle wants to talk but I'm not so sure.

He says, You should call her. She just got tired, John. She loves you, but she's tired. Be fair to the reasons that led up to the split. It's okay. Ultimately, this won't be about blame no matter what happens.

221

DAY FIVE

Mom comes home from the hospital.

With the caretaker in my childhood bedroom there's four of us in the house plus the two dogs and everything feels a bit close.

I sleep in the living room.

The tension ratchets up when Mom gets out of bed.

Uh-oh. Where's she going? What's she doing?

I hear her headed for the kitchen. She uses the walker and makes a horror-movie sound as she inches across the tile: plant walker, drag foot, plant walker, drag foot, plant walker, drag foot.

She pulls a bowl out of the cupboard and drops it.

It shatters.

Dad yells at her, GODDAMMIT! STAY OUT OF THE KITCHEN!!

I try not to listen. My whole body convulses. I walk out onto the back patio while they yell at each other.

I get dizzy.

My hands curl into fists.

DAY SIX

I meet Elle in Laguna Beach for dinner.

We have an awkward few minutes before we're seated where I don't know what to say.

When we take our seats she starts to cry.

We order drinks.

She toasts to the future.

The future?

John, I got it in my head you were going to hurt me. Like kill me or something, in a rage.

Oh great, I say.

Don't be defensive, she says. I'm trying to explain. I know now that's not true. I expected you to react violently when I asked you to move out, to punch walls and break things. When that didn't happen, I realized I was wrong about that. Okay?

I blew up maybe ten times in the five years you've known me, I say. Maybe six of those blow-ups were directed your way. I broke an inanimate object or two—

John, I know you wouldn't hurt me physically. But that's where my head was when I asked you to leave. I love you. But we've got *Chase Manhattan Bank* calling the house every five minutes—

—over a measly two thousand dollar credit card bill, I might add.

It doesn't matter how much, she says. The bills have to get paid.

You know what, I say. This what-have-you-done-for-me-lately attitude really stinks. I helped you raise your daughter! I made money. I know it came in sporadically and I didn't handle it well but you know what I can do. I don't know why I feel so messed up, why I can't concentrate, why I feel like I want to drink a gallon of scotch right now just to calm my breathing down—

You're getting all worked up, she says. It's been confusing from the beginning.

Exactly. I'm figuring it out now. I never hid my distress from you, I say. I've been trying to figure this out the whole time. For you to just throw me away like this, like a piece of rancid meat—this is what I was afraid of, this is why I didn't want to get married again—

Oh come on, she says. We're here now, aren't we? I love you. You're the most amazing man I've ever met. If I'm not with you I'm gonna be alone. I told my counselor that we had a—a transcendent relationship.

Transcending what? Chase Manhattan Bank?

Please, John.

I'm sorry, I say. I thought we were transcendent too. But do you know how embarrassed I am? I made Orange County my home. I adopted your friends, your family as my own. Now they all think I'm some free-loading wife beater—

They don't think that. It's not like I've told them details of why—

Don't play it down, you've got to have made yourself out to have really good reason to do something this drastic. I can't look anyone in the eye anymore. My life is over down here. You've branded me a head case.

Nicole isn't doing well with it, John. She shook and cried when I told her. She asked if she could pretend you're on a business trip. She said you're like a real father to her.

She did?

I want you to come home, Elle says. But you have to do some things first.

I don't have to do anything, I tell her. My mother is dying. My father's on the verge of closing his business. He looks like he hasn't slept in a year. I owe creditors what, about twelve thousand dollars? I could make that much money in a month or two if I had a free hand. But I don't have a free hand now do I?

Why don't you move out of your parents' place?

I can't move out. Why don't you take me back? You threw me into the street on ten minute's notice. I'm negative five hundred bucks in my bank account. I have two dogs, one of whom is ginormous and landlords hate him. I'll need to rent a whole house for crying out loud—my credit's going down the tubes.

Will you please stop saying I threw you out? You did so many bad things by that point—

Bad? Like a little boy or a dog? You threw me out and maybe I deserved it but I'm not going to phrase it in some more agreeable form for you—

I don't think you should stay at your parents' place, she says. It's dangerous for you.

You're damn right it's dangerous, thank you very much.

Just pay the bills off—

I'll pay down the bills that are bothering you if I can do it under this crazy scenario. But if you want to try and work this through, we'd better stick with our marriage counseling. That's one bill I'll pay right now even if I have to borrow the money.

DAY SEVEN

I take a nap in my old room while the caretaker is out for the afternoon. I find an empty bottle of whisky in the closet. So she's been driven to drink too? What, are she and Mom drinking buddies now?

I'm gonna die here.

DAY EIGHT

At dawn I wake to yelling and slamming noises from down the hall.

Mom's incontinent and doesn't seem to care.

Dad yells at her in the morning about it.

GET UP, he yells. GET IN THE SHOWER!

NO, she yells.

GET UP RIGHT NOW, he yells.

FUCK YOU, she yells. FUCKY FUCK FUCK FUCK! ALL YOU WANT TO DO IS CONTROL ME!

Dad yells, THE BED IS SOAKING WET! HOW CAN YOU NOT CARE?

He grabs at her.

She screams.
My engine howls.
Should I get out of bed?
Intervene?
The room is abstract and whirring.
Louise has her ears pinned back in fear.
Of me?
I start to get up but stop.
I hear the shower running—

I'm Ten.
Father Gannon's coming over for dinner tonight.
This is something priests do, I'm told.
And since he's from Ireland, and Nana, who just died,
was from Ireland, he's coming over to pay a visit. A nice
visit, but—
Dad's been out of town and Mom really hit it hard.
It's worse now with Nana gone.
I don't know what to do.
I'm out of practice.
I couldn't get her sobered up in time.
So Dad came home and there was a lot of yelling.
A lot of yelling at me this whole week.
I've been bad, too.
Really bad in school.
I just can't do it.
Just can't do it—
Something else happened today that I'm gonna get in
trouble for, some note that was sent home, something about
my writing the word Help on a spelling test, throwing it
away, and Sr. Dawn Marie pulls it out of the trashcan, and
now there's this whole big thing—
Dad's home.
I'm running away.
Not sure where.

226

I think I'll go to Rocketship Park and think about it.

It's close to Kevin's house, maybe I could stay there for a few days.

Nah, I can't just show up there.

I'll stay at the park tonight.

But it's raining.

It's January.

I walk a mile to the park.

And I have nothing with me.

Rain, rain, rain—

I'm soaked through.

The lights at the foot of the hill are hidden in the wetness.

I climb the rocketship itself and sit in the very top section near the big steering wheel.

It's kinda cool, being up here all alone in a rainstorm.

But I'm gonna freeze to death, just plain freeze to death in Southern California.

And there's this annoying whistling sound because the very top of the rocketship has a hole in it, a tiny hole, and the wind rips across the top of it and it sounds like a Piccolo Pete on the Fourth of July.

It hurts my ears.

It bothers me so much that I sit on top of the steering wheel of the rocketship and plug the hole with my index finger.

This is ridiculous, absolutely ridiculous.

I've been gone forty-five minutes.

Time to go home and take it like a man.

DAY NINE

Mom attempts to make dinner.

She puts a whole bunch of raw meat into a casserole dish and turns on the oven.

Her hands are filthy, stained with nicotine and smeared with poo.

Dad comes home.

He says, WHAT'S IN THE OVEN?!

Mom made dinner, I say.

YOU LET HER DO THAT?!

She just started—

Goddammit, he says.

Dad throws open the oven door, pulls out the casserole dish and tosses it on the counter.

WHAT THE HELL IS THIS?

Mom says, I'm making dinner—

Dad says, YOU RUINED TEN DOLLARS WORTH OF MEAT!

I slink out of the kitchen. My whole body twitches.

I walk to the back of the house but I can still hear them.

I'M NOT EATING FOOD THAT YOU DON'T EVEN COOK RIGHT—THAT YOU JUST RUINED—

I walk out to the back patio and stare at the sea but I can still hear them.

LOOK AT YOUR HANDS, COVERED IN SHIT, HERE, LOOK AT THIS MEAT!!!

I'm going all hazy, the edges of my field of vision are starting to blur—

Something in my upper thorax shatters.

I head toward the kitchen in slow motion.

I feel as though I'm watching myself.

My whole body's sprung taut.

When I see the two of them standing there I explode.

SHUT THE FUCK UP, I scream.

I grab the casserole dish and throw it into the sink.

It lands with a thud and breaks in half.

DON'T TALK TO HER LIKE THAT YOU MOTHERFUCKER. I'LL KILL YOU, DO YOU HEAR ME? I'LL

FUCKING KILL YOU. WHAT'S WRONG WITH YOU MOM?
WHY DON'T YOU WASH YOUR HANDS?!

Dad yells, GET OUT OF HERE YOU LUNATIC.

He moves toward me.

I put my hands up like I was taught.

I strike first, throwing a soft right at Dad's gut.

It barely connects.

If I touch him again I'll kill him.

I flip a chair over.

I'm screaming, my voice is quickly hoarse.

I can't hear myself.

I can't see, can't think, can't feel.

I slam an open drawer as hard as I can.

It pops back out and contents go flying, rubberbands
and pencils.

Dad yells, WHAT ELSE ARE YOU GOING TO BREAK
OF OURS?

I can no longer speak.

I grab the dogs and evacuate the house.

I go somewhere I used to go when I was small—Frog
Canyon.

I stay down here until nightfall, huddled in the canyon
with the dogs. They look at me funny—what are we doing
down here they want to know.

At midnight we go back to my car and stay out all
night, sleeping in the car on a quiet cul-de-sac near my
former house in Palos Verdes, the house I sold five years
ago for a million two.

We're homeless now, I think.

Homeless.

DAY TEN

Nothing much happens.

I drive around.

229

I have no phone so I've no idea if anyone is trying to reach me.

DAY ELEVEN

I go to my parents' house.

I have nowhere else to go.

Dad says, The caretaker is leaving.

I ask, Do you want me to stay?

John, I can't take it when you behave like that. You're really out of control.

I'm out of control?

Yeah. And you've got boxing training now.

I'm sorry, I say. Please let me stay.

DAY TWELVE

Mom manages to call a cab and get to the store at around one o'clock in the morning.

She wakes me up when she comes home.

Dad gets up.

We spy her in the front yard sitting on the retaining wall drinking wine from a plastic cup and smoking a cigarette.

Dad yells at her.

I yell at her.

He pulls her inside the house.

She's disheveled and filthy.

GODDAMMIT, he says. WE'RE GOING BACK TO THE STORE RIGHT NOW AND YOU'RE GOING TO RETURN THIS WINE. AND THIS OTHER CRAP YOU BOUGHT. JOHN YOU'VE GOT TO BE ON THE SAME PAGE WITH ME!!!

We all pile in the car.

When we get to the grocery store I can't believe we're going to do this. I want to wait in the car but that seems unmanly.

Plus, I might get in trouble if I don't support this endeavor.

I might get kicked out again.

Really, I don't think it's the store's fault.

Mom should be under lock and key somewhere.

Dad confronts the night manager who says they don't take liquor back.

The manager is resistant and Dad starts to make his case—

Suddenly, I snap at the manager.

LISTEN TO ME YOU JAGGOFF. TRY AND SELL MY MOTHER WINE AGAIN AT ONE O'CLOCK IN THE MORNING AND SEE WHAT HAPPENS TO YOU—

Dad intervenes and says, JOHN, WAIT IN THE CAR—

My blood is surging, coursing.

I feel a deep sickly familiar shame, a seventies kind of shame.

Like when I wet my pants on the pitcher's mound kind of shame.

I could beat the crap out of the night manager, Dad, the counter clerk, Ernest and Julio Gallo—

What's the word?

Thunderbird!

Bastards!

I grab Mom by the upper arm and hustle her out the front door. On my way out I shove a greeting card rack display and it screeches across the floor.

I put Mom in the front seat, strap her in, slam the door, and lean against the back of the car.

Dad comes out and says, He gave us a gift certificate equal to the value of the wine. No thanks to you, Dad says. You've really got a problem with your temper—

DAY FIFTEEN

They yell at each other much of the time.

231

My whole being seizes.

DAY SIXTEEN

First day without the caretaker.

She abandoned ship, went back up North.

My father blames me for it, for intruding, invading the house with my dogs and cumbersome self, all because I failed to make a go of my marriage, failed to make a living, failed, failed, failed, failed, failed—

Mr. Most Likely to Succeed, a failure.

Finally the truth comes out.

The three of us are alone now.

Father, mother and child.

I'm back in my childhood bedroom.

Dawn.

Doors slam.

Not again.

GET UP, he says.

NO!

GET IN THE SHOWER, he says.

I'M NOT GOING ANYWHERE YOU ASS, she says.

He grabs at her.

She screams.

Blood pounds in my temples.

I get up and walk across the floor.

I put my hand on the doorknob.

I can't turn it.

My hand won't move.

I'm frozen.

I go back to bed and put my head under the pillow like I used to.

DAY SEVENTEEN

Mom's a chain-smoker now.

232

She wants a cigarette every five minutes.

We have to ration them out Dad tells me.

We have to set the timer, and he'd better not see me give her a cigarette on less than hour and a half intervals.

The whole day revolves around the smoking.

She begs and pesters, begs and pesters.

I mete them out.

I light them for her because her hands don't work.

She puffs on them like her life depends on it.

She staggers back to the bedroom and lies down until she gets the urge to smoke again.

Twenty more minutes, I tell her.

Oh come on, she says. Pleease! That's hardly any time at all—

MOTHER!!! Go back to bed. You break Dad's rules you jeopardize my life. I'd just as soon cram all these cigarettes down your throat and light them at once, but if he says an hour and a half then it's an hour and a half.

DAY TWENTY-ONE

A Thursday.

Or is it Tuesday?

Who can keep track of such things?

They wake me up at dawn with their yelling again.

Poo, cigarettes, a mess in the kitchen.

The same stuff over and over and over.

I stay in bed while he hoses her off in the front bathroom.

A few minutes after her shower while Dad mops up I give Mom a cigarette too early and Dad flies into a rage.

JOHN, I JUST GAVE HER ONE. LOOK AT THE CLOCK. YOU HAVE TO FOLLOW THE RULES—

I snap again.

WE'RE TRADING SHIFTS, I'M STARTING FRESH—

HOW DARE YOU—

233

HOW DARE *I*, I say, HOW DARE *I*?

GET OUT OF HERE HE SAYS, YOU WORTHLESS PIECE OF SHIT. I'M ASHAMED OF WHAT I RAISED. CAN'T MAKE A LIVING, HAVE NOWHERE ELSE TO GO. GO LIVE ON THE STREET, he says.

I can't believe my ears, I tell him. I oughta kill you where you stand you scumbag. I'm here bailing you out of the worst time of your life after all you did to me?

After all I did to you—

Yeah—I've done $250,000 worth of legal work for you, saved you hundreds of thousands of dollars—

OH BULLSHIT, he says, YOU HAVEN'T DONE ANYTHING.

BULLSHIT? I step toward him.

I will surely kill him with one blow.

GET OUT, he says.

I'LL GET OUT, I tell him.

I head to the back bedroom.

I grab the dogs' single lead, a six foot leather strap.

I burst into the garage.

On my way in I shout, I'M GONNA HANG MYSELF NOW YOU MOTHERFUCKER!!! I HOPE YOU ROT. I'LL SEE YOU IN HELL—

Oh Christ, I've really done it now.

I have to go through with it.

Can't make a threat like that if you're not going to do it.

I want to die anyway, fuck.

I grab the step ladder.

It stands on the very spot where Mom nearly bled out in 1985.

I loop the leash around the rafters.

I pull it tight.

I hook the other end to the clasp halfway up the strap.

I put my head through.

It's not quite a noose exactly, more of a loop.

Maybe my head will slip out.

Is he going to come in here and try to stop me at least?

Jesus.

I'm going to die now.

I'm really going die.

I'm doing this.

I readjust the lead so that it makes a bonafide noose.

I stand on the stepladder.

Okay, I'm doing this.

I might have one last chance to pull myself up with my hands after I kick the ladder out—

The door to the garage bursts open.

It's Dad.

Thank God.

He runs toward me.

I kick the ladder out from under me.

He grabs me and pulls the ladder back.

He stands on the bottom step and yanks the leather loop from around my neck.

I black out.

A few hours later Dad's gone to the office.

I'm trying to cook Mom breakfast like I do every morning, like the caretaker did, eggs over easy, bacon, sourdough toast, but Mom just can't wait. Here I am just damn near killed myself and there she is grabbing at the toast, grabbing at this and that, grabbing at the canned cranberry sauce again, she can't stop eating the same strange foods over and over, cottage cheese and cranberry sauce. She gets the cranberry sauce all over the counter.

I grab the bowl away from her and it slips from my hand onto the kitchen floor. It shatters. Shards of glass shoot everywhere. Cranberry sauce runs like oxblood through all the grout in the tile, bits of cottage cheese splatter against the low cabinets and the freezer door—

MOM, GODDAMMIT, SIT DOWN!!

What, she says, and keeps grabbing—

GODDAMMIT, SIT DOWN SIT DOWN SIT DOWN SIT DOWN!!!

I grab her and push her back toward the kitchen table.

She stumbles forward and catches her shin on the corner of the chair.

AAAAAWWWWGGGGRH!

I look down at her pajama bottoms.

A large red bloom appears through pale green silk.

Oh god oh god, I think, I've torn her leg open. It's the steroids and that friable skin, like tissue paper.

Now I've done it.

She yells again, AAAAAHHHHHHGHHH!

Sit down Mom, I'm sorry. I'm so sorry, let me go get a bandage.

I go pull the first aid kit out of the bathroom.

I bring the pajama bottom up over her knee and the wound is unbelievable, like nothing I've ever seen, down to the bone. It's disgusting. How can this be? The corner of the chair isn't even that sharp. I did this to her!

I use butterfly bandages and non-stick gauze.

She bleeds right through the gauze for a while until finally I apply a layer that seems to resist the blood soaking.

I sit on the floor and look her in the eye.

She has a strange vacant look about her considering what just happened.

She asks, What? Why are you looking at me like that?

I look around at the floor running reddish purple with that horrible canned cranberry goop.

I look at the glistening pieces of the splintered glass bowl.

I look at the field-medic dressing I applied to her leg.

I notice I have a huge cut on my ring finger and I bleed profusely onto my shirt, my jeans.

I start to cry and shake uncontrollably.

This little excuse for a family is off course again in that bleak landscape *scraped flat by the roller of wars, wars, wars—*

I never thought I'd see this rocky dungeon again.

DAY THIRTY-FIVE

Dawn.

Yelling.

GET UP, Dad orders.

NO!

GET UP RIGHT NOW AND GET IN THE SHOWER!!!

I have a floaty feeling.

I don't have the strength to put the pillow over my head.

I hear him coming down the hall.

Oh God, he's coming into my room. Oh no—

He throws open my door.

YOU'VE GOT TO HELP ME, he says.

Help you do what?

GET HER IN THE SHOWER.

He goes back down the hall.

I can't move.

I'm pinned to the bed *like a patient etherized upon a table.*

SHIT, he says. YOU SNUCK OUTSIDE FOR A CIGARETTE, he yells after her.

He slams the door to the bathroom and stomps out to the deck to retrieve her.

PUT IT OUT, he yells. PUT IT OUT!!!

AAAAARGH, she yells.

He's got her and he's pulling her back toward the shower.

NO YOU DON'T, she yells. YOU CONTROLLER!!!

She's yelling and screaming more than usual.

I can't take it.

I rise from the bed.

I start for the hallway.

If I go down there someone is going to die.

It could be me.

It will have to be me.

I'm going to hang myself for real this time.

My mouth opens.

I yell, STOP IT STOP IT STOP IT STOP IT STOP IT STOP IT STOP IT STOP IT STOP IT—

I pound on the dresser in my room until my right fist throbs.

Silence.

Then Dad: There he goes again!!!

The sound of his voice is sickening to me, the mockery in it, the derision, the sense that his is somehow normal behavior that I should be expected to endure, the yelling and screaming first thing in the morning like I'm not even here. I'll kill him if I go down there—

I reach for the phone.

I dial 911.

I can't speak, the dispatcher is yelling at me to calm down, trying to get me to say what's wrong. I mumble something about elder abuse, about suicide, about something or other—

Then I call Elle.

Dad comes back to my room.

I'm on the phone with Elle.

I'm sorry, Elle. I can't make it. I'm going to kill myself now. I loved you. Thank you—

I brush past Dad when I hear the sound of sirens.

Three cop cars roll up.

I hang up on Elle.

One of the cops creeps up the driveway with his hand on his gun.

I come outside with my hands up.

They yell at me to move over toward the retaining wall.

I sit down and start crying.

A lady cop comes up and asks what's wrong.

I say I think I want to die.

She says, Okay, I'll stay with you.

The other cops talk to my Dad.

It's all confusion.

I don't know what's happening.

I can't see/hear/think.

Everything is pulsing and red.

Suddenly I'm cuffed and in the back of a patrol car.

The lady cop says, So you're going through a divorce huh?

Yeah, I say. And, well, there's this—

Me too, she says.

She starts to drive away. .

I look back over my shoulder and the cops are handling Wendell and Louise—

Listen, this isn't worth it, she says. I'm telling you, whatever the problems with your parents, whatever the problems with the woman you're married to, you need to forget about them all maybe. Just forget about them and move to a new town. Start completely over if you have to.

I would, but I—thanks, I say. Where are you taking me?

Harbor UCLA, she says.

Oh, I say. The psych ward?

Mm-hm. It's the only thing I can do, she says. You were talking suicide.

What're you going to do with my dogs?

They'll be safe, she says.

When we get to the hospital she checks me in, says goodbye and wishes me luck.

I'm in a holding room with a big Latino dude on a cell phone.

He's in an argument with someone.

He gets off the phone and looks at me.

What's up, I say.

Oh man, my life's such a mess, he says.

Yeah? Mine too, I say. I almost offed myself yesterday.

I been thinking suicide too, he says.

I ask him, Anything in particular?

It's a lot of things. Problems with my lady mainly, he says.

Me too, I say.

He asks, What do you do?

I'm a lawyer, I say.

A lawyer?

Yeah, I say.

Wow. What does your lady do?

She's a prosecutor.

A prosecutor?

Yeah, I ask, what do you do?

I'm a drug dealer, he says.

Really? What kinds?

Whatever, he says. I know it's not right, but I've done pretty good at it. It's stressful even though I've never caught a case.

I bet, I say.

Wow man, he says, I always thought on that level, professionals or whatever, you'd never end up in a place like this—

Yeah, I say. I can see why you might think that but you'd be surprised. I probably should've been a drug dealer.

Go to med school, he laughs, and do it all legal.

A young, attractive woman of Indian descent comes in and introduces herself as a psychiatrist.

Hello, I say.

Hi, she says.

The big guy gets up to excuse himself.

My ride's here, he says. Good luck.

Thanks, I say. Don't kill yourself.

I won't if you won't, he says.

The young doctor says, John, are you really suicidal?

Yes and no, I say. If I could get a handle on everything that's happening to me I think I'd want to stick around. I had a horrible fight with my father—well, the whole family situation is—

Do you live with them?

I guess I do. My wife kicked me out a month ago and I ended up back home. My Mom's got cancer—it's such a long story. I honestly don't have the strength—

You don't seem suicidal.

I don't want to die, I say. I'm in a lot of pain though. Do you know of a shelter or something where I could go, maybe with my dogs, just to get away from them? When my Dad's mad he orders me into the street—

Not really, she says. Not for you. What you're thinking of is like a motel. There's motels all over the city.

I don't have a dime.

Yeah, that's a tough one, she says.

So, I ask, if a person finds themselves with no money for some brief period in their lives, there really aren't any resources for them are there?

She says, If you leave your bed in a shelter you'll find someone in it when you get back.

How does one become homeless, exactly?

You're doing it, she says.

That's nice. So it's back to suicide I suppose.

No, no, no, she says.

Yes, yes, yes, I say. I've been on every drug you guys have to offer. I've been to counseling. I've been back to

Church. Still, I wake up in the morning and I can't breathe and you all have no idea why or what to do about it. So the natural next step is death, don't you think?

No, she says. I'd like to talk to your wife.

My wife? What for? She kicked me out. She's done with me.

What's her number?

I give it to her.

The doctor leaves for a few minutes.

When she comes back she says, Your wife wants me to keep you on a 5150 hold. She's very concerned about you.

That's great. My wife throws me out, my father screams at me, threatens me, I can't breathe, think or see straight, and now I end up on a 5150 hold because my wife tells you to keep me? Everyone's concern is really touching—

You have insurance, yes?

Yeah, for the moment.

Do you know *Del Amo Hospital?*

Oh great. Mom went there once or twice to detox when I was a kid. Also, every now and then some nutjob from the South Bay I hear about gets sent there. Is that where you're gonna put me?

Yes, she says. For a few days.

Apple don't fall far from the tree, I think.

DAY THIRTY-SIX

When I get to the little single story mental hospital they give me crazy-person pajamas and introduce me around.

They give me a couple pills and I start to feel really weak.

I go to sleep for a few hours.

When I wake up they send me in to see the psychiatrist on staff.

Hi John, he says.

Hi.

I've been looking at your chart here. I've talked to your father.

Uh-huh.

I don't know what to say to you, he says.

That's candid, I say.

I understand you were a very good runner.

Still am, I say.

Still running?

I'm here, aren't I?

He smiles.

You're very accomplished, he says.

For someone on a 5150 hold, I suppose.

I was a runner too, he says. At *Stanford.*

He asks, Do you remember when we were in college—running in the mornings?

Yeah, I say.

In Palo Alto I used to get up early and run in the mist, he says. I had that fire. I was gonna be a *doctor*—

I ran in tule fog in college, I say.

You remember that feeling you had inside, that yearning?

Yeah, I say.

You need to get it back somehow. I don't know how. We can give you some drugs, some counseling, but to get better—you're gonna have to do it yourself. You're gonna have to dig deep—

An honest psychiatrist, I say.

Later that day I hang out in the day room with all the other mental patients and we have a sing along with one of the staffers who plays the guitar.

It's fun.

There's a bunch of alcoholics, drug addicts, suiciders and other assorted desperados.

I like them.

Everybody's on the *Ativan* they pass out twice a day and sort of wraithlike, floating across polished floors in their hospital gowns.

We all go out for a smoke break.

I smoke a cigarette and don't cough.

Pretty good for my first one.

Why do crazy people smoke so much?

We talk politics and baseball with the big male nurse in charge of the smoke breaks.

He's cool.

One of the patients is an attractive woman who checked herself in. She said she and her husband are a couple of rich but poor alcoholics and she's afraid she's going to drink herself to death.

My roommate is a drunk lawyer.

He shakes all over.

Nice guy, knows a lot about classical music.

He and the attractive lady and I walk back in for meds.

Here's to no guarantees, I say, and chase another Ativan with a paper cup full of tap water.

I'll say one thing for scotch: it finishes better.

DAY THIRTY-NINE

In the morning we have a little group therapy which doesn't really work because nobody knows each other and there's no time to develop any trust or context.

Then a somewhat annoying nurse gives a chalkboard lecture on how we all have to learn how to get comfortable with being uncomfortable.

Yeah. Maybe so. But why, might I dare to ask, are we so damned uncomfortable in the first place?

DAY FOURTY

They let me out at the end of my three day hold and give me a bottle of *Ativan* and a bottle of sleeping pills.

That's great.

They've provided an alternative to hanging which, when you think about it, is such a ghastly way to go.

Dad picks me up.

He doesn't know what to say.

We ride in silence back to the house.

DAY FOURTY-ONE

The counselor who did the EMDR with me calls me up and says, John, counselors' practices go down when their patients commit suicide. Please promise me you won't commit suicide.

I won't commit suicide, I say.

You need to come back to therapy.

Okay, I say.

DAY FIFTY

I'm free of the mental hospital.

The frightening daily routine with Mom resumes.

Tonight I have counseling with the EMDR lady and marriage counseling with Elle down the hall.

I insist on paying for the marriage counseling myself since everything is my fault.

I'm still taking 8 milligrams of *Ativan* every day.

On my way down to Orange County from Redondo Beach I stop for gas.

I misjudge the distance between my front fender and the raised island upon which the gas pumps sit.

I ram the edge of the concrete and demolish the right corner of my bumper.

Oh well.

The turn signal lamp hangs by its wiring.

I yank it off and throw it into a trash can.

I show up to counseling in a blue haze.

You're under the influence, my counselor says.

I'm just taking what they gave me, I say.

It's not good for you, she says.

Apparently not.

I sleepwalk through the EMDR session, sleepwalk through the marriage counseling session.

I'm vaguely aware of the marriage counselor and Elle haranguing me about something—

You've got to take this seriously, one of them says.

I am taking it seriously, I say.

I hand Elle a folder full of photographs I developed from the shots I took out in the canyons before we split up.

These are for you, I say.

DAY SIXTY

I learn a few cases I was handling have been dismissed for failure to prosecute.

That's nice.

Now I'll lose my license.

DAY SEVENTY

I go to Federal Court with a declaration of attorney fault and get the cases that lapsed reinstated.

How embarrassing.

My practice has dwindled to next-to-nothing and it needs to stay that way until further notice.

I'm not taking anyone else down with me.

But there're some things I have to finish for people, nobody else will do it—

DAY SEVENTY-FIVE

Mom takes a turn for the worse.

The oncologist says her bloodwork shows active myeloma again and she's not responding to her old medications.

He has an experimental treatment he says we can try.

We sign all the paperwork and she starts with bone marrow tests and a bunch of other stuff.

We're at *Cedars* two or three times a week and I'm the one who takes her most times since Dad is working.

One day on the car ride home she passes out in the front seat.

I try to wake her up but she won't wake up.

I hold her forehead with my right hand and drive with my left.

Her breathing slows.

Finally we hit a dip in the road and it jars her into a sluggish consciousness.

She asks me, At my funeral would you play *Amazing Grace* on your saxophone?

Sure Mom, I say.

DAY EIGHTY

I think this is it for Mom, I tell Dad.

Yeah, like the doctor said if these new drugs don't work—

She'll be gone by the end of the Summer, I say.

DAY EIGHTY-EIGHT

I miss an EMDR session and the counselor wants me to pay up immediately right over the phone.

I tell her I have eleven dollars in my bank account. I can't afford this and anyway, I don't think I'm necessarily getting better anymore. I'm kind of stalled out. EMDR did some good things for me, but it seems somehow incomplete.

And in its false promise of completeness, it's as dangerous as all of the other genuinely false modalities.

I stop going.

I've got Wellbutrin and Lithium, neither of which seems to do much at this point. And forget about raising the dosages. They're plenty high.

The shrink at the mental hospital was right: I'm on my own.

DAY NINETY-FIVE

Not practicing much law. Just trying to finish what I've got. The parents still yell each other. I can't get started.

DAY NINETY-NINE

Elle and Nicole and I go to a baseball game.

We're still trying to work things out against all odds.

The baseball game resembles something I used to call fun.

That's something.

Of course, I sneak over to the hard liquor bar between innings to buy a shot of eighty-proof goodness and come back with a beer or two for cover.

Beer...

That's what I drink when I'm not drinking.

DAY ONE HUNDRED

I go far out onto the Southward cliffs of Palos Verdes to a new resort. It used to be a place the kids would park and make out. I sit in the bar and have a *Maker's Mark* Manhattan, up.

It's really pretty out.

I wish I had some idea how to move on.

DAY ONE HUNDRED TWENTY

I don't blow up very much anymore.

I mostly do the same thing every day now.

Wake up early, take the dogs out, try to get back by zero dark thirty so Dad can go to Mass at dawn.

Then I make Mom eggs, bacon and toast, monitor the cigarettes, wait for the caregiver to show up, go to Dad's office and try to work, or rather, try to do as little damage as possible, leave at three in the afternoon to take the dogs to the dogpark, stop and get a bite to eat, get home by five, take over for the caregiver, maybe give Mom a shower or clean her up a little bit, do something about dinner, wait for Dad to come home and pray for peace when he does.

Then shortly before bed I call Elle.

That's my day.

Over and over and over and over and over—

And every now and then something really shocking happens.

I can no longer see the beginning or end of this tunnel.

DAY ONE HUNDRED THIRTY

Mom takes too much pain medication and ends up in the hospital because her breathing slowed to nothing.

It's my fault. I was on meds duty this weekend.

They do a brain scan as a matter of course and call us in for a conference.

The doctor says the CT scan shows white matter deterioration.

I ask, What's that?

Her brain has atrophied in general and lost volume. And in the deep frontal lobe, the doctor says, there's a whole bunch of tiny strokes seen throughout that area. They've been there for a while now, accumulating. It looks like she might have vascular dementia—

Dementia? Like Alzheimer's?

That's the one everybody knows about and, on some level, dementia is dementia. But Alzheimer's works on a completely different principle. In your mother's brain little blood vessels stroked over time, some brain tissue died, but the outcome is different for everyone. The patient with vascular dementia develops what we call patchy deficiencies. In her case it could explain the apathy, the indifference to basic self-care, the impulsiveness, the childlike wanting, the cravings for specifc foods—

I guess she's fortunate the cancer is coming back, I say.

Actually, the doctor says, her myeloma is stable. Whatever they're giving her at Cedars is working. There's no detectable evidence of cancer in her blood.

Outside I sit on a bench for a while.

Holy smokes. What is she, going to be the first person in the country to be cured of multiple myeloma? It killed Dean in two years.

Maybe drinking and not giving a damn about the cancer is the way to go. Forget juicing, forget prayer, forget anything but finding the best doctor you can and checking out—

Mom's not just a cancer patient and an alcoholic, she's a dementia patient. And now her cancer's stable. She's outliving her brain!

What're we gonna do?

So much for easing her gentle into that good night—

She ain't going nowhere.

All this time and we don't find out until now she's got dementia?

Four and a half years in?

No wonder everyone's losing it.

DAY ONE HUNDRED FIFTY

The choir keeps me going.

Today we sing a sublime setting of that ancient prayer, the *Anima Christi:*

Anima Christi, sanctifica me.
(Soul of Christ, sanctify me.)
Corpus Christi, salva me.
(Body of Christ, save me.)
Sanguis Christi, inebria me.
(Blood of Christ, inebriate me.)
Aqua lateris Christi, lava me.
(Water from the side of Christ, wash me.)
Passio Christi, conforta me.
(Passion of Christ, strengthen me.)
O bone Jesu, exaudi me.
(O good Jesus, hear me.)
Intra tua vulnera absconde me.
(Within Thy wounds hide me.)
Ne permittas me separari a te.
(Separated from Thee let me never be.)
Ab hoste maligno defende me.
(Against the malignant enemy defend me.)
In hora mortis meae voca me.
(In the hour of my death call me.)
Et iube me venire ad te.
(And bid me come unto Thee.)
Ut cum Sanctis tuis laudem te.
(That with thy Saints I may praise Thee.)
In saecula saeculorum.
(Forever and ever.) Amen.

251

DAY ONE HUNDRED FIFTY-SEVEN

Mom says, I want to go see where Christopher is buried. Do you want to see your brother's gravesite?

I say, Sure, you've never seen it?

No, she says.

What happened when Christopher died?

It was very hard, she says. You were two. He was premature. He lived for several hours. It wasn't my regular doctor. He just said he didn't make it. They kept me in the hospital for a few days and by the time I got out, he was already buried. I couldn't ever make it out there.

Did you get any counseling or anything like that?

They gave me this phone number to call when I left the hospital. There was a center in the Midwest for women who lost live-birth babies. But when I called it was just this nice woman who talked to me for an hour, not really a center or a program or anything.

What did you talk about?

I don't really remember. But she was very nice.

DAY ONE HUNDRED FIFTY-EIGHT

Dad, I ask, What happened when Christopher died?

Which part?

Well, the whole thing. What was going on between you and Mom, in the business—

You were two. We were just about to move into this house. We were in escrow on it, actually. And we took a road trip up to Northern California a month before. That's something we shouldn't have done. We should've kept Mom in bed. She had a weak cervix. But we went. We were closing escrow in a matter of days when her water broke. So she went to Little Company of Mary and Christopher died. You were there. Anyway, he was very small and lived for just a little while. Your grandmother and I and a couple other people buried him out at a Catholic cemetery up near Culver City. Then Mom came home from the hospital and we moved into our new house.

What did Mom do when she got home?

She took to her bed.

For how long?

For a long time, John.

What were you doing?

I was covering a lot of territory for the company I worked for. They had me in Oregon, Utah, Arizona, San Francisco. I traveled a lot.

Do you think Mom had started drinking heavy yet?

He pauses.

I would call home some nights and the phone would be off the hook, he says. That was her way.

Wow, I say.

I didn't know what to do, he says. I had to work.

I know, I say. I don't blame you. You provided well. It's just—I was two and alone with her so much. I remember all her drinking starting from the time I was five, but there were many years before that?

Yeah, he says. Do you really think it affected you?

DAY ONE HUNDRED FIFTY-NINE

We head out to the cemetery to find Christopher's grave.

It's Sunday so the cemetery office isn't open to help us.

We drive around and around the cemetery looking for his grave but it all looks the same.

We can't find it.

People are having little picnics near headstones, playing music from boom-boxes for their departed relatives.

We vow to come back but I hope we never do.

Or at least I hope I'm not on booze-watch the night we find the headstone.

I'll have to sleep in front of the door.

DAY ONE HUNDRED EIGHTY-ONE

Elle and I have a fight.

John, all I wanted you to do was pay off those outstanding bills and come home, but now so much time has passed, I have a routine with Nicole—

A routine?

Yeah, the thought of you coming back and living with us is starting to seem—

Don't worry. Enjoy your routine, I say. I have one too and it involves bedside nursing, cooking, laundry and lighting Mom's fucking cigarettes. Just wait until your parents get sick, just wait—

Sorry my mother's not dying on time—

DAY TWO HUNDRED TWENTY

I'm trying to work again but it's tough.

I have to cram everything into five or six hours a day.

Plus, I'm exhausted and getting numb by the minute.

But is that really the problem?

No.

I'm all seized up and it has nothing to do with time or the lack of time, just the palpable dread and haywire vital signs that start before I even hit the shower.

I seem to be moving further from Elle, not closer.

I'm drifting.

But Elle thinks we're finally making some progress.

She says, Maybe you could be back home by Valentine's Day?

Yeah, that's three months from now. That's a pretty good goal, I say. Valentine's Day. Ten months.

I love you, John. I want you to come home.

But when we hang up I'm concerned.

I'm not better.

I owe about $6,000, down from the $12,000 that upset Elle so much, but for me the resolution of this period is not about paying off a few more late bills, it's answering the central question of my life: Why, exactly, do I wake up every morning feeling like some kind of a—a prey animal?

Yes, that's the question.

I've become a prey animal.

I've always fought the sensation—even at my best—but now it's upon me fully, flung around my neck and thorax like a grasping vine.

Everything's an effort.

I spend the whole day confronting this swirling dread, this paralytic toxin.

I've got three months to resolve it.

I can't go back to Elle and Nicole unhealed.

I can't go back broke.

But the psychiatrists, psychologists, therapists and other assorted medical professionals seem to have nothing further for me.

How many psychiatrists does it take to screw in a light bulb?

Only one, but the light bulb has to really want to change. Ha!

DAY TWO HUNDRED FIFTY

The choir rehearses the Christmas Mass.

I call Elle and say, I sure hope you can come to Midnight Mass with Nicole and your Mom.

We'll do that, she says. She asks, But what about Christmas Day?

CHRISTMAS DAY

It's bad, man.

Ever hear of a *Charlie Brown Christmas?*

This is a *Charlie Sheen Christmas.*

My folks come over to Elle's house and Elle's parents are there.

My parents start fighting and I flip out.

Okay?

I flip the hell out, alright?

In front of Elle's parents, Elle and Nicole and the dogs and cats.

NEW YEAR'S DAY

So coming home next month is totally out now.

Elle doesn't want me there.

Neither does her father.

Nicole's still supportive, but she's ten.

Elle's mother, cautiously so, but wants me to get straightened out.

I'm a head case.

I'm bad.

I mean, so what if my parents want to fight right in front of me at my wife's house with her parents there?

On Christmas Day.

After I'd been up till two in the morning singing Midnight Mass.

My parents fight.

That's just what they do, Elle and her mother tell me.

Sure.

Why can't I just handle that without getting that strange bitter taste in the back of my mouth that I tried to drown out with root beer, funny how much root beer I drank that night when they first got there, watching Mom look at all the wine glasses, no thought in that group that maybe they shouldn't drink out of kindness, I mean, why ruin their Christmas after all, so then Dad comes in and tosses me that pad to put down on the sofa after all the pissing and crapping and screaming I live with now, he walks into my wife's house and tosses me the pad, I'm on poo duty now, did he think for one minute that maybe I was hosting this too in a way even though it wasn't my house, but then he's just all pissed off, walks by Elle's father hardly saying a word, and perhaps it's hard for all of us because the last time we all three were in that house Elle kicked me out with her Dad's and my Dad's able assistance, so this is a reunion of sorts, survivors of a plane crash perhaps, but still, that wouldn't excuse the way my hands shook when Mom and Dad rang the doorbell, even before they walked in I knew they'd been fighting, I wish they hadn't come, oh Mom's headed for the food straight away, gonna shovel down like a cave man (a cave man with vascular dementia) but that's ok, we're all family here, at least in that Southern California way where divorced parents still hang out with their kids together on Christmas and you can be separated for ten months and still—but it's family and why can't I be totally calm in the face of Mom's publicly desperate craving ways?

I mean, hell, I was made to return wine to the grocery store at two in the morning with her, so how bad can this be?

I'm just a menace I suppose.

Temper temper temper—

John you've got to take responsibility for your own reaction, Elle and her mother tell me.

So to throw my parents out a few minutes after they got there (and Dad was glad to go) was really just déclassé and over the top on my part, to refuse all consolation thereafter, but to keep from putting my fist through the wall a feat for which I will never receive accolades—oh i am so sorry to have had the old thoughts in my head the thoughts about shame and how I'm gonna die and stuff like that but that's how it feels—

Didn't you see that?

They tried to kill me!

DAY TWO HUNDRED FIFTY-NINE

One last detail about Christmas.

Mom looked very sick, but Nicole went up to her anyway and gave her a big hug.

I didn't want to embarrass Nicole by commenting on it, but it was a gift to me. I remember how scary sick older people seemed to me when I was little, the stale smell, the weird patchy skin, the crazed look in the eye—

It was hard to touch them even though they wanted to be touched.

But Nicole did it consciously and without prompting.

I could see a slight hesitation.

It required bravery on Nicole's part.

I wonder if she thought about it ahead of time.

The hug was enthusiastic, genuine.

This ten year old girl hugged my mother like she were a real grandparent when everyone else in the world wished she would just go away.

That is to be remembered and commended.

What a great kid.

I will never forget it.

DAY TWO HUNDRED SEVENTY-FIVE

I've showered, dressed, changed and smoked Mom out with her favorite cigs. She's in bed. Dad doubles back from work. He comes in and starts in on her about something. It gets heated. I'm shaking. I resent the hell of out him for

Christmas Day. It was a betrayal. He brought Mom in to my wife's home and messed up my shit. And now he's all upset again. I just cleaned crap out of Mom's ass crack and he has nothing good to say, well listen up buddy Ima tell you something about the way it was, about the way you THREATENED TO BREAK MY FINGERS WHEN I WAS TEN YEARS OLD!

And he says, I WAS TRYING TO GET YOU TO DO YOUR MATH!

My hands are clenched again.

I look over at Mom sick in bed.

She's staring at us with that slightly vacant look she has now.

I look at this man before me and I realize, *he remembers!*

And he stands by it!

Stands by threatening to break a fourth grader's fingers.

My hands uncurl.

I back out of the room like I've seen a ghost.

He says, John, John! Where are you going?

I've forgotten my lines.

I quietly take my keys.

I'm not angry anymore.

A certain peace washes over me.

I see it now.

Doesn't matter about blame.

It's what happened.

No wonder I can't breathe in here.

I creep down the sidewalk in shock.

I'm leaving now.

DAY TWO HUNDRED SEVENTY-SIX

I roll out with two thousand dollars cash a client was good enough to advance me, two dogs, and a beat up

Cadillac with a broken back passenger window and expired tags.

I find a live-work space to rent about five miles away from Elle, deep in the heart of Laguna Canyon, behind a tow yard, up against the hill, the same property Timothy Leary occupied when he operated his *Rainbow Shack* and got half of Laguna high on windowpane.

Elle and I have to make a decision now.

If she takes me back I'll use the new place as an office.

No furniture, everything echoes in here, including the clopping of Wendell's Clydesdale hoofs.

Wendell, Louise and I head for the dingiest bar in Laguna.

DAY TWO HUNDRED NINETY

Anxiety is love's greatest killer. It makes one feel as you might when a drowning man holds onto you. You want to save him, but you know he will strangle you with his panic.

— Anaïs Nin

DAY THREE HUNDRED

It's late. I'm alone and drunk again on cheap blended whisky, and phenomenally high. I've blazed more weed than the *Wu Tang Clan*. I write an angry and absolutely unforgivable poem:

Re: Mom, why won't you just die already?
Dear Mom,
Why won't you just die already?
I can't stand watching this anymore
Medicare and Blue Cross and Cedars-Sinai
Stand between you and what's next

(her true brilliance was the way she used Calder, Mondrian and Miro to teach school children to love art)
Mom's in the hospital again—
Stole Dad's car at two a.m.
Wrote a bad check for six bottles of wine
Broke them open, drank them all
Fell down the hill and broke her hip
Shit all over her legs and back
She said Help me I said Not this time
Paramedics hosed her down and scooped her up
When the sun was higher and the day warmer
I held my hand over the heavy earth where the body hid
I said to the impression in the moss or no one really that
In modern times we make sure the body outlives the brain
(her Catholic school classmates voted her Most Ideal Senior)
Pull your pants up! Don't you have any sense left at all?
You think I enjoy talking to you like a child?
(she made the scout troop behave when the dads couldn't do it)
I'm all punched out, see—
I've watched you bleed, piss, crap, puke and pass out
I've seen you stuck, punched, cut, drugged, and drunk
I've changed, bathed and swatted you
Your teeth are falling out
If you'd just brush them—
(you said in all the years you'd known him dad never did anything unethical)
If you get wasted
One more time
You're going into a Home
(she used to say, If elbows had labels they'd say please don't
put me on the tables)

Goddammit I want another Marlboro she bellows
You just had one five minutes ago you crazy bitch
(when I was twenty she took me to the Chicago Art
Institute
and showed me The Banquet by Magritte)
I could've died right there
On the museum floor
From aesthetic arrest
That was enough for me
Haven't found anything better
Except the old Mass
There's nothing else to see here
So Mom, for the good of all mankind—
Why won't you just die already?

Part Eight: The Clearing
Season: Spring into Summer
Locale: Laguna Canyon
Preferred Handheld Device: Martini Glass
Dominant Theme: What—is beyond—the veil?

105

I wake up thick tongued and half blind.

Wendell thwacks me with his giant paw, ready for his morning trek.

I lie on an air mattress in an echo chamber of a rented painter's studio in Laguna Canyon. I take a good look around at the place I rented in such a frantic rush, moving in under cover of darkness. It's actually rather pretty and not cheap, fourteen hundred bucks a month. I'll have to scrape it together.

The property is snug up against a five-hundred foot hill full of wildflowers, annual grasses, deer, coyotes, hummingbirds, lizards, mountain lions, dragonflies and bobcats.

Not only do I not have much furniture, I don't really want any.

I wonder how long a man can survive on an air mattress?

Can it be like, you know, just your regular mattress?

It's better than a heating grate.

This one deflates in the middle of the night and I wake up with a hip pointer or with my face stuck to the vinyl where the sheet pulls off the corner.

So, yeah, I probably need a real mattress at some point.

And some socks.

I don't ever have any clean socks anymore.

Or clean matching ones anyway.

Why do I keep ending up in canyons listening to coyotes feed?

Lying here staring up at the beams I realize if I don't figure out what's wrong with me and get fixed up I'm gonna hang myself from one of them.

I won't screw it up next time.

106

I call a man I used to work with. He's a very smart lawyer, very strategic, great with rules and tactics.

He was a military officer and knows a lot about a lot of stuff.

I tell him about my horror show of last Christmas, and the horror of the last few years really.

I tell him I split from my parents' house and worry about what's going to happen up there now but if I stayed a minute longer I'd be dead.

I tell him I want to try and win Elle back but it seems like a long shot.

He says, Whatever else may be wrong with you, you've got PTSD.

PTSD, I say. Are you sure?

Yes, he says. I think it's your primary problem. You're probably also a drunk like your mother. Those things together just make each other worse. Did you have a bitter taste in the back of your mouth on Christmas?

Uh, yeah, come to think of it. I kept drinking root beer to drown it out.

Right, he says, that was inappropriate adrenaline you were tasting in the back of your mouth. Your reaction far exceeded the threat.

Well what do I do?

You were already doing cognitive behavioral therapy?

Yeah, EMDR. It was a lot of let's-take-the-scared-boy-out-of 1983-and-put-him-in-the-present-where-he's-safe.

How did that work for you?

Elle kicked me out when I was about ten sessions in.

Right, my old colleague says. So the *scared boy* re-learned that he wasn't safe in 1983 and he's not safe now.

Mm-hm.

Excellent, he says. What a mental health disaster. Truth is, he says, you're *not* really safe now. I'm not sure I could say you have post-traumatic stress disorder because you're actually being re-traumatized *now*. You're living it again. Mom's drinking, falling down, terminal, Dad's raging, you're supposed to do something about it and can't. It would be like I tried to take a man under my command who came back from a hostile theatre and fired an AK-47 over his head during therapy. And one other thing. When you were a child alone with your drunk mother you tried to keep her alive for your survival. Now that she's dying you sense you will die too.

Wow. That's heavy.

Yes. But be aware of it. Her death does not mean your death. Let her go, he says.

Every few days it seems there's some crisis, I say.

Yeah, he says. There is. I don't have a lot of good answers for you. I think you should stop drinking and using drugs though. You think they're helping your anxiety, but they're actually causing a lot of it. I used to be in charge of a bunch of guys, I remember a group of airplane mechanics, not even front line troops—they'd sometimes have personal problems or severe issues from foreign deployments and I'd tell them, *look,* we can't do everything at once. We'll get you some help, you'll have time to heal, but in the meantime can you just fix the damn plane?

What happened?

Sometimes they could and sometimes they couldn't. Just behaving normally can be its own treatment. Contrary action and all that. Can't really baby people on active duty, though. If they couldn't make it they got boarded out. I think that's a good thing. When someone hits a limit, they hit a limit. You're going to have to do the best you can. But I repeat, you have a very good chance of becoming a drunk and a drug addict if you're not one already, he says. Whatever you do, you should try to treat the underlying trauma and not just chase symptoms. That's the problem with psychiatry and most psychology. You can't drug it and you can't just talk it out. Something more is required. Some form of action. I'm not a religious man but some people go there. You're going to have to work it out through trial and error.

He says, The thing about PTSD is there are two types, shock trauma and complex trauma. Shock trauma is like a car accident or a rape or something. It's bad, and the trauma can kill people, but it's isolated and easier to treat. You're an adult child of an alcoholic. All that means is you have Complex PTSD. Go look up the laundry list of traits they use to describe the malfunctions of adult children of alcoholics and then go to the DSM and look up Complex PTSD. It's the same stuff. Complex PTSD results usually when a person is traumatized over time by something from which they cannot escape. That's what it's like growing up in an alcoholic home. Some are worse than others. Some people are more sensitive than others.

Complex PTSD requires a lot of different things to treat it, he says, like hypnosis, talk therapy, group therapy, like I said, I'm not religious but I've heard prayer and meditation and things like that help too. I'm not so sure about the meds, especially in your case.

You should read some Peter Levine. He's a shrink who wrote a book called *Waking the Tiger*. Pretty good. But he seems to be better with shock trauma than complex trauma. He promised another book on complex trauma but I haven't seen it yet.

Why, I ask, do you know so much about this?

I was bored a lot on duty and it was just one problem after another with these guys. I just wanted them to function. And I realized a lot of guys have trauma but the military compounded it with highly traumatic deployments. I could really see the dysfunction on the surface. So I had to understand it or half my guys would have been boarded out or in the brig.

So what do you think of my situation?

If you were under my command I'd be worried about you. You seem pretty far gone. But the fact is you used to be very successful in some ways and that didn't happen by accident. So there's hope for you. But many people in your condition eventually kill themselves. We'd see about twenty military suicides a day now in the United States. That's the endgame for untreated PTSD or treatment-resistant PTSD. My feeling is many of the people who kill themselves are comorbid with alcoholism. You've gotta consider knocking the sauce off ASAP.

Oh and there's a thing called the *Holmes and Rahe Stress Scale,* he continues. They list all these stressful life events and assign them points. If you have a certain number of points you're at a statistically higher risk for death and disease. I think you have like five of them. Divorce is number two on the list after death of a spouse. You're in the red zone my friend. Part of it is you just have to weather this. Those risks go down with the passage of time after the stressful events.

Wow. Thanks. I wished I'd called you a few years ago.

Nah, he says, you wouldn't have listened then.

107

The days pass slowly because I'm not seeing Elle very much, my Dad and I only talk every so often now, and I only have one or two clients left. I'm short on friends in Laguna so my main companions are drunk tourists and bartenders.

I don't think my old colleague is right about my being a drunk.

I enjoy it entirely too much.

That wouldn't be fair if I were a drunk. Without the chemical release I get from the brown liquor and the grass I think I'd be dead by now. It's a lot better than all the pills they gave me. None of that stuff worked at all.

I become a regular at a few gin joints around town. One high end, one low end, and one somewhere in the middle.

I have so little money at this point I shouldn't be dropping it on anything but food and gas and rent.

But there always seems to be a few extra bucks available for booze and grass.

The first time I hear the word *regular* at a bar, as applied to me, I'm startled. I never thought of myself as a *regular* at a bar.

I'm not sure I like the sound of it.

That Joni Mitchell tune comes to mind.

All good dreamers pass this way some day.
Hiding behind bottles in dark cafés.
Dark cafés.
Only a dark cocoon before I get my gorgeous wings and
fly away.
Only a phase, these dark café days—

Bartenders seem to come in two varieties, the set-em-up-joe type and the mystics.

I tend to favor the mystics.

At a minimum, the bartenders are armed with a central nervous system depressant and horse sense.

Until further notice the bartenders are all I've got and they beat the psychiatrists by a country mile.

108

I want to see Elle every day, or at least talk to her.

But I don't.

I've declared my intention to work it out.

She knows I'm down the hill.

I've got to let her come to me.

One day she calls me up and says Nicole has an interview at a Catholic elementary school.

Elle says, She's gonna transfer. Would you like to come and check it out? You know all the Catholic stuff.

Yeah maybe I know a thing or two, I say.

At the interview Nicole's grandmother tells me that Nicole said she thinks she's Catholic. She says Nicole said her father is Catholic, her step-father is Catholic, and her grandfather is Catholic. Her grandmother said she laughed at Nicole and said but Nicole, you're not Catholic, you haven't been baptized.

I ask, Nicole hasn't been baptized?

No, Elle says, When she was born I asked her father if he could give me one good reason why she should be baptized and he couldn't give me one.

This jars me.

I wonder how I would fare, even coming into the Faith a wee bit as I now have—how would I answer that question if it were put to me. Why *should* Nicole be baptized?

The principal gives us a tour and afterwards Nicole says she's going to write an essay on the saint they named the school after to put with her application.

Elle says it's not required but Nicole says she wants to do it anyway.

We go to dinner and then Elle goes back to her house and I go to my Laguna Canyon hideaway.

I lie here on my leaky air mattress and stare at the ceiling.

I ponder the question, *Why should a person be baptized?*

109

A few aimless weeks later it's Saturday night again.

High Mass tomorrow.

I decide not to go out drinking and sit there with strangers tonight.

I need to get serious.

I need to review.

What really happened the last seven years?

I take out a pencil and a yellow legal pad.

I write down every major event that occurred in my life.

Mostly it reads like a series of shocks.

But then I write, *Discovered the Latin Mass—*

I stop with that last one.

Through the last two and a half years, through the collapse of my psyche, through the inability of anyone at all to address it with me, through Mom's turn back to hardcore alcoholism by way of dementia and terminal cancer, through disillusionment and confusion, there was the Mass. A phenomenon I hardly understand.

I don't even take Communion.

I do some late night reading, looking into the history of the Mass, thinking maybe I should know a little bit more about it before I walk back into one tomorrow. I read things I was somehow never told in twelve years of Catholic school. The earliest surviving account of the celebration of the Mass in Rome is that of *Saint Justin Martyr* who wrote about it in 148 *Anno Domini:*

On the day called Sunday, he wrote, all who live in cities or in the country gather together to one place, and the memoirs of the apostles or the writings of the prophets are read, as long as time permits; then, when the reader has ceased, the president verbally instructs, and exhorts to the imitation of these good things. Then we all rise together and pray, and, as we before said, when our prayer is ended, bread and wine and water are brought, and the president in like manner offers prayers and thanksgivings, according to his ability, and the people assent, saying Amen; and there is a distribution to each, and a participation of that over which thanks have been given, and to those who are absent a portion is sent by the deacons.

He also described the change in the bread and wine which Christians of that day believed to occur on the altar:

For not as common bread nor common drink do we receive these; but since Jesus Christ our Saviour was made incarnate by the word of God and had both flesh and blood for our salvation, so too, as we have been taught, the food which has been made into the Eucharist by the Eucharistic prayer set down by Him, and by the change of which our blood and flesh is nurtured, is both the flesh and the blood of that incarnated Jesus.

I'm struck by the awesome durability of the basic structure of the Mass, divided *now* as *then* into the *liturgy of the word,* where prayers are prayed, scripture is read, instruction and exhortation are given just like Justin Martyr described in 148, and the *liturgy of the Eucharist,* a series of prayers leading up to a consecration, wherein the priest prays the words of Christ over bread and wine and they are thereafter said to contain the body, blood, soul and divinity of Jesus Christ, and to have salvific value for those who partake of the consecrated matter.

I stop and think about this for a minute.

No wonder people don't believe it.

On its face, it's one of the craziest things I've ever heard. But there at the Mission, I witnessed for the first time an *ad orientem* consecration of the Eucharist. *Ad orientem* technically means *to the East,* but in liturgical practice it means that the priest faces the same direction as the congregation. This is what I heard about when I was an altar boy, that they got rid of the old Mass because the priest turned his back on the congregation and mumbled in Latin. But now I find the actual experience of it altogether breathtaking.

As an attorney the *ad orientem* posture of the priest makes perfect sense to me: he stands in the breach. The Mass is not a human performance, the priest is our advocate and more than that, a victim, a proxy for Christ. His focus is on the re-presentation of the atoning sacrifice offered through him by the timeless action of Christ. We face God together, but the priest intercedes. And of course the *ad orientem* consecration emphasizes the peculiar reality of the holy sacrifice of God the Son to God the Father, an event so strange it would seem no man would have made it up, and if a man had made it up, it seems no other men would have kept it alive for two thousand years like our spiritual lives depended on it.

Something about this old rite of Mass makes this indelibly plain to me. Through the *ad orientem* posture, it seems the idea of the priest as *in persona Christi* is made clearer somehow, perhaps paradoxically because the countenance of the priest himself is obscured except when he preaches and a few other times.

I realize now that even though I cannot yet partake of the Eucharist, what I observed, or really discovered, in the *ad orientem* consecration over the past couple years was the fulfillment of a need I did not know I possessed: a deep, unshakable desire to *worship*.

Unlike a rock concert, where the crowd *idolizes* the performer, or really any other kind of man-to-man presentation, in this liturgy—the offering of God the Son back to God the Father—we are truly *doing this in commemoration of Him* but also acknowledging the force of His words over bread and wine that *This **is** My Body; This **is** My Blood*—as though they mean what they say.

Maybe Catholics are the true fundamentalists after all.

I read that throughout Church history there was some variability in the practice of consecration *ad orientem* or toward the people, *versus populum*. However, what I've observed of late highlights an aspect of the theology of the Mass that had been heretofore hidden from me—an undeniable emphasis on the re-presentation of Christ's sacrifice and our metaphysical participation in it.

It's very, very late. Mass is in four hours. I do not yet understand the full impact of John 6 and the shocking, terrifying, hopeful proclamations contained in it—that *if we do not eat of His body and drink of His blood, we. have. no. life. in. us.* (John 6:53) Or the converse—His promise that if we do eat of His body and drink of His blood He will *raise us up on the last day.* (John 6:54)

But some dim awareness is beginning to open before me like a Japanese folding fan.

I try and absorb it. The shock of those initial words—the *necessity of eating* His body and *drinking* His blood lest we are lifeless—is followed by an extraordinary promise. If we *do* eat of His body and drink of His blood, Jesus proclaims, He will *raise us up on the last day.* This strange practice is thus understood by the Church to be tied *directly* to salvation. The only way around it is to argue metaphor, and there's no evidence elsewhere in Scripture, or in the history of the Church, that these solemn decrees of the Messiah were ever understood to be mere metaphor.

Saint Paul seemed to think the Corinthians needed to receive the Eucharist *worthily* and if they didn't it would make them *sick* and *weak* or worse. This would be an unlikely thing to say about a mere symbol.

But let a man prove himself, Saint Paul instructed, *and so let him eat of that bread and drink of the chalice. For he that eateth and drinketh unworthily eateth and drinketh judgment to himself, not discerning the body of the Lord. Therefore are there many infirm and weak among you: and many sleep.* (1 Corinthians 11:28-32)

Even Martin Luther affirmed the supernatural reality of the Eucharist. Luther realized that the whole of the early Church understood some form of the doctrine of the *Real Presence* of Christ in the Eucharist and so he challenged his newly Protestant fellows, who were already splitting from him on this point and many others: *Before I would have mere wine with the fanatics,* Luther declared, *I would rather drink sheer blood with the Pope!* And we know how he felt about the Pope.

As Flannery O'Connor, the great Catholic short story writer from Georgia, famously remarked when put on the spot at a dinner party in the deep South by some challenging Protestants: *If the Eucharist is just a symbol,* Ms. O'Connor said, *to hell with it.*

Under the long illuminating shelter of the elevated Host after the *ad orientem* consecration and its reverent presentation to the communicants, kneeling, on the tongue, touched only by consecrated hands, I know exactly what Ms. O'Connor means.

Why *wouldn't* God communicate with us in some ways that are quite simply beyond words? If the Real Presence is good enough for Jesus Christ, Saint Paul, Martin Luther and Flannery O'Connor, maybe it should be good enough for little old me.

110

This morning I sit in the choir loft more attentively, even though I'm sleep deprived from staying up half the night reading about the *Real Presence* of Christ in the Eucharist.

Today I follow the prayers of the Mass closely. I remember when I was a kid the liturgy of the Eucharist was always *the boring part,* the part that never changes, while at least the readings during the liturgy of the word were a little different and the preaching might be good. But here today I focus almost exclusively on the prayers leading up to the consecration of the bread and wine.

I'm struck by two words that come toward the beginning of the Eucharistic prayers: *Sursum corda* in Latin, translated as *Lift up your hearts* in the modern Missal. The translation at the beginning of the missal I have from Celia says, *Hearts aloft!*

I find this translation for *sursum corda* compelling. The priest issues this as a kind of command: Sursum corda! Hearts aloft! And then proceeds with the prayers of consecration. As he elevates the host after the consecration, displaying the Eucharistic Christ, it *does* feel as if *my* heart and *all* the beating hearts of the congregation rise with *Corpus Christi,* rise in an offering of God back to Himself, rise in true *worship.*

The stakes are high on this point, unless of course there is no God or God doesn't care what we think or do. One thing is clear. Christian Scripture, and Apostolic tradition and teaching regard the Eucharist as *the* vital core of Christian worship. If the Christians got this wrong from the beginning—this *Real Presence of Christ in the Eucharist* business—what are the chances they're right about the fantastic claims concerning the divinity of Christ?

If Saint Paul and the early Church and all Catholic theologians are wrong that the Eucharist is a channel of sanctifying supernatural grace—that it's a *necessary* and *indispensable* way Jesus left Himself with us—then they're undoubtedly wrong about His divinity too.

If they're wrong about the mystical character of the Eucharist, none of their other ideas should be trusted, especially considering the centrality of Eucharistic theology in the apostolic Church. If the Church is wrong about the Eucharist, She must be wrong about Christ.

And thus, we'd be engaged in a dual idolatry, idolizing first a mere historical figure as divine and secondly believing the false promise that the eating of Christ's Body and drinking of Christ's Blood is salvific.

It occurs to me that the Eucharist is the perfect corollary to a being who was fully human and fully divine, existing as the Eucharist now does—or at least is believed to—in both a fully natural and fully supernatural way.

That's as far as I can go with it, at least for now. But I'm starting to come around. God left us more than a Church, more than a Church that would produce a New Testament and prayers, He left us means of corresponding with Him that are truly, truly above and beyond language. No wonder men shove it aside, no wonder they cannot see these truths with the eyes of faith. These realities are so clearly above our nature we'd have to *have* supernatural grace to apprehend them.

I sit in the choir loft somewhat forlornly now as the rest of the members shuffle down the two hundred fifty year old brick staircase for Communion. I flip through the 1962 Missal, the little booklet that contains the prayers and instructions for the Mass. I'm struck by the fervency of a prayer entitled *Thanksgiving After Communion*. It's meant to be said privately. It's not part of the Mass, but suggested as something that could be prayed after Communion in private devotion:

My good Jesus, the prayer reads, *I pray You to bless me; keep me in Your love; grant me the grace of final perseverance.* **Help me to become a Saint.** *Safeguarded by You in soul and in body, may I never swerve from the right road, but surely reach your kingdom, where, not in dim mysteries, as in this dark world of ours, but face to face we shall look upon You. There will You satisfy me with Yourself and fill me with such sweetness that I shall neither hunger nor thirst forevermore: Who with God the Father and the Holy Spirit lives and reigns, world without end. Amen.*

Help me to become a Saint? Really? Doesn't that seem like a bit much? I never saw a prayer like that before. It never occurred to me to ask to *become a Saint.* But sitting up here in the choir loft at the Mission among those who just fervently received Communion in such great faith, the

277

whole idea of *saints,* united to God in the particular way He intended, in communion with Him, seems at least possible.

111

After Mass the choir goes out to breakfast.

Today there's a special guest with us, a woman who's introduced by another member of the choir as a Dominican nun from Peru.

She's dressed in a full white habit with a black veil and has a certain animated quality.

I listen to her speak for a moment and realize: she's not a real nun.

She's pretending to be a nun, but she's not one.

I can't quite articulate the reason why I know this to be true, but I know it to be true.

The fake nun talks excitedly about how she's travelling because there's some problem or other in the region where she was and how the government and the embassy might not be hospitable to the Dominicans anymore, and she talks about a dying woman whose hand she held before she left the world and tells us that the dying can teach right up until their very last breath.

I actually like this person, but she's a con artist.

She doesn't have that certain quality—which I cannot at present seem to name—that other authentic Catholic nuns and priests seem to have.

What should I do though?

You can't go around calling nuns fake.

What if I'm wrong?

But what if I'm right and this nice lady from the choir is housing a killer?

I know the fake nun is not a killer though. She wants to be a nun. She wishes she were a nun. And she needs a place to stay.

I'll just have to let it ride for a bit.

At rehearsal after breakfast the pseudo-nun sings with us and passionately points out that this *very part* of the Mass we're rehearsing was sung by the sixteen Carmelites who lost their heads to the guillotine in the French revolution. One by one, she says, they were marched up to have their heads chopped off and this *very Mass part* is what they were singing!

I think I'll have to research that, along with the Dominicans in the part of Peru where our guest claimed to have been!

My research more or less confirms my suspicions.

She ain't no nun.

The next week the habit-clad guest does not come to Mass and so I ask her hostess, my choir mate, where she is. She says she has her working out at her ranch and I think that's good. Something about her response tells me she knows the nun is not a real nun now and is distancing herself from her.

Excellent.

No need for me to mention it.

A few weeks later we're all at breakfast after choir and somebody asks where the nun went, and my choir mate explains that she just moved on.

At this point I can't resist anymore and I ask, *Was she entirely who she claimed to be?*

Everyone at the table turns and looks in my direction at the stunning implication of my question.

The hostess to the fake nun says, You hit the nail on the head. *How did you know?*

The problem is I can't really answer that question.

I can't say *how* I knew, I tell the long table, I just knew.

Another one asks, Why didn't you say anything?

I say, It's kind of like asking a woman if she's pregnant. I don't know you well enough to run around calling your nun friends *fake.*

The choir's impressed with me now, like I have some special gift for spotting impostors.

112

After breakfast the woman who housed the fake nun pulls me aside and says, *Honey, I'm worried about you. You've been with us over two years and you haven't made your general confession and you're not taking Communion. You really need to get that going. It's very dangerous what you're doing, like standing out in the middle of an intersection. You need to come all the way over to the other side of the street. Have you ever heard of the Confessions of Saint Augustine?*

No, I say. But I've heard of Saint Augustine.

I think he would be good for you now, she says. He's one of the greatest Doctors of the Church.

What's a—*Doctor of the Church?*

Oh—well, she says, there're thirty-three of them, soon to be a few more. They're Catholic Saints, typically Saints that wrote something of enormous assistance for Christians of all times. They wrote timeless works, usually judged by the Church well after the fact to be classic statements of the Faith. Outside of Scripture, there's really nothing like the writings of the Doctors of the Church. They're all saying the same thing from different perspectives; they shine light on different aspects of the Faith.

I'm somewhat stunned by this. After all, I graduated with a doctoral level degree from a Catholic law school and I'd never even heard of these so-called *Doctors of the Church.*

At best, I knew a few of the major names, like Saints Augustine and Thomas Aquinas. But I didn't know there was this cluster of thirty-three who had been vetted through the centuries. I'd heard vaguely that Augustine said something about the *God shaped void in the heart*. I always liked that. But it never occurred to me to see what he did about it. I thought of him and the others more as philosophers, stating problems without very satisfying solutions.

I ask her, Why don't more people know about this?

She smiles sadly and says, There's been a profound loss of faith. The reasons are complex. You will learn more in time. But most people are living in a state of mortal sin and that darkens the intellect and weakens the will. God just can't break through to most people anymore. And we are being divided into the sheep and the goats. The goats are in the vastly greater number. Be glad, she says, you've received great graces to be here with us, to be learning as you are. But John, you need a priest. Go see the community up on the hill. You need confession, you need spiritual direction. And you so badly need the Eucharist. Please. It's time.

She gives me her copy of the *Confessions of Saint Augustine* which she had in the car. It seems old and boring at first glance. I'm not looking forward to reading it at all, but I thank her nonetheless.

It's a hard read, she says, but it's thought to be the world's first true autobiography. I think you'll relate.

113

A few days later I get an email from the soprano who gave me the rosary and the novena booklet. She writes:

Dear John, I hope I am not being too forward here, but I would encourage you to use this time away from Elle to get right with God. If you were to actually be married to her, you'd have to do it according to God's law, and that is going to be very, very difficult. I hope you can start praying the Rosary soon. Also, there's a concert with the Orange County Symphony coming up featuring the priests that live up in the hills. They are going to sing some chant and the conductor of the symphony, who is a Catholic convert, is going to give a talk. Then the symphony is going to play a piece by Anton Bruckner, a Catholic composer. I've got an extra ticket if you want to come.

I'm startled by the email.

I can tell it took her some courage to write it.

I can picture her swirling a glass of red wine in her hand and then deciding to give it to me straight.

One thing I've learned about these people is they really believe in God and they really believe that God has a *law*.

A year ago I smirked a little bit at the notion, even while finding myself enamored of the Mass. One day we went over to a choir member's house for breakfast and our priest was there blessing the food. Half the people were on their knees, even one of the men I considered to be *normal*. But even he had such a deep look of prayer on his face, eyes closed, head upturned slightly. I thought then they were vaguely ridiculous, but now I'm not so sure. *God's law*, I think. *Marriage according to God's law.* I wonder what that would even look like. *Holy Matrimony?* That always sounded like more of a punchline to me. But it's a sacrament. *Many marriages are not good, and they do not please God,* Our Lady of Fatima is reported to have told her young seers in 1917.

I'll buy that.

I write back and thank the soprano and accept her offer of that extra ticket to the symphony.

114

The night of the concert is galvanizing. It's held at the major performing arts center in Orange County. We stream in and see some of the habited priests in the foyer, munching cookies, drinking wine little plastic cups and chatting with some of the Catholics they know as the large general audience heads for their seats.

We choir members sit in the high mezzanine, far from the stage. After the lights dim, the priests process in from the back, singing an absolutely luminous chant. They walk perfectly spaced, voices rising and falling, and take the stage in a large semi-circle. There are about forty of them. The house lights are slightly lavender, which gives their habits an otherworldly quality.

The priests continue singing prayer, standing in a semi-circle, standing in front of their chairs. I feel a palpable heat coming from the stage. They're doing something ferocious, like a martial arts display, but no one would confuse it as such. They finish, and sit in perfect unison, palms facing upward on their laps. They're relaxed but they don't move a muscle.

See, *this* is the quality that I've found in authentic Catholic clergy. I don't know what to call it exactly, but it seems to be a deep reserve, an interior quietude. Whatever it's called, these priests have that certain quality the fake nun lacked.

The symphony conductor takes the stage. He thanks the priests and begins to introduce the piece by Anton Bruckner. He speaks of Bruckner's deep Catholic Faith, and he speaks of how if one listens closely, one can hear the profound *Thou* in Bruckner's composition, as opposed

283

to the brash I one often hears in the compositions of other composers, like Tchaikovsky, for example.

The conductor talks for at least twenty minutes.

But my eyes are on the priests.

Not one of them moves.

Not one of them scratches an earlobe or looks out at the audience, or down at their shoes. This demonstration of relaxed prayerful stillness is profoundly fierce. The priests have something special. They've achieved something extraordinary in order to sit like that for that long. I've seen military discipline, sporting discipline, but this is different. Whatever it is they've done with themselves to get to that point, however they are the way they are—deeply serene—I want to be like that, me who can't sit for five minutes without looking around or fidgeting, me who can't leave the same station on the car radio for more than two songs in a row, me who's been driving around with a rosary and prayer booklet stashed in my center console for five months—

What am I doing? These people in the choir, let's face it, they have things I don't have: intact marriages, children, a certain peace. And the priests are on another plane altogether it seems. Am I ready to *really try* the Catholic Faith, instead of lurking up in the choir loft like a voyeuristic Mission swallow?

That means confession, that means at least trying this Rosary Novena thing, it means reading the Gospel and these so-called *Doctors of the Church*. Maybe I'll try it for real now, to really practice the Catholic Faith like I believed it. I mean, what else am I doing that's so special?

115

Something about the concert gives me hope. I think maybe I can make it somehow. A few days later I have enough confidence to call Elle and tell her I miss her, that

I'd like to spend more time with her and see if we can get reacquainted.

There's silence on the other end of the phone.

John, she says, what if I *can't?* I might like to, but I don't think I can. There's just been so much upheaval. We've been apart for almost a year. You feel like a stranger to me now. I don't know what you're going through, but it's just too intense for me. I'm afraid.

I stare out at the hillside, not entirely surprised.

That's okay, I say. *I'm sorry. I'm so terribly sorry.*

Later that night I go down to my favorite bar in Laguna and order a big vat of gin. Bring it to me in a tub, I say, half joking. They serve me martini after martini, dry as a bone.

I stumble out of the bar and very nearly into traffic. I can't find my car for what seems like hours. I've sobered up very slightly by then and drive to a liquor store. I buy a bottle of cheap blended scotch called *Canadian Mist* and drive back up to my lonely room. Wendell and Louise look at me funny.

I swill that so-called scotch straight out of the bottle. I finish about half of it and throw the bottle toward a cluster of rocks up the hill from my place. A man of my taste shouldn't profane my palate with this rot-gut. It tastes like *Night Train.*

The empty bottle of Canadian Mist shatters with a deeply satisfying popping sound. I picture the disgusting syrupy brown liquor seeping down the face of the large round stones, anointing them.

I pick up the copy of Saint Augustine's *Confessions* and open to a random page. It's blurry and incomprehensible. I throw it at the wall.

Waves of nausea sweep over me. I vomit in the general direction of the toilet for a minor eternity. I wash my mouth out with tap water and lie on the floor. The dogs amble over dumbly and inspect my corpse.

116

I speak to no one for days, maybe weeks. I lose time in great clumps now. The money runs low, but I go back to the bar, back to the liquor store. I stare with vicious contempt at a new bottle of *Canadian Mist* on my countertop. I recall with bitterness the New Mexico trip Elle and I took and the twenty-four dollar a shot scotch we drank by the fire.

Oh how the mighty have fallen, oh how pride cometh before the fall, oh if my classmates could see me now, Mr. Most Likely to Succeed, Mr. President of This, President of That, Editor of the Law Review, what a joke, I'm a dead man. Dead dead dead dead.

If you do not eat of My Body and drink of My Blood, you. have. no. life. in. you. (John 6:53)

The words of Jesus pop into my head like a buzzing mosquito.

Aaaaarrrrrggghhh! Blech! How can any of that be true?!

I grab the keys and Wendell and Louise's leash.

I'm thinking of driving off a cliff.

When I slide behind the wheel, I rev the engine, getting ready to peel out into Laguna Canyon and head for a high jumping off point. I glance at Wendell's goofy face. How many times has he prevented my demise? I stop myself for a minute. I pull the rosary and the novena booklet out of the center console. I drive to the beach, half drunk. I get out with the dogs and begin walking down the beach, leash in my left hand and rosary and novena booklet in my right. I begin to say the Novena prayers out loud like a madman, like one of the hairy homeless people who dot the Laguna landscape near dawn and dusk. I don't care who hears. If this doesn't work, I'm going to kill myself. I really wish this religion could be true, I really do, but look around! These couples on the beach don't believe it. They're having a perfectly fine time. And here I am, staggering around like a drunken pirate. What good is all this religion doing me?

Whatever.

Fine, so here goes: Day One of the Fifty Four Day Novena, The Joyful Mysteries, beginning more or less with *The Apostle's Creed,* which I recite aloud:

I believe in God, the Father Almighty. Oh do I now?

I believe in Jesus Christ, His only Son, our Lord. Really?

He was conceived by the power of the Holy Ghost, uh-huh

and born of the Virgin Mary. Okay, whatever you say.

He suffered under Pontius Pilate, was crucified, died and was buried. At least now we're standing on some historical ground.

He descended into hell. Wow.

On the third day He rose again from the dead. This better be true.

He ascended into Heaven and is seated at the right hand of the Father. Look, we're already so far out on a limb we might as well.

He will come again to judge the living and the dead. Anytime now.

I believe in the Holy Ghost, the Holy Catholic Church, the Communion of Saints, the Forgiveness of Sins, the Resurrection of the Body, and Life Everlasting. Amen. They sure throw in a lot of stuff there at the end. I'll have to look some of it up. What's the Communion of Saints anyway?

The Joyful Mysteries, I say out loud, competing only with the hiss of surf rushing up the wet sand.

The First Joyful Mystery: The Annunciation, I continue.

287

Sweet Mother Mary, meditating on the Mystery of the Annunciation of our Lord, when the Angel Gabriel appeared to thee with the tidings that thou were to become the Mother of God; greeting thee with the sublime salutation, Hail Mary, full of grace! The Lord is with thee! *and thou didst humbly submit thyself to the will of the Father, responding:* Behold the handmaid of the Lord, Be it done unto me according to thy word, *I humbly pray...*

Our Father, who art in heaven, hallowed be Thy name.
Thy Kingdom come, Thy will be done, on Earth as it is in Heaven.
Give us this day our daily bread and forgive us our trespasses,
As we forgive those who trespass against us.
Lead us not into temptation but deliver us from evil. Amen.

Okay, now I'm supposed to meditate on *The Annunciation* while I pray these next ten *Hail Marys*. Phew.

Hail Mary full of grace, the Lord is with thee! (Luke 1:28)
Blessed art thou among women and blessed is the fruit of thy womb, Jesus. (Luke 1:42)
Holy Mary, Mother of God, pray for us sinners now and at the hour of our death. Amen.

two, three, four, five, six, seven, eight, nine, ten—

Glory be to the Father and to the Son and to the Holy Spirit, as it was in the beginning, is now and ever shall be, world without end. Amen.
O my Jesus forgive us our sins, save us from the fires of hell and lead all souls to Heaven especially those most in need of thy mercy.

I bind these snow white buds with a petition for the virtue of charity and humbly lay this bouquet at your feet.

You gotta be kidding me! I've got to do this four more times, plus more prayers at the end, then every day for the next fifty-four days?!! This is no joke.

Toward the end of it there's a place where I'm supposed to make my petition—the first twenty-seven days are in petition and the second twenty-seven days are in thanksgiving.

I stop for a moment and look out at the sea.

I ask to be healed from my distress, that if it's PTSD I have to please make it go away, to enable me to move on in life without all this chaos swirling around me and all this interior pain. I ask to know how to feel better somehow.

Wendell pulls on the leash to sniff a passing Dachshund. I almost drop the rosary and sustain a burn from the leash slithering across my wrist.

Funny thing though, by the time I'm finished about forty minutes has passed. And that anger I had in the car, the sense I wanted to drive off a cliff, is a distant memory. I suppose it's just from the concentration that's in this practice, but I'm totally soothed out. Tired, but soothed out. I feel like I've been somewhere. I'll have to look into this prayer and see what it's all about. But for now I make a note not to miss it the next fifty-four days even if I'm tired or lazy, which is most of the time.

117

The days pass like a gelatinous goo now. I hardly know if the weekend is upon me. Weekends are good days to avoid the beach itself in late Summer. I can't walk Wendell down the block in Laguna without posing him for pictures. The crowd is intense, crushing, and my cue to head toward the local mountains, away from the beach for our daily dog-walking treks.

One evening, since I'm up by Saddleback Mountain anyway for Wendell's sake, I decide to stop into the Abbey. At eight o'clock every night they have Eucharistic Adoration, along with their evening prayers, as part of the ancient daily cycle of prayers called *The Liturgy of the Hours.*

It's nice to see and hear the priests up close and personal not just like at the performing arts center when they were so remote. The public is invited to all their prayers in the chapel. It's really quite an extraordinary thing to see. The pews are only about half full tonight, but everyone there looks deeply devout.

People wait in line in the back for something.

Confession?

I gather they do three things at the same time every night at eight: They expose the consecrated Host for adoration. They sing their prayers, and they hear confessions.

I kneel with everyone else when the priest displays the Host in the monstrance. The Gregorian chant washes over me like rosewater. But I can't stop thinking about what's going on behind me, all those civilians in line for confession.

I find myself getting up and getting in line behind the last person, not remembering what to do or say when I get in there. The line moves slow, which is good. The priests finish singing their night prayers for the moment and take seats in the pews with the faithful.

Everyone kneels in the pews or sits quietly in the presence of the Eucharist on the altar, and some appear to read the Bible or some other kind of religious text. Suddenly, I'm next in line. My palms sweat.

Eventually the door opens and I find I'm face to face with a serene looking young priest, probably thirty. I make the sign of the cross and say, Father, forgive me but I've not been to confession in about twenty years. I've been told I should make a general confession and I know this probably isn't the time to do it. But I didn't really know how to go about it so here I am.

He smiles broadly.

First of all, he says, welcome back. It's a wonderful thing that you're here. I'm sure you have a story to tell. The second thing is, here's a little booklet that you can look through which will help guide you to make a good confession. My name is Father Polycarp. After you read through the booklet, consider writing down your sins. Keep it succinct, but be thorough, starting from your earliest childhood memory. Don't hold back. We want to get it all, like a surgeon going after a cancer. Lying, cheating, stealing, murder, I don't care. God wants your repentance and He wants you back, He wants to forgive you. When you're ready, leave me a note at the front desk, and I'll call you and we can make an appointment. In the meantime, why don't you say an Act of Contrition here and I'll give you a blessing.

He hands me a little slip of paper.

Instinctively I kneel down and read:

Oh my God I am heartily sorry for having offended thee. And I detest all my sins because I dread the loss of heaven and fear the fires of hell, but most of all because they offend Thee my God who art all good and deserving of all my love. I firmly resolve, with the help of Thy grace, to confess my sins, to do penance, and to amend my life. Amen.

Father Polycarp makes the sign of the cross over me and gives me a short blessing in Latin.

291

Nice to meet you, he says. Don't wait too long.

Thanks, Father.

I walk out to the car feeling like I'm finally getting something accomplished. I don't know how many more Sundays I can go to the Mission without receiving Communion.

118

I do the bare minimum where work is concerned, just enough to pay the rent and buy a few groceries and keep gas in the car. The rest of the time I read the Doctors of the Church or Scripture, then go into town at about six or seven for some time at one of my hangouts. Some nights I go back up to the Abbey for holy hour. I pray the Rosary Novena every day. I feel somewhat better, even considering now I'm not waiting for Elle, other than for her to file some papers. I'm alone here in Laguna Canyon living on circular time, dawn and dusk, dusk and dawn. I picture the priests up there praying at dawn, and then at mid-morning, and then at noon, and then at four, and then at eight. It gives me great comfort. I feel somehow joined with them at all times. If they can live a quiet life full of prayer and sacraments with some work in between and go back to their cells and sleep alone, so can I. What is this life I've got, a hermitage? I've come across that in my reading, the hermitage as a valid spiritual practice. I seem to have the makings of one.

119

Fall comes and Dad calls.

His tone is grave.

John, he says, Mom is dying.

Now?

Soon, he says. I know we aren't getting along these days but I'd like you to come home more for her. I've been holding it together with the platoon of nurses we have, but it's getting down to the wire. We got a bad report from the oncologist. They're running out of options and she's getting weaker and weaker.

120

A few days later I go up there and Dad's at work. Mom's at home with a nurse. She looks terrible. I see what Dad meant. She's just so weak. She has a fairly vacant look in her eye at times, but she still knows all about current events and wants her cigarettes and her favorite foods.

I sit there with her not feeling like talking. There's a knock at the door. It's a so-called extraordinary lay Eucharistic minister from Saint Lawrence Martyr coming to provide Mom Communion. He comes into the room. Mom is polite. She receives the Host somewhat perfunctorily. It's a bit of an effort for her to swallow it. Her teeth are loosening and one of them's has just fallen out.

Oh honey, she says, would you get me some ginger ale. My mouth is so dry.

I oblige.

I'm touched by the visit. It calls to mind that passage of Saint Justin Martyr who described the early Eucharist, noting that *to those who are absent a portion is sent by the deacons.*

Nearly two thousand years later, a *portion* of the Eucharist was sent to my own mother, who was *absent* from Holy Mass.

The tradition of which Justin Martyr wrote in 148 A.D. continues here in Redondo Beach, California in our lifetime. Maybe there really is something to it.

I drive back to Laguna Beach, content not to see Dad on that trip. I wonder how long Mom has left. Weeks, months? I brace myself. I give Big D a call.

Hey man, he says. How're you doing?

Eh, I'm alive, I say.

That's good.

Mom's dying, I tell him.

Ah, sorry to hear that bro. She's really lasted a lot longer than you all thought though, huh?

Yeah, not sure it's been the best thing for all of us, but that's how it is.

How do you feel?

Not so good, I say. I'm kind of hoping she dies suddenly and I just get the call after she's gone.

Oh, I don't know about that, he says. I think it would be good for you to be there, to see it through if you can. You know I found my Dad's body the day after he died. I'm glad I was the one who found him. I wish he'd have healed up and had a natural death. Some cultures say an important passing of the spirit occurs between a parent and child when the parent dies.

Well, I don't think I want any part of my mother's spirit, not the way it is right now at least.

Don't be scared, he says. It'll be okay.

Thanks, I say.

121

One night I drive into town to go to my favorite Laguna bar. I order a big gin martini, dirty, and a decadent gourmet hamburger topped with duck and melted Gruyère cheese. I haven't had much to eat or drink all day and I'm famished. They set the martini in front of me and I prepare to slurp it down when, over the bar, a strange set of letters appears. They're arranged in a sort of translucent grayscale font. I can read it. It's a sentence. It says:

YOU SHOULD FAST.

Just like that. I can't quite hear the words in my head. But if they were to have a voice attached it would not be an emphatic voice but calmly objective, neither male nor female, simply saying, *You should fast.*

I look around furtively to see if anyone else can see the hanging sentence. All the patrons at the high tops behind me are chatting and drinking and eating without a thought.

I look back up above the bar and the words are gone.

Just then the waitress slides the giant steaming duck burger in front of me. The bartender gives me a smile and says, looking good Mr. Carmichael, as usual.

Yeah, I say, distractedly.

He says, Is everything okay?

Yeah, yeah, sorry. Why?

You don't look well, he says. Like you've seen a ghost.

Ha! No, nothing like that, I say. I just remembered something I'm supposed to do at home. I gotta make this quick.

I want to ask the invisible purveyor of the hanging sentence instructing me to fast some follow up questions like, Can I even finish the duck burger? Or drink this martini? Or maybe, Who are you? Or, Why *fast?* Or, *How* does one fast, exactly, just stop eating? For how long?!

I'm actually rather annoyed.

I slam the martini, pound the duck burger, pay the bill and split. I'm unnerved by the image of that peculiar sentence. I head home and the thought of it refuses to leave me. I smoke a fat joint and drift off to sleep, listening to the crickets.

The next day the memory of the strange message at the bar lingers, but I don't really know what to do about it. I

295

walk Wendell and Louise and pray the Rosary. I made it to day fifty! That's something.

I wonder if I'll ever get an answer to my prayers.

122

A few days go by and I show up to the Mission for Sunday Mass. After our seven o'clock morning rehearsal we're walking over to the Junipero Serra Chapel. The choir director stops me and says, John, you know my husband just died.

Yes, of course, I say, I'm very sorry.

Thanks, she says, but that's not why I'm stopping you. I saw a certain book the other day in the drugstore and thought of you. I need a breakthrough in my life to keep going. It seems perhaps you do too. Anyhow, I wanted to see if you'd like a copy of this book I bought. Maybe it's something we can work on together.

Okay, I say, What's it called?

She says, *Fasting.*

Fasting?

Yes, that's the name of the book, she says.

I feel like asking her if she's been following me, if somebody put her up to this.

She says, it was written by a local Protestant who takes his congregation through a fast every year. He discusses all the Biblical fasts: the half day, the one day, the three day, the seven day, the ten day, the twenty-one day Daniel fast, the forty day. Anyhow, it just seemed like something I was supposed to share with you.

Wow. Okay.

After Mass she gives me a copy of the book.

I pore over it most of the rest of the day.

On Monday I decide to start a one day fast.

By three o'clock I feel bizarre, like an astronaut outside his craft, cut adrift, threatening to float off into deep space.

By six I'm famished and drive into town and pound a bunch of sushi and wash it down with Japanese beer. I couldn't face the prospect of going to bed hungry.

I call my choir director and tell her I'd like to try a few day-long or three day fasts together. We use the buddy system and call each other when we feel weak. Both of us take broth and other juices.

I find when I fast I don't drink alcohol or smoke. It's as if the fasting induces a similar response in me as the grass—kind of ethereal, dreamy—but I'm not driven to hedonism like when I'm high. When I read spiritual material in this state it seems to lodge in my brain with treble hooks. I feel profoundly honest by day two of a fast, more loving, more open, more vulnerable. There is a cost for the enlightenment of this altered state however, the cost of hunger, the fear of hunger, the sense of being cut adrift. How strange though, the idea that one could go days and days and days without eating solid food. It's mysteriously empowering.

On another note, my fifty-four day Novena ended a few days ago. I wonder yet if my prayers for healing will be answered.

123

December.

Mom goes to Cedars-Sinai for what may be the last time. I meet Dad and Mom at the hospital. She's been admitted. We wait for the oncologist. He comes in.

Hi there, he says.

Hello doctor, Mom says.

We've used all our frontline therapies on your myeloma at least twice, he says. It's been seven years. We tried an experimental drug but didn't get much mileage out of it. There are one or two other things we could try, but I'm concerned because you're so weak.

What would you advise, doctor?

Well, if it were me, he says gently, I would probably stop treatment.

Okay, Mom says.

Mom, I ask, are you afraid?

Oh no, she says, quite convincingly.

Thank you for all you've done doctor, Mom says. Thank you.

The oncologist looks a bit sheepish, this heroic figure, having extended a thirty-six month prognosis by more than double. But that's the way it goes as a myeloma man, a lot of goodbyes.

124

I head back to Laguna Canyon. We have a hundred year flood. Water rushes down the canyon overflowing the creek and smashing everything in its path. The water rages and pours off the cliffs in giant torrents. It's a majestic catastrophe. Downstream, it floods one of my favorite subterranean bars, turning it into a fish tank for a few hours. No martinis in this town until they mop up. I decide to split and head back to Redondo Beach.

125

A day later Mom comes home from the hospital for the last time.

It's her birthday, Christmas Eve.

She arrives by ambulance.

The attendants help her to her room.

298

She eyes the new hospital bed warily, not knowing or caring to know that it was delivered by *hospice*.

She told us she did not want to hear the word *hospice* spoken in her presence.

So we quietly ordered up their services, knowing Mom would most likely not be returning to any hospital.

It was Mom's wish to die at home and it appears as though it's going to be granted.

Though, truth be told, it seems to be her wish not to die at all.

126

Mom quickly settles into her old routine of asking for things—food, cigarettes, but not cigarettes so much because she's on oxygen and knows she can't smoke inside. The effort is nearly too great for her to get outside.

And then she stops asking.

I have to leave and drive to the Mission to sing the midnight Mass for Christmas. I wish Mom a happy birthday, say goodbye to Dad and head South for the night.

The midnight Mass is eerie and haunting this time through, considering now this is Mom's last Christmas on Earth. I feel a certain shadowy presence in the Mission courtyard after Mass at two in the morning. Some say it's haunted. I wouldn't doubt it.

I drive back to Laguna Canyon from the Mission at three a.m. to survey the flood damage. It's massive, the canyon is covered in silt and the landscape is dotted with *Caterpillar* tractors and land moving equipment. A great torrent washed through the gully that I call home. It seems to portend a change somehow, this flood, turbulent, destructive, violent, but oddly cleansing.

A couple weeks later, Mom loses consciousness.

I go up to the house.

Dad calls the pastor from Saint Lawrence parish who shows up with another priest.

Mom regains consciousness long enough to receive extreme unction, also known as the last rites.

I stand outside her room.

The priest asks her if she's sorry for all the sins of her life. Her head lolls back and forth, seeming to say yes, or something like it, but she seems elsewhere, distracted, wishing they would just get out of her room. They administer the rest of the sacrament.

They leave.

I walk into the room.

Mom says, *I have no intention of dying.*

This is a woman who's *not ready.*

She loses consciousness again.

The next day Dad has to leave the house for a few hours. I'm alone with Mom and various friends who pop by. One of them shows up and tries to speak with Mom but Mom waves her off, saying, *Oh honey I'm sorry I can't talk right now,* and turns to her left where she appears to be focused, eyes closed, on some other sort of conversation. I observe what appears to be a preoccupation on her part. I sense that the people in the room are a distraction to her because she is elsewhere, trying to listen to something or someone. But it doesn't seem like a hallucination to me, it seems that she's really receiving information from somewhere and doesn't want to be interrupted.

A friend of mine stops by, a beautiful woman who has an affinity for the dying. We dated briefly once and have warm affection for each other. She alighted on my shoulder the past few months and she's by my side today. My friend is quiet, I am quiet, and we sit and observe Mom on her deathbed.

Mom's eyes are closed as if she's in a light sleep. But she makes strange motions with her hands, especially her right hand, as though she were gesticulating, or gauging distances she had never before seen. The movements do not seem purposeless but rather like the movements one might make in an actual conversation.

Another friend of the family stops by. She's had some experience in hospice. She says it looks like Mom has less than twenty-four hours to go.

Dad makes it home around sunset.

My friend and I go out for dinner.

We need a break.

I order a Manhattan.

I don't think Mom would begrudge me a belt or two.

Here at the bar we're disoriented.

My friend flirts a little bit, as if it were a normal night out.

It's a gift to me.

We have an odd thirty minute interlude, but after a couple drinks the solemnity of death returns to our faces and we know this most definitely is not a date.

Mom's still in extremis, *dying by degrees.*

We finish our drinks and head back to the house.

128

When we get back to Mom's beside the hospice nurse is there and my Dad's sister is there. My sweet friend gives me a hug, wishes me well and heads off into the night.

Dad, his sister, the hospice nurse and I all stand around Mom's bed. She's beginning to gasp for breath.

Mom opens her eyes for the last time.

They appear to be a different color, an olive green.

Mom looks right through me, as though she were looking on a vast expanse, an endless distance.

It's as though she wants to speak, as though if she could she'd say something like: *the immensity,* or *it's all real.*

Suddenly she reaches up and grasps Dad's hand.

She exhales and speaks Dad's name at the same time, *John, John, John,* she says.

Mom uses what remaining strength she has to pull Dad forward—not toward her, but forward, as if she wants him with her as she proceeds into whatever reality lies ahead.

I'm quite convinced Mom's looking into another world.

Having exhausted herself, she releases Dad's hand and falls into unconsciousness again, and her breathing steadily relaxes.

Dad, his sister and the nurse migrate into the living room.

I decide to stay with Mom.

I'm frightened.

I think of her wishy-washy response to the last rites the night before. I wonder if she ever made a good confession.

I don't know where these thoughts are coming from, since I don't think like this, but I start to feel a growing sense of dread. I run to the car and grab the rosary and the novena booklet out of the center console.

I kneel at Mom's bedside, peering at her through the hospital railing, listening to the dull whirring sound of the air circulating through the clinical mattress.

I begin by making the sign of the cross:

In nomine Patris et Filii et Spiritus Sancti, I intone.
I believe in God, the Father Almighty!
I believe in Jesus Christ, His only Son, our Lord!
He was conceived by the power of the Holy Spirit—

I pray the Joyful Mysteries, thinking I should've gone with the Glorious instead, but I'm fumbling with the booklet, trembling as I speak the prayers. I'm astonished at the scene, dimly aware that I'm kneeling at my mother's bedside praying the Rosary like our lives depend on it.

The second part of the Ave Maria comes into razor sharp focus as I ask the Mother of God to pray for my own poor mother:

Holy Mary, Mother of God, *pray for us sinners...now and at the hour of our death. Amen.*

Holy Mary, Mother of God, *pray for us sinners...now and at the hour of our death. Amen.*

Holy Mary, Mother of God, *pray for us sinners...now and at the hour of our death. Amen.*

Mom, who is truly now at the hour of *her* death, the *very moment* of it, makes exhausted groaning noises. She's fading, *fading.* As I enter the last decade of the Rosary, Mom begins to turn toward me, eyes closed, her face appearing ghastly gray and lined with pain through the bars of the hospital rails.

The rails appear to me as prison bars, separating us by a gulf, a vast chasm. I want to touch her so I reach through the bars and place a shaking hand somewhere on the dull lump under the bedding.

I finish the last few prayers:

Holy Mary, Mother of God, *pray for us sinners,* now *and at the hour of our death!*

Holy Mary, Mother of God, *pray for us sinners,* now *and at the hour of our death!*

Glory be to the Father, to the Son, and to the Holy Ghost, as it was in the beginning, is now, and ever shall be, world without end. Amen.

O my Jesus, forgive us our sins, save us from the fires of hell, and lead all souls to heaven especially those most in need of Thy mercy!

With that Mom appears to take her last full breath as though she *waited* until the Rosary was complete before she absented her ravaged body.

I call out to the living room, *Hey, I think you'd better come in here! I think she just died!*

The hospice nurse flips on the overhead light which strikes me as glaring and harsh, having just been in deep prayer for the past twenty minutes. She checks Mom's pulse, Mom's breathing and says, *yes, yes, she just passed.*

We stare at Mom's body which looks small and gnarled on the bed. She went through so much in this agonizing seven year illness.

The nurse straightens Mom's corpse out and cleans her up a bit. Dad goes to call the funeral home.

I cannot leave the room.

I stare at her body for a good long while, wondering what it was I just witnessed. I have the strong, overwhelming sense that she still exists, though I know not where.

I place the wooden rosary around her neck.

The hospice nurse stares at me.

She says, This kind of death only happens when there's prayer in the house. I'd love to talk to you about your faith sometime. I'm a Christian, and I tend to feel very alone.

Sure, I say, staring back at her blankly, wondering why anybody would want to talk to me about *my* faith, so weak and paltry as it is.

She says, It was good to see the men by the deathbed. Most men stay out on the patio, as far away as possible. I'm very impressed by you and your father.

Really?

Yes. You did a good job here. I was at a death last night with a ninety-two year old woman and everyone was screaming and crying and carrying on. It was terrible. Like I said, this kind of death only happens when there's prayer in the house.

The nurse leaves.

The funeral home attendants arrive.

They tote a large black body bag on top of their stretcher.

They place Mom's body into it and zip it up.

The wheels on their cart make a rattling sound as they rumble across the tiles in the foyer.

Dad, my aunt and I sit stunned, exhausted, numb.

I'm rather alarmed by the experience of Mom's death. It was very different than what I expected. It seemed to have a *content* to it, a *context* of some kind that was much broader, much beyond the mere expiration of corporeal energy. It really did seem, well, *spiritual,* and not entirely comforting. If the hospice nurse counts that as a *good* death, I'd hate to see a *bad* one.

Mom's spiritual condition, at least that which I understand now from the Church, in an objective way, was perhaps not so good.

Dad and his sister retire for the night. I stay up thinking.

Confession, confession, confession, confession.

I'm filled with a burning desire to get back to Father Polycarp as soon as I can arrange it.

I've got to make a general confession.

What the hell have I been waiting for?

129

A few days later, Mom's funeral.

We do the best we can in that span of time.

We plan a Catholic Mass with a viewing and Rosary at Saint Lawrence Martyr.

The Rosary has a special significance to me now.

I help lead the thirty or forty people present in it and I tell them that we'll pray the Joyful Mysteries since that was what I prayed with Mom a few days before at the hour of her death.

The classic Catholic funeral usually includes a Rosary the night before or hours before the funeral. I grew up dreading them, meeting in the creepy funeral home, praying in the same room with the body, often exposed in an open casket for viewing. But now, *now,* I stand next to Mom's open casket like I belong here, like a lieutenant.

Darn right we're praying the Rosary, troops! Buck up. It takes twenty minutes. Do you think you can manage it for my dead mother?

I even find myself reassuring the attendees that they don't need to actually *have* a rosary to *pray* the Rosary. I start it like a pro and everyone seems to feel like I know what I'm doing. I find myself thanking God we're all gathered here to pray a serious prayer for the repose of Mom's soul. And the comfort of the Rosary at the hour of Mom's death seems to link it now to *this* Rosary, and all the subsequent ones I'll pray, leading up even to the hour of my own death whenever it may arrive.

It's been said that when a parent or a loved one dies, we receive a grace. Hundreds of thousands of people can perish on the other side of the globe but because our hearts are hardened, or because we simply can't take it all in and live ourselves, the reality of death bounces off our consciousness. But a mother's death, well, Saint Alphonsus Ligouri, in his famously stark exhortation, *Preparation for Death,* put it like this:

Imagine that you behold a person who has just expired. Look at that body still laid on the bed, the head fallen on the chest, the hair in disorder and still bathed in the sweat of death, the eyes sunk, the cheeks hollow, the face the color of ashes, the lips and tongue like iron, the body cold and heavy. The beholders grow pale and tremble. How many, at the sight of a deceased relative of friend, have changed their life and retired from the world?

We carry the casket in procession from the funeral home to the Church. The handles dig into our white gloved hands. After the Mass, I give a short eulogy and one of Mom's friends speaks about her life.

As I look out over the assembled group there, mostly Catholic, mostly lapsed or lukewarm, I want to scream.

I want to scream: *It's all real!!!*

There is life after death.

Sister Aloise Mary gave it to me straight thirty years ago right here at Saint Lawrence Martyr, thirty feet away in what was the first grade classroom.

After death, judgment.

Then heaven or hell or purgatory.

We've got three priests here...

Grab your purple stoles, Fathers!

Confessions for everyone tonight!

But of course I can't say that.

Instead I spend my few minutes charming everyone, recalling *Carol Carmichael,* a woman who shunned her first, given name of *Mary,* thinking it what, too common? Too traditionally pious?

And there I was at the hour of Mom's death, begging Mary for intercession. What fools we've all been. The time of our salvation is now, *now* people. The first word out of Christ's mouth when he began his public ministry was

Repent! And here we sit in a Catholic Church, everyone allergic to the confessional.

I wish I could tell them the truth. I don't know what I saw the night of Mom's death, but it didn't fill me with a warm glow. I'm quite convinced she met a supernatural fate of some sort, and she was scared when it came into view.

130

At the reception, a striking woman taps me on the shoulder.

Oh, hello there, I say, and give her a hug.

This is the family friend that appeared out of nowhere the day I found Mom bleeding out in the garage after her fall those two and a half decades ago.

I ask, How are you?

I'm good, she says, under the circumstances.

It's nice to have everyone together, I say.

Yeah, she says.

I ask her, Do you remember the day you came over and found Mom on the garage floor?

Oh yes, she says. How could I forget it? Twenty-three years ago now, isn't it?

I've always wanted to ask you something about that day, I say.

Mm-hm, she says.

How is it you came over to our house at that precise moment? Because I just got home from school and found Mom lying there a few minutes earlier. I walked to the back of the house in a daze not sure what to do but then the doorbell rang and there you were—

Oh, she says, I can tell you exactly what I was doing—I was baking, which I didn't really even like to do, but I was in the middle of it and had flour and eggs all over the place.

Suddenly I got a jolt of some kind. I said to myself, There's something wrong at the Carmichael house.

Whoa, I say. I always thought you were just coming home from the store and happened to stop by—

No-no. It was very specific, she says. I was compelled. Then I drove over there and found your Mom in the garage. How long had you been home?

Two minutes, I say. A very long two minutes.

Part Nine: The Field Hospital
Locale: A New Dimension
Subject: Angels and Demons
Age: 40
Occupation: We'll see about that
Condition of Soul: Scrubbed and raw

131

A few weeks after Mom's funeral, I have a startling dream.

It's like watching a bright, overexposed, eight millimeter home movie.

In the dream I'm standing in the living room at my parents' house.

I hear sirens racing up the street.

I assume it's a stress dream about Mom's illness, the many times she was rushed off in an ambulance.

But then a single car arrives, a red sedan, with a sole flashing light on top. A man is driving. He parks on the street and kills the engine and the siren.

Silence.

The man hops out of the car.

He's wearing a crisp white shirt and dark slacks and a white captain's hat. He appears to be a Fire Captain.

He rings the doorbell.

Just then Mom glides down the hallway from the backrooms.

She looks elegant, about forty, just as I remember her when I was young, no trace of the devastation of her final seven years.

She opens the door without concern or complaint and lets the mustachioed Fire Captain in the house.

She walks into the kitchen and turns to stare at me directly, calmly, breaking the fourth wall of this strange dream. She says nothing but places her hands behind her back, all the while maintaining a serene eye contact with me.

The Fire Captain moves behind Mom and calmly places her in a pair of handcuffs that he pulls dutifully from a utility belt just like he's done this a hundred times before. Mom gives me a Mona Lisa smile and nods her head, as if she were expecting him to take her into custody.

He calmly, gently turns her toward the door and leads her out of the house. They approach his red sedan.

My last thought before I come out of it is—*arson investigation—she's to be* detained *for a while.*

The dream ends.

I wake wide up, alert, like I've just seen a movie, not a regular dream, but a kind of—appearance. Strike me dead if I'm making this up. That was my mother. That was a message.

Purgatory?

132

I call up the soprano, the woman who gave me so much, the rosary, the novena, her prayers, her love, her patience. I ask if she'll meet me for dinner.

We meet at a dark bar near the train station in San Juan Capistrano.

I order a giant martini and some appetizers for us.

The soprano has a glass of wine.

I tell her of my eerie dream.

She says, *Purgatory?*

Or worse, I say.

Mm-hm, she says. But the emphasis on your Mom *being detained* is interesting. She may be asking for your help. There's a lot written on this John. I'll give you some things to look at.

This Godly soprano doesn't fight me here, none of that *Oh your mother's with God, she's in a better place* business, *she's an angel now,* nothing like that. My friend knows hell is always a possibility and, as I would later conclude, a probability, for most. She knows purgatory is a gift, only for the saved, an extremely likely passage for the *few* Christ spoke of who would find salvation.

For my own part, I *know* that dream wasn't an ordinary dream. Just like I *know* I didn't imagine those words above the bar telling me *I should fast.* After all, that *imagining* was quickly reinforced and confirmed by a very real book on fasting thrust into my hands three days later.

Things are getting weird.

The soprano tells me that a child has a high obligation to pray for a deceased parent. She tells me of various devotions that take place on All Souls Day. She tells me to pray for the repose of my mother's soul every day and have Masses offered for her.

She and I are well aware of the cacophony of outcry about purgatory. We will have none of it. That doctrine can be defended scripturally, historically and experientially, through volumes of writings by the greatest and holiest saints, who give startlingly consistent depictions of it. But this is not a time for apologetics. It will take me years to back up that which I am being shown through a heavy handed application of grace.

Oh yes, I've been reading about *grace,* that pretty word, so very, very pretty, like butterflies and unicorns flitting about the meadow, something sweet for old ladies and the weak minded.

For hard cases like me there's a rougher brand of grace, one that collapses in on us like a brick outhouse, cracking noggins and knuckles: the rough grace God applied to a killer named Saul, knocking him clean off his high horse, blinding him, infantilizing him, chastising him, and pulling him into His service; or the rough grace God applied to a young playboy from Assisi, who was minding his own business throwing opulent parties at his father's house and luring young women into the back rooms until he was thrown in prison for rattling his puerile saber at the toughs from Perugia; or the rough grace God applied to a virile Spanish soldier, blowing his legs through with a cannonball, laying him up behind enemy lines, forcing him to read holy things for once.

Yes, I'm coming to understand grace in a whole new light, a searing light that exposes all my schemes and ulterior motives.

133

Confession, confession, confession. It's all I can think about. I drive up to the Abbey the next day and put a note in Father Polycarp's box. I leave my number and ask him to call as soon as he can. *I'm ready,* I write.

But I'm not quite ready. I never read that little booklet he gave me. *What* is *sin exactly?* I have to examine my conscience. I know the obvious things like lying, cheating, stealing. How many times *have* I lied? Hundreds? Thousands?

I'll have to make a good estimate and confess those lies by their number:

I'm thirty-nine. I've been able to talk for thirty-seven of those sin filled years. I've been able to lie for probably thirty-three of them. It's very possible I've told at least one lie a day every day for thirty-three years. I could see that. Little things, cancelling a meeting with a lie about a crowded schedule, telling a client a project is further along than it is. And, sadly, some big ones too.

365 x 33 = 12,045 lies including so-called white lies if there are any such things, but not counting *Good Morning* or *Hello.* I stare at the number. 12,045 lies. To be safe I could double it or triple it.

I'll confess the major whoppers individually.

I hope Father Polycarp has a few hours.

134

I'm so depressed by the thought of what a liar I am I drive aimlessly and find myself back down at the Mission. Increasingly I live my life between the Mission and the Abbey, the Abbey and the Mission. No wonder some monks take vows of silence: no talking, no lying.

I'm not religious!

Why is this happening to me?!

I meant to go home to Laguna Beach, back to my cave, but somehow my car pointed me here. Wendell and Louise are excited. They think they're getting a second walk. But I can't walk them right now. I need a drink.

I grab the little booklet Father gave me, *Preparation for Reconciliation,* and stop in at the old train station bar which everyone swears is haunted.

It's two in the afternoon, so I can justify a drink.

Patrón, double, salt, I say.

The young barmaid is friendly but seems to pity me.

I try to play it off like I'm a tourist killing time before a train but she knows I'm just a local guy who drinks double shots of tequila at two in the afternoon.

It does feel a bit drafty and ghostlike in the place.

I ask her to tell me the story of why they say this bar is haunted.

She's told the tale a hundred times before, but she obliges.

She tells me something about something and a murder and a long time ago.

It makes no sense.

I'm disinterested in ghost stories.

I'm living a real supernatural encounter sure as I sit here sucking down this last drop of blue agave juice.

I gulp a crisp Mexican beer to chase it, pay up, and leave.

I'm done making eyes at young barmaids.

I walk across the train tracks to a small park.

I pull the little booklet on confession preparation out of my pocket.

The cover bears a haunting, classic image of the face of Christ.

I open to the introduction and begin to read. It starts with a long quote by Pope John Paul II who wrote on the subject of sin in 1984, further quoting Pope Pius XII from 1946:

THE LOSS OF THE SENSE OF SIN

Over the course of generations, the Pope wrote, *the Christian mind has gained from the Gospel as it is read in the ecclesial community a fine sensitivity and an acute perception of the seeds of death contained in sin, as well as a sensitivity and an acuteness of perception for identifying them in the thousand guises under which sin shows itself. This is what is commonly called: the sense of sin.*

This sense is rooted in man's moral conscience and is as it were its thermometer. It is linked to the sense of God, since it derives from man's conscious relationship with God as his Creator, Lord and Father. Hence, just as it is impossible to eradicate completely the sense of God or to silence the conscience completely, so the sense of sin is never completely eliminated.

*Nevertheless, it happens not infrequently in history, for more or less lengthy periods and under the influence of many different factors, that the moral conscience of many people becomes seriously clouded. Have we the right idea of conscience? I asked this question two years ago in an address to the faithful. Is it not true that modern man is threatened by an eclipse of conscience? By a deformation of conscience? By a numbness or deadening of conscience? Too many signs indicate that such an eclipse exists in our time. This is all the more disturbing in that conscience, defined by the council as the most secret core and sanctuary of a man, is strictly related to human freedom. For this reason conscience, to a great extent, constitutes the basis of man's interior dignity and, at the same time, of his relationship to God. It is inevitable therefore that in this situation there is an obscuring also of the sense of sin, which is closely connected with the moral conscience, the search for truth, and the desire to make a responsible use of freedom. When the conscience is weakened the sense of God is also obscured and, as a result, with the loss of this decisive inner point of reference, the sense of sin is lost. This explains why my predecessor Pius XII, one day declared, in words that have almost become proverbial, that **the sin of the century is the loss of the sense of sin.***

I sit on a concrete bench. The hand that holds the small booklet drops between my knees like it's holding a lead brick. I am slumped, overcome, rendered mute by the sheer genius of that final zinger from Pope Pius XII. When did he reign again? Up through 1958? And even by then he said we'd lost the sense of sin, twelve years before my birth. What chance did I have?

Time stops.

All the nervous energy drains from my shoulders out through the soles of my feet.

That is the truth.

Sin. That's what's been bothering me my whole life.

The *wages of sin* really *are* death.

And as my sin became more acute in the past five years through my drinking-partying-carousing lifestyle, through my idle and mischievous hands, I courted an *actual physical death* from sin, not just a spiritual one.

How close have I been to an eternal death, dangling over an open alligator pit, doing little with my vainglorious life except waiting around to get thrown in the fire?

A train, the *Surfliner,* pulls into the station with a deafening rumble.

The lifelessness I feel...the deadness in me, the cotton between my ears, the gray soapstone that passes for my heart—

I *am* dead.

Dead to sin.

That's a fact, Jack.

Holy God.

135

The next day Dad calls. He says he has a few things of Mom's and wonders if I want any of them.

Sure, I say, and drive the sixty miles North to claim my inheritance.

I walk in and there's an obvious tension between us.

He's upset with me and and I'm upset with him.

Ice.

He shows me some clothes of Mom's. I'm not interested.

He shows me some books of Mom's. I take one.

It's called *Theology and Sanity.* The title intrigues me.

I take another one. *Alcoholics Anonymous* by Anonymous.

I take Mom's pewter ashtray, that crucible of pain for the whole lot of us the past so many years.

It's a nice ashtray.

She used the hell out of it.

If anything contains her spirit, it's this damned ashtray.

I want it.

I'll never forget her when I gaze upon it.

Dad says, That's it? That's all you want of hers? Two books and an ashtray?

Yeah. What else is there?

Oh Carol, he says, and his eyes brim. The night she died I saw a bright light in the back of the house, Dad says, a radiance.

I could cry with him, I could try and comfort him, but there's a hard feeling in me. *Oh now you get sentimental,* I want to say.

Oh yeah? I didn't see any glow, I respond coldly. I saw a frightened woman who was looking into another dimension.

You're so smart, he says. Why don't you go display your genius somewhere else—

It doesn't take much for me to start shaking with anger.

I can't speak. I can't articulate all the reasons why. But I'm not listening to one more drop of venom directed my way. I don't deserve it.

I'm ashamed of you, he says. I'm ashamed of what I raised.

I slam my fist into his wall, careful to hit a part of it I know is bolstered by studs. My hand does not break. The wall shows a slight depression. The force must have been immense. I don't even feel it.

Get out of here, he yells.

Gladly, I say, and I walk away from him.

Then I turn, and the words that leave my mouth come from elsewhere. I could not speak them of my own power alone:

I'm not talking to you again until you go to confession, I shout.

He looks at me, stunned and angry.

I'm not the one, he says. *I haven't done anything!*

The loss of the sense of sin, I say.

Get out, he bellows.

I tear out of the driveway, tires squealing, Wendell and Louise rock and roll in their seats. Burning tears stream down my face. What have I done? Was that necessary? Oh God. God help me. God help us.

136

A few days pass in silence.

Lent.

I get a call from my choir director.

She says, John, how would you like to do a serious fast with me?

I would, I say. How long?

As far as we can go into Lent, she says.

Starting tomorrow?

Yes, she says.

What are the rules?

Well, you know, we make up our own rules. We have to be safe, she says. For my part, I'm going to take water, broth and juices. If I need more I'll have some kind of soup.

Okay, I say. I'll do the same. But I may have to add whole milk and syrup occasionally so I can function.

319

We begin the fast.

The first thing I notice is I don't want to drink liquor or smoke.

It's as though I'm lifting off the deck of a ship and watching it steam away without me. It's a terrifying feeling, rising high above the sea.

I feel the hunger pangs, but not as bad as some of the shorter fasts we tried before Mom died. I can *do* this, I think.

Some nights, when it's just too much, instead of breaking the fast with a meal I go ahead and mix some maple syrup in with a mug full of warmed whole milk.

I know milk is more of a food than a liquid but it's what I have to do to keep going. I'm a novice.

Three days pass, five days pass, I'm praying the Rosary.

Enough money comes my way so I don't have to talk to too many people.

137

On day seven of the fast, Father Polycarp calls me up.

Hello Father, I say, nice to hear from you.

Yes, well, sorry for the delay, he says. We're not too big on the phone up here.

Sure, sure, Father, I understand. Maybe the timing is right.

So when can you come up and see me?

Let me check my calendar, I say. Looks like I'm free all year.

Ha! Okay, he says. Tomorrow, five o'clock. Meet me in the chapel.

Oh, he says, a lot of pressure may come upon you to cancel this meeting. Be careful the next twenty-four hours and resist anything that gets in your way of being here as we agreed.

138

I've written all my sins down, all the ones I can remember anyway, by name and number.

I've read accounts of near death experiences where people are shown the film of their life—doesn't everyone always say *my life flashed before my eyes*—when they have a brush with death?

To prepare I recline in a dark room on my leaky air mattress trying to play the movie of my life as it might appear at the end of it, as Mom's life might have appeared to her in those unsettling hours before her death where she appeared to be undergoing a review of sorts.

There I am at five, sitting in the living room, watching Mom walk through the bathroom door drunk. When I knocked her over did I sin? When I denounced the idea of God a few months later did I sin? When in doubt I'll confess it and let Father work it out. He's had ten years to prepare for this. I'm sure he knows more about it than I do.

The time for living according to *my* terms has passed. Never have I seen a creature as helpless as my dying mother, except maybe animals in cages awaiting euthanasia.

There she was, bound to her bed, seemingly unable in that late desperate hour to recall her sins, to form contrition, to make a proper repentance, to receive absolution, except through that shaky exchange during the last rites. O God may it cover her, may our prayers assist her in Your sight, may she be purified and not eternally damned.

When I enter the chapel for confession Father Polycarp is playing the organ gently, skillfully, perhaps preparing for holy hour later in the evening. I'm impressed my confessor is also an organist. I don't know how anyone in human history ever mastered the organ. It's a beast of an instrument.

He finishes up, gathers a purple stole from the organ bench as well as a few small books and meets me in the back near the confessional.

Hello, he says, nice to see you.

We enter the confessional and sit across from one another. I place the sheaf full of papers bearing my dirty deeds on my lap. He has a big smile on his face, not giddy, but anticipatory.

In nomine Patris, et Filii, et Spiritus Sancti, I begin.

Forgive me Father, for I have sinned. It's been twenty years since my last confession. These are the sins of my life, for which I desire God's forgiveness and mercy.

I do my best to simply state the sin and the number of times I committed it, to properly accuse myself, but Father Polycarp interrupts on occasion and inquires more deeply.

Especially concerned he seems to be with two things: my suicide attempt and my sessions with the psychic. He wants to know everything about them, my state of mind before, during and after the sessions with the psychic, any sense I had of *becoming a different person* just before the suicide attempt, and the intensity of the drug and alcohol use before, during and after that period.

My head is spinning. His line of inquiry unnerves me. He strikes me as very bright, like one of the top flight associates I used to work with at high rise law firms in Century City, whip smart, like he could have done anything with his life, but chose to do *this* instead.

We go for about an hour and a half and at the end I say, I think that's it.

Good, he says. Well thank God for a good confession. But I need to say a deliverance prayer over you so, if you'll follow me into the library, we'll suspend the confession for a moment, and I'll pray the deliverance prayer, and then grant you absolution by the power of Christ.

Uh, okay, I say.

Did he just say—deliverance?

I thought that was like an Appalachian thing, like a snake-handling, backwoods type deal.

Deliverance?

Right here above suburban Orange County?

I hope it doesn't hurt.

Father Polycarp removes his purple stole, picks up his two small books and some holy water and puts his hand on the door knob of the confessional.

Father, I say, light headed and breathy, it's just so hard for me to believe that any of this—is *real.*

He opens the confessional door. Without even looking over his shoulder he says, *It's all real, John.*

He says this with an offhanded objectivity, like he was saying *the parking lot is crowded or there's rain tonight or we're having stew for dinner.* The perfunctory affirmation that the *Catholic Faith* is *all real* seems to this brilliant young man a fact no more exotic than blue skies or gravity.

Of all the testimonies, of all the declarations of faith I have ever heard, Father Polycarp's is by far the most terrifying, the most compelling, the most withering, because he was not trying to persuade me of anything.

The Church doesn't *need* me.

I need the Church!

I'm ten paces behind him and he turns to look at me.

He nods his head sideways as if to say, *C'mon, it's only a deliverance prayer.*

The comedian Jerry Seinfeld once quipped that you never want anything done to you in a hospital that makes doctors say to *other* doctors, *Man I gotta see this.*

Does everybody get the *deliverance prayer* at their general confession? I would think not, otherwise he would have had the book in the confessional with him. Clearly aspects of my confession have caused him to think he needs to *cast out demons* or worse.

Demons? In me? Well why not?

I've behaved like a demon lately.

140

We enter a small alcove near the library.

We're a full service monastery here, he says with a smile.

Kneel down, he says.

Kneel down?

Yes.

I kneel down.

With great authority and calm self-assurance, he extends his hand over my head. He holds a large bound tome with the other.

He begins praying a long prayer over me in Latin.

Kneeling here, this is almost more than I can take.

I *do* feel something.

This is not a parlor trick.

He's decidedly un-theatrical about this entire affair. He's just doing his job, which makes it that much worse in my mind. I'm undergoing a, a—*procedure:*

Exorcizo te, omnis spiritus immunde, he reads, *in nomine Dei Patris omnipotentis, et in nomine Jesu Christi Filii ejus, Domini et Judicis nostri, et in virtute Spiritus Sancti, ut descedas ab hoc plasmate Dei John Carmichael, quod Dominus noster ad templum sanctum suum vocare dignatus est, ut fiat templum Dei vivi, et Spiritus Sanctus habitet in eo. Per eumdem Christum Dominum nostrum, qui venturus est judicare vivos et mortuos, et saeculum per ignem.*

I'm teetering a bit as he finishes. There's something substantial going on here. This ain't a sweet nothing. He closes his book and asks me to read and pray the *Act of Contrition,* which I do:

O my God, I am heartily sorry for offending Thee, and I detest all my sins because I dread the loss of heaven and the fires of hell, but most of all because they offend Thee my God, who art all good and deserving of all my love. I firmly resolve, with the help of Thy grace, to confess my sins, to do penance and to amend my life. Amen.

Then he pronounces the words of absolution in Latin from memory:

Deus, Pater misericordiarum,
(God the Father of mercies,)
qui per mortem et resurrectionem Filii sui
(who through the death and resurrection of His own Son)
mundum sibi reconciliavit
(reconciled the world to Himself)
et Spiritum Sanctum effudit
(and poured out the Holy Spirit)
in remissionem peccatorum,

325

(for the forgiveness of sins,)
per ministerium Ecclesiae
(through the ministry of the Church)
Indulgentiam tibi tribuat et pacem
(may He grant to you pardon and peace...)
Et ego te absolvo a peccatis tuis
And I absolve you from your sins,
in nomine Patris, et Filii, et Spiritus Sancti.
(in the name of the Father, Son, and Holy Spirit.)

He smiles at me and says, *I foresee great holiness for you.*

I stare dumbly, blinking.

I want to respond but the words don't come.

Holiness? What is that exactly? That's one of those words people use. I don't know quite what it means.

And great *holiness* for *me?*

What would that even be like?

I just say, *Thank you Father.*

Sure, John, he says. Let's pray for each other, okay?

I'm struck by this parting act of humility. As if my prayers could further his spiritual life, he of the white habit and serene spirit, gliding through his divine office and sacramental ministry.

Okay, I say, dazed and somewhat weak.

141

I wander out to my car through a light mist that's settled on the dark hilly landscape. The faithful are arriving for the eight o'clock holy hour and benediction. I wonder for a moment if I should join them, but I'm too tired.

I sit in the quiet interior of my car and wish I could cry from the catharsis of it all.

But it wasn't exactly cathartic like a counseling session.

In fact, the young priest didn't do much counseling at all. Instead I feel a sensation I can't entirely name: a sweeping, dawning acknowledgment of where I've been and where I am now.

The tears begin to fall, but I can sense they're not tears of relief, not tears cried at the culmination of a long battle. In this precise moment I suddenly realize I'm not at a finish line, but at a *starting* line. This awareness confuses me in my exhaustion. *Now what,* I think.

I confessed an awful lot of sins, some things I didn't think were all that bad until I read that little booklet on confession and did some research. But *now,* now after having spoken them aloud, to have accused myself, and to have received the sign and sacrament of forgiveness, I really do believe there is such a thing as a *soul* and that the soul can be stained, occluded, ruined by sin.

I can feel the seriousness of my sin, the danger of it, its residue. I suppose it is the case that through some peculiar mechanism, I have recovered the *sense of sin* that the Popes have reckoned man has more or less lost of late. I see the sense of sin not as a burden but as an immense benefit, something that would have been impossible for me to come to on my own.

Do I feel lighter?

Somewhat.

But more than that, I feel *aware.*

I experience a groaning awareness of the horrific condition in which I was languishing, like a man waking up in a burning building, coughing from inhaling acrid smoke and looking for an exit.

I'm unnerved by my confessions of illicit drug use, drunkenness and sexual impurity. I realize I made a *promise* in my *Act of Contrition.* I *promised to amend my life.* To walk right back out and get lit after I get home just wouldn't be right. But I don't drink for the taste of the stuff. I'd just as soon have a lemonade on ice with muddled mint, or a *Pellegrino* with lime or even a chocolate milk if flavor and texture were all that mattered to me. I fancied myself a scotch connoisseur but who would ever savor the taste of that rank and peaty carcinogen if it weren't for the eighty-proof kick in the pants? I drink to get good and drunk. If I'm going to stop getting drunk I'm going to need some help. I'm not sure the confession is enough, though Saint Augustine informed me recently that *the beginning of good works is the confession of evil works.*

I go to put the key in the engine and something arrests me. This time, not a field of grayscale Arial letters like over the bar that one time, but it's the same voice: calm, impassive, interior. I don't see it this time so much as I *hear* it. The voice says:

GOD NEEDS YOU SOBER.

I feel like I didn't hear the verb correctly. *Need?* God *needs* you sober? How about *want* instead? Why would God *need* anything, especially from me, if God is God? Now I doubt myself, not the voice, but the verb. Was it *need* or *want?* I know from my first experience with this strange phenomenon that there will be no follow-up questions allowed.

And whose voice was this that spoke of God in the third person? It didn't strike me as God speaking exactly, but an emissary of sorts. Yet I'm quite certain it was the *same* voice that spoke and displayed the suggestion that I *fast* in the bar so many months ago.

Finally I start the engine and proceed down the hill.

I stop the car on the steep incline.

A shock wave concusses my electrified body.

It hits me: *I'm—an alcoholic.*

And a drug addict.

Oh Dear God.

I was so caught up by the verb that I didn't properly contemplate the implication of the word *sober.*

I know *exactly* what it means in my case: *stone cold sober.* It means *never again,* not a wee drop, it means a stark reversion to my tea-totaling youth.

So I *am* a drunk, just like Mom.

It *looked* different, it *felt* different, but alas my drunkenness was no less alcoholic than hers. Look at me! I don't even have clean socks!

I betrayed Nicole.

I betrayed Nicole!

I'm suddenly stricken with the thought of Nicole. Elle, yes, of course, but Nicole—I managed to betray a child who was placed rightly or wrongly into my care, into my sphere of influence. What have I unwittingly taught her through my betrayal? The same thing Mom taught me? That people are unreliable, not to be trusted. Or worse, that *there is no God?*

Oh God, I am heartily sorry for having offended Thee—

Sober. Never again. No booze, no drugs, no mind or mood altering chemicals of any kind, just life straight-up without anesthesia. I'll have to go through all that recovery crap with those black-coffee swilling drunks at those ratty clubhouses. Maybe I'll have to go to a treatment center or some madhouse like that.

Oh this is terrible. I feel like Harrison Ford as *Indiana Jones* when he looked down into the pit to see what was guarding his treasure and saw snakes.

Snakes, he murmurs, *why'd it have to be* snakes?

Sober, I think, *why do I have to be* sober?

142

I call my choir director the next day and tell her I don't think I can take the fast much longer. We're on day twenty-

329

one, that's the length of the *Daniel fast* I tell her. Oh, and by the way, I made a general confession yesterday, I say.

She's *ecstatic* for me, and nearly squeals with delight, as much delight as someone who hasn't eaten solid food for twenty days can have anyway.

For once I think I'm starting to understand these people and the bizarre things they get so excited about.

143

The next day I break my Lenten fast with one of those pre-cooked supermarket chickens and a four pack of *Boddington's*. I bring the chicken and the beer back to the bat cave and tear at the bird carcass with my hands. Wendell and Louise look up at me forlornly, having been denied the opportunity to beg for food for twenty-two days now.

Dogs do not understand Lent.

I shovel the chicken into my mouth with my hands and take clumps of meat and toss them to Wendell and Louise. They become wolves.

I look at the Boddington's like a dare. *Drunkenness* is the sin, not mere drinking *per se*. I can drink the beer without sinning. I just fasted for twenty-two days for Pete's sake and made a general confession in the middle of Lent. Those strange voices, *You should fast* and *God needs you sober*—I mean what is that? How can I really be sure those aren't just my own impulses, my own passing thoughts? I don't see how a man can go without a beer from time to time.

I haven't had solid food in my system for twenty-two days, let alone ethyl alcohol.

So the Boddington's hits like crack cocaine.

I'm swacked, crazy as a March hare, swaggering around my pad like a gangster on PCP.

I reach for the second one and shotgun it just for spite.

I grab my waterpipe and blaze up the crispy ganja that's all crumbly and dried out.

It burns my throat.

Smoking a giant column of unfiltered smoke from a water pipe suddenly seems like a hideously violent and reckless act.

My lungs burn.

It's a rough hit and a bad high.

I'm immediately paranoid and sick.

I try to drink another Boddington's but halfway down I feel violently ill and up comes the chicken and the beer all over the living room floor.

It's a revolting mess.

The dogs go for the chicken but find themselves repelled by the taint of the alcohol and my stomach acid. Wendell grabs a big piece out of the pile and retreats back to a safe corner. Louise, a much daintier beast, sniffs the vile undigested heap of chicken marinated in the beer and vomitus and heads for her perch high up on the top cushion of the couch.

I've only one and a half Boddington's left and I won't touch them.

It's as if suddenly they're marked with skull and crossbones.

I can't drink them.

The water pipe looks like a menacing object of the occult.

I walk toward it, grab it at the top, walk out onto the patio and hurl it end over end at the rock pile.

It shatters.

My throat still rasps from that harsh hit.

I feel like my head is turned inside out and the slick red shiny inside part is burning.

I'm having a seriously bad trip.

I collapse on the air mattress and fall asleep until the next day.

144

When I wake up I feel grotesque, like an alien.

The beer and chicken stick to the floor and stink up the place.

It smells like a frat house.

The Boddington's sits warm on the counter.

I pour the last can and a half down the drain.

What a waste. Who could pour Boddington's down the drain?

Surely not I.

145

Later that afternoon I lie down on the air mattress and a great darkness settles over the room.

I feel defeated.

The confession was such a pinnacle and nadir all at once.

I so don't want to give up drinking and dope.

I'm lying on my side facing the wall.

I feel something like talons digging into my right arm.

It isn't as *literal* as the two messages I received about *fasting* and *sobriety*. It seems to be more from my imagination, but it's a horribly creepy sensation. I picture a giant vulture, or some black winged thing perched on my arm, a demon really. A great ravening beast—

I flash back to my first drink alone in the swanky hotel room in Beverly Hills, the beer and vodka from the mini-bar. I remember something I said to myself that day, to a God I didn't believe in, to no one in particular and everyone all at once: I said, or thought, or felt, or formed the notion that if there *was* anything out there, anything like a *God* or a *divine energy* or a *protective spirit,* it was going to have to prove itself to me, to *catch me,* because I was going to jump.

And I remember more deeply, further back, my five year old self standing in the driveway with hot tears in my eyes deciding there was *nothing and no one* out there or in me, giving up even on the very possibility of God.

And now this *thing* perched atop me laughs, cackles even, *You thought you could come into my house and beat me at my own game? I'm tired of toying with you. I'm going to eat you now, devour you like a rabbit the coyotes misdirect and rip to shreds up in the hills. You nothing.*

I picture the hideous thing in human form some years ago, like John Waters in an ascot, inviting me into a velvety sitting room, asking me to rest my feet, making me feel at ease. *Come into my parlor said the spider to the fly.* Now, some years later, the *thing* returns in unfamiliar and monstrous form, ready to peck my eyes out and collect its due.

I spring up off the floor, looking at the hideous mess of the place and feel a rushing urge to flee. I grab the keys and the dog's leash and we're the three of us out the door like a shot.

146

I feel a little calmer in the car.

I decide to go to my favorite bar one last time to have one last drink.

I think God means it. I think He *needs* me sober.

But one last drink, *please God,* grant me that.

Just to say goodbye.

It's two o'clock and my bar is empty except for one older woman reading the paper and a new bartender. Blond hair, green eyes, classy.

She smiles like she's been waiting for me.

Hi there, she says.

Hello, I say.

What can I do for you?

I'd like a *Pearblossom* please, I say.

It's a special cocktail they make with vodka and pear juice.

I enjoyed it in the early afternoons on many an occasion.

She makes it perfectly and sets it before me like a golden chalice.

The restaurant manager comes down the stairs and lights up like a Christmas tree when he sees me.

Hey John, he says. *Great to see you.* He slaps me on the back.

Green-eyes takes note that I seem to have some *status* with her new employer.

Just then a distinguished, virile, older gentleman comes in with his silver headed girlfriend and they sit down next to me. He wears a supremely elegant red and white striped dress shirt with silver Tiffany cufflinks in the form of the scales of justice and white pants.

I used to have a pair of cufflinks like that.

If I still had them I'd try to pawn them.

Red-stripes' ladyfriend sits between us.

They order hard drinks and the bar starts to fill up a bit.

I sip my Pearblossom and then ask for another.

Red-stripes is a lawyer and he's trying to impress his date with tales of his derring-do in court. He makes me want to puke. I hate guys like this. I'm listening to every word he says and suddenly he reaches in front of his ladyfriend, grabs my right forearm, and says, *Are you enjoying our conversation?*

I turn my head slowly and look at him, half-stunned.

I say, *Take your hand off my arm or I'll throw you through that window.*

A black rage wells up inside me.

I picture how I'd grab him by his fancy shirt with my left hand and by the belt buckle holding up his white slacks with my right, and hurl him through the bay window onto the brick walkway.

It's a terrifying sensation because I'm fully committed to it.

If he doesn't release my arm there will be blood.

Silently I begin to count to three.

He slips his hand off my forearm and says, *I'm so sorry. I don't know what came over me.*

He picks up his drink and his lady's drink and moves to a high top about twenty feet away. He looks at me as if he'd had a terrible fright, as if he saw reflected in my eyes the vivid, violent fantasy I entertained.

I'm horrified. I've never had a bar fight and certainly never an interaction like that with anyone at this bar, this high class bar, the sacred spot of my odd message to fast. This is certainly not what I had in mind for my last drink. I feel the presence of evil here today, in him, in me.

I've got to get out of here.

Just then Wendell starts barking out the window of my parked car at a passing dog. I jump up from the bar to go calm him down. The barmaid leaves her post and follows me out. We stand on the street together.

That's a beautiful dog, she says.

Thanks. He's a bit much for city life as you can hear.

I've always wanted to live in the country, she says.

She stands with her hand on her hip like she's wearing a country dress in a Summer rain.

I'm overcome by her sensuality.

She says, *Come back inside. I wanna talk to you.*

Okay, I say, and follow her like a horse on a halter lead.

I regain my perch at the bar and she says the next drink is on her.

Honestly, I say, I really only came in to have one.

Then today's your lucky day, she says.

I think she's coming on to me. I know bartenders play a game with their patrons but it seems like she's putting a little extra mustard on it.

She pours me something of her own making, a vodka cocktail to follow up the Pearblossom. It has citrus in it which I hate. I think citrus should be reserved for furniture polish.

I smile politely and thank her for this foul cocktail that assaults my palate.

Some other customers leave.

Now it's just her and me at the bar and a few patrons at the high tops, including Red-stripes who turned his back to me completely.

I don't like this, I think.

She asks, What do you do?

I'm a lawyer, I say.

Ohhhh, she says. That would explain the fancy car and the fancy dog. Do you live in one of the fancy houses up on the hill?

No, I say. I'm separated and I live like an animal.

She arches her eyebrow. *Really?*

Yes.

I'm so sorry to hear that, she says insincerely.

We get to talking about the state of the world and the state of marriage and romance and I tell her I think we're headed for the apocalypse.

She says, *In that case, why don't you take me out for a drink tonight? We can split a bottle of wine at* Tommy Bahama's *next door.*

I hate that place, I think to myself: who wants to mix clothing and cuisine?

I'd love to, I lie, but I have to go up to Sacramento on business.

Okay, she says, *but when you get back I'd really like to talk to you about the end of the world.*

Mercifully, Green-eyes is summoned by Red-stripes. She pours whatever it is he's drinking and exits her station behind the bar to bring it to him. As she passes behind me, she takes a single finger and runs it along the length of my shoulders, left to right. It's one of the most erotic moments of my life. I'm instantly aroused. I have enough money to buy her a bottle of wine and get a hotel room across the street—

What the hell is going on?

I've got to get out of here.

If I split that bottle of wine with her I'll be lost. Totally lost.

I throw down forty dollars and slip out the back door without taking so much as a second look at her or the bar itself. I run for the car like Lot's wife.

Don't look back, I think. *Don't look back.*

I fire up the engine in a near panic.

I fly up the hill and get back to the relative safety of my hovel.

I clean up the mess like I'm preparing for a military inspection.

I look at Wendell and Louise.

Pups, I say, I think that really *was* my last drink.

They stare back goofily with their semi-vacant brown eyes.

147

I fall asleep for about sixteen hours and wake up early. I drive to the Abbey for *Lauds,* the morning prayer. I spot Father Polycarp in the choir stall. After the priests finish singing their gorgeous hymns I corner him and ask him if he's got a minute.

He looks busy but says, Fine.

We step outside and sit on a bench.

Father, I say, I need to tell you about a couple things that have gone on since my general confession.

I tell him of the voice in the parking lot that said *God needs you sober.* I tell him of the voice in the bar that said *You should fast,* which I didn't happen to mention during my confession. I tell him of the strange experience with the conclusion of my fast and my allergic reaction to the beer, and my urge to go back to the Laguna bar and my unsettling encounter with Green-eyes and Red-stripes, which both together seemed to portend sex and violence with an unreasonable intensity.

I take a breath.

He smiles and says, Remember the other night when I said I foresaw great holiness for you?

Yes.

Well, that's only half the story. Have you ever heard the phrase *Catholic formation?*

No.

Right, well, that's because you don't really have one. That's a sad reality these days.

He stands up and says, Come over here with me.

I follow him around to the back of the chapel a few feet away.

He says, This is a statue of Saint Michael the Archangel.

Funny, I say, I chose Saint Michael as my confirmation saint.

Oh *really,* he says. That's interesting. A bold choice. Why?

Because he had a sword.

Father Polycarp laughs. Yes, he has a sword. It represents his role, his function: he's a warrior. You identify with that?

Yes, I say.

What else do you see in this depiction?

Wings.

Mm-hm. When you see wings on an angel remember that they are there to depict or connote speed, celerity. Angels are pure spirit. Doubtless they do not need actual wings. But when humans depict them this way it suggests their properties—that if they need to be what for us is a hundred miles away they can do it in an instant.

He snaps his finger.

I think of our family friend's tale of dropping her rolling pin because she was prompted that there was *something wrong at the Carmichael house.* A guardian angel-to-angel request perhaps? A call for backup? That's far too complicated a story to tell Father Polycarp now.

He asks, What else do you see?

Well, Saint Michael seems to be stepping on Satan's head.

Right, a victory! He is your confirmation saint. John, in case no one's ever told you this before, you are at war. A spiritual war. A war for your soul. As a disciple of Jesus Christ you are called to fight the world, the flesh and the devil. The Catholic Church on earth was traditionally referred to as *The Church Militant,* as opposed to the *Church Suffering* in purgatory or the *Church Triumphant* in heaven, where we both hope to be.

Spiritual warfare?

Yes, he says.

The term burbles up from the depths.

I've heard of spiritual warfare, I say.

That's good, but you don't know the rules of engagement. You don't have the Catholic formation you need to fight this battle. You need some spiritual direction. I'm a bit too busy to help you with that now, but we'll find you one of the other priests here to direct you. You've received great graces. There are theological terms for what you're experiencing. For example, those two messages you received; about *fasting* and *sobriety*. Those are called *locutions*. They're reasonably rare, but yours come right out of a textbook on spiritual theology. They were short, unforgettable to you, did not sound like your own natural inner voice, and came on their time, not on yours. But both followed acts of immense spiritual warfare—your long Novena and your general confession. You see, John, the instruction to fast and your trip to the confessional *were the answers to the Novena you prayed.*

I'm rocked by this awareness. *Of course! Of course!* It fits together so neatly. My appetites were raging. I fed them and they only got hungrier. The fast makes so much sense now. It's not what I wanted, it's not what I ever would have chosen for myself, but it's what I needed.

He says, I will recommend you to read Saint Teresa of Avila on locutions at some later stage. For now, just know you've received two. You will never forget them.

Thanks, I say. I have to tell you, I'm still blown away by what happened after confession. I'm a little freaked out actually. Why is confession so powerful? What is it exactly?

It's a channel of supernatural grace, he says, of sanctifying grace, like all the sacraments are. Later today, read John 20:19-23. But your impulse to confess, that came directly from God, that's the Holy Spirit granting you an *illumination of conscience, convicting* you. As I said, these seemingly strange experiences you're going through *have names,* theological descriptions. Theology is a science

John, a metaphysical science, a way of knowing. Other people have gone through exactly the same thing as you, praise God.

Okay, I say.

Now John, I can't overload you right now but here are some quick instructions for you, one warrior to another. First, I want you to read *Imitation of Christ* by Thomas a Kempis. Secondly, read the four Gospel accounts. Don't worry about any other Scripture yet, just the Gospel. Third, I want you to come to confession every other day. You must *avoid the dangerous occasion.* Stay out of the bars. You may try a 12 step program. I love the 12 step programs; it's desert father spirituality, but you must have confession and Communion. Have you taken the Eucharist yet?

No.

Why not?

Well, I just didn't. Can I receive the Eucharist even though I'm divorced?

Your second relationship, he asks—the so-called civil *marriage*—is over, right? You're not living with her, sleeping with her?

No, I haven't lived with her for over a year.

And you're not going to?

No.

Then yes, you are divorced, so you cannot licitly remarry without an annulment or receive Communion if you are not chaste. But you may receive Communion provided you're in a state of grace, meaning you've been to confession and have not committed any mortal sin in between your confession and Communion. This is very serious, John. Receiving Communion in a state of mortal sin is worse than not receiving it at all. You can read Saint Paul on that one. He warns us that doing so can make us sick or even kill us.

I think I read that, I said.

341

Okay. So that's your battle plan, some offense—prayer, Scripture, and the sacraments—and some defense, avoiding the dangerous occasion. Try to come to Mass every day. Now pray with me:

Saint Michael the Archangel, defend us in battle, be our protection against the wickedness and snares of the devil. May God rebuke him, we humbly pray, and do thou O prince of the heavenly host, by the power of God, cast into hell Satan, and all the evil spirits who roam about the world seeking the ruin of souls. Amen.

Father Polycarp smiles and heads back to the chapel.

I stand there next to the winged statue of Saint Michael the Archangel.

It suddenly occurs to me I just had a serious conversation with another full grown man about *the properties of angels.*

148

I drive to a Catholic bookstore next to the Mission and buy a copy of *Imitation of Christ*. I also buy a Bible—the Douay-Rheims Haydock edition—and head back to Laguna Canyon for a little light reading.

Halfway home I turn the car around. Father pointed out that my locutions regarding fasting and sobriety came on the heels of the Rosary Novena. I can feel the connection now as sure as breathing. I've got to learn more about Mary, her role, what the heck is happening to me.

I look over at *Imitation of Christ* and *The Holy Bible* on the passenger seat. I think of how perfectly Father Polycarp diagnosed my weird encounter at the bar, and how mind blowing the possibility of spiritual warfare truly is—a fight against *the world, the flesh and the devil* for the salvation of my individual soul and a greater fight of some kind, between good and evil, between God with his angels and saints on the one hand and the devil and his legion of demons and all people who serve them on the other.

Wild stuff.

And yet it seems more plausible to me by the hour.

It's as if I'm now watching an artist paint a massive mural before me on the side of a fifty foot wall, the shapes and colors at first indistinct, but coming ever more clearly into view. The artist is working to communicate something to me, something highly specific—in the case of a mural, a seascape perhaps—but in the case of the strange events of the last few years, well, a question blossoms in my mind above all else:

Are you telling me—
—that the Catholic Faith—
*—is **true**???*

True in an actual, literal, hard, real sense—not merely a *metaphor* for the truth, or some collection of teaching stories?

But *true,* true. Like Father said so offhandedly, *It's **all** real, John.*

Conceived by the power of the Holy Spirit and born of the Virgin Mary true?

On its face, well, it sounds pretty far out.

All I know is I prayed for Mary's intercession and got a highly specific answer to my prayers that was nothing I would have ever thought of myself—*fasting*—on day fifty of the fifty-four days and then received a book on fasting four days later, as if dropped from the sky. It never would have occurred to me to voluntarily stop eating.

We're talking prayers with answers here; *instructions,* a map and compass, *signal graces* I think they're called.

343

To think I had so easily dismissed Jesus and His Church like they were nothing.

I don't feel particularly joyful about it at the moment. Indeed, a certain anger rises in my throat about the way in which the Faith had been presented to me between 1975 and 1988, my formative years.

Yes, *formation,* Father Polycarp said! *Catholic formation.*

How carefully descriptive the word *formation* is. Not *training,* not *brainwashing,* but *formation.*

I was not properly *formed.*

I guess that means I was *malformed.*

I have the shambles of a life to prove it, in spite of all my gifts, all my talent, all my early promise.

I grew crooked.

The number and intensity of things that are basic to the Catholic Faith—and I mean *basic* Catholicism 101— about which I'm just now finding out are actually rather hard to digest, like a force-feeding of farm fresh produce after a lifetime of eating processed food.

Why? *Why* if the Church has all this—*truth*—did She not scream it to me, considering what's at stake?

It's almost as if somebody doesn't want us to know.

149

I get home and drink water and ginger ale, as my stomach is churning from the previous day's activities.

I set three books on the cardboard banker's box I'm using as a nightstand next to the air mattress: *The Holy Bible, Imitation of Christ* by Thomas a Kempis, and *True Devotion to Mary* by Saint Louis de Montfort. I feed Wendell and Louise and decide to take a shower. Afterwards I put on the least disgusting loungewear I can find, blow up the air mattress to a healthy firmness, and get under what is left of a comforter for some reading.

First of all, I'm curious about confession. I want to see what the Bible says about it, having been inexplicably shaken to vibrancy by my experience with Father Polycarp in confession.

He told me to read John 20:19-23:

Now when it was late that same day, the passage begins, the first of the week, and the doors were shut, where the disciples were gathered together, for fear of the Jews, Jesus came and stood in their midst, and said to them: Peace be to you. And when he had said this, he showed them his hands and his side. The disciples therefore were glad, when they saw the Lord. He said therefore to them again: Peace be to you. As the Father hath sent me, I also send you. When he had said this, he breathed on them; and he said to them: Receive YE the Holy Ghost. Whose sins YOU shall forgive, they are forgiven them; and whose sins YOU shall retain, they are retained.

Ohhhhhhh, so *there* it is. Right there in black and white. The Christ, post-resurrection, is said to have appeared and given *certain men the authority to forgive or retain sin!* And seriously, people run around asking why Catholics confess to men? Pshaw. Especially when put next to the authority to bind and loose Christ granted Peter and the Apostles, and the power of the Keys to the Kingdom given to Peter alone, like it or not the idea of confession as a sacrament instituted by Christ to be carried out through His Church makes sense, assuming the first premises are true.

I think a little differently about my own general confession now—it's certain it was not a counseling session. Given the result, the stark change in my awareness and desires, it must have been of a distinctly supernatural character or it was nothing at all. I wasn't

345

responding to mere *advice* or unburdening myself, which I had done many times before with secular counselors.

I close the Bible, driven to later find the basis for *all* seven of Christ's sacraments in the New Testament, which is, of course, a collection of Catholic books.

Imitation of Christ is absolutely shocking. I've never read anything like it. It's buckets and buckets of ice water. I can only take so much. I stop after the first ten pages because it's just so rich, so intense, like eating five chocolate truffles in a row.

I'm exhausted.

I flip through the book at random. At nearly every page my eye falls upon a passage that raps me against the side of my head:

Go where you will, the passage begins, seek what you will, you will not find a higher way, nor a less exalted but safer way, than the way of the holy cross. **Arrange and order everything to suit your will and judgment, and still you will find that some suffering must always be borne, willingly or unwillingly, and thus you will always find the cross.**

I think of my floundering attempt to create a heaven on Earth in Palos Verdes with my pretty wife and perfect job and Cadillac car and food finer than the kings of old could have eaten—

Yet I found the cross straight away, right from the get go, not a trivial surface level suffering but a deep soul stretching sense of disappointment and confusion with every new achievement, every new pleasure come and gone. The emptiness.

Tell me more, Thomas a Kempis:

Either you will experience bodily pain or you will undergo tribulation of spirit in your soul, he says. At times you will feel forsaken by God, at times troubled by those about you and, what is worse, you will often grow weary of yourself. You cannot escape, you cannot be relieved by any remedy or comfort but must bear with it as long as God wills. For He wishes you to learn to bear trial without consolation, to submit yourself wholly to Him that you may become more humble through suffering. No one understands the passion of Christ so thoroughly or heartily as the man whose lot it is to suffer the like himself.

The cross, therefore, is always ready; it awaits you everywhere. No matter where you may go, you cannot escape it, for wherever you go you take yourself with you and shall always find yourself. Turn where you will—above, below, without, or within—you will find a cross in everything, and everywhere you must have patience if you would have peace within...

If you carry the cross willingly, it will carry and lead you to the desired goal where indeed there shall be no more suffering, but here there shall be. If you carry it unwillingly, you create a burden for yourself and increase the load, though still you have to bear it. If you cast away one cross, you will find another and perhaps a heavier one. Do you expect to escape what no mortal man can ever avoid? Which of the saints was without a cross or trial on this Earth? Not even Jesus Christ, our Lord, Whose every hour on Earth knew the pain of His passion. It behooveth Christ to suffer, and to rise again from the dead...and so enter into His glory. How is it that you look for another way than this, the royal way of the holy cross?

The whole life of Christ was a cross and a martyrdom, and do you seek rest and enjoyment for yourself? Indeed, the more spiritual progress a person makes, so much heavier *will he frequently find the cross, **because as his love increases, the pain of his exile also increases.***

*Yet such a man, though afflicted in many ways, is not without hope of consolation, because he knows that great reward is coming to him for bearing his cross. And when he carries it **willingly, every pang of tribulation is changed into hope of solace from God.** Besides, the more the flesh is distressed by affliction, so much the more is the spirit strengthened by inward grace.*

It is the grace of Christ, and not the virtue of man, which can and does bring it about that through fervor of spirit frail flesh learns to love and to gain what it naturally hates and shuns.

*To carry the cross, to love the cross, to chastise the body and bring it to subjection, to flee honors, to endure contempt gladly, to despise self and wish to be despised, to suffer any adversity and loss, to desire no prosperous days on Earth—**this is not man's way.** If you rely upon yourself, you can do none of these things, but if you trust in the Lord, strength will be given you from Heaven and the world and the flesh will be made subject to your word. You will not even fear your enemy, the devil, if you are armed with faith and signed with the cross of Christ.*

I can't take anymore. I close the book. This writing is not like ordinary writing. These so-called *Doctors of the Church* bring a fierce brand of medicine. I know it must be medicine because it doesn't go down easy.

I'm wiped out from reading that one passage alone.

I drift off to sleep for a while.

When I wake up a half hour later, I pick up de Montfort's *True Devotion to Mary* and thumb through it somewhat apprehensively. I'm gobsmacked. I expected a sweet little book about sweet little Mary. It's nothing of the sort. It's bracing, even more militant than Imitation of

Christ. The introduction discusses de Montfort's view which he summarized eventually as, *To God Alone, by Christ Wisdom, in the Spirit, in communion with Mary, for the reign of God.*

Father Polycarp didn't tell me to read *True Devotion to Mary,* but when I doubled back to the Catholic bookstore and asked the clerk for an introductory book on Mary, this is what she recommended. Frankly, if I had not such startling experiences after that Novena I don't think I'd care one whit about Mary. I'd be over with the Protestants saying *any woman would do! Why would you ask dead people to pray for you? What can they do? It's idolatry! It's necromancy!* So much for the Communion of Saints.

I asked Mary to pray for me, just as I would a living person. And I got some real, highly specific, very old school kind of help that brought me to her son. *Do whatever He tells you.* I'm open to hear what the Church has to say about Mary, and about this *communion of the saints* proclaimed in the Apostle's Creed. Isn't anybody interested in going beneath the surface of things anymore?

I recall what my choir mate wrote in the novena booklet. She wrote: **All for Jesus,** *through Mary.* Saint Louis de Montfort addresses that in *True Devotion to Mary* using plain but soaring language. I can understand the Marian controversy, but because of the extraordinary leading I received through asking for Mary's intercessory prayers to God, whom she is not, I have no trouble believing the following is at least possible. Saint de Montfort wrote:

With the whole Church I acknowledge that Mary, being a mere creature fashioned by the hands of God is, compared to His infinite majesty, less than an atom, or rather is simply nothing, since He alone can say, I Am He Who Is. Consequently, this great Lord, who is ever independent and self-sufficient, never had and does not now have any absolute need of the Blessed Virgin for the accomplishment of His will and the manifestation of His glory. To do all things He has only to will them.

However, I declare that, considering things as they are, because God has decided to begin and accomplish His greatest works through the Blessed Virgin ever since He created her, we can safely believe that He will not change His plan in the time to come, for He is God and therefore does not change in His thoughts or His way of acting.

The world being unworthy, said Saint Augustine, to receive the Son of God directly from the hands of the Father, He gave His Son to Mary for the world to receive Him from her. The Son of God became man for our salvation but only in Mary and through Mary. God the Holy Spirit formed Jesus Christ in Mary but only after having asked her consent through one of the chief ministers of His court.

God the Father imparted to Mary His fruitfulness as far as a mere creature was capable of receiving it, to enable her to bring forth His Son and all the members of His mystical body. ...St. Augustine, St. Ephrem, deacon of Edessa, St. Cyril of Jerusalem, St. Germanus of Constantinople, St. John Demascene, St. Anselm, St. Bernard, St. Bernardine, St. Thomas and St. Bonaventure [all agreed] that lack of esteem and love for the Virgin Mary is an infallible sign of God's disapproval. On the other hand, to be entirely and genuinely devoted to her is a sure sign of God's approval.

Saint de Montfort spends a good long while here establishing the role of Mary as a mere creature, but one to whom unique graces and attributes must have been granted, as spouse to the Holy Spirt and Mother of God the Son. She was closer to God than any human person could have ever been if you accept the premise—why wouldn't she have a special role now?

And so de Montfort then considers that special role and what it is increasingly toward the fullness of time. He envisions a group of disciples who will have a special devotion to Christ under a particular inspiration and guidance from Mary and will call many to conversion, even as they themselves are pilloried for it. Saint de Montfort wrote:

But what will they be like, these servants, these slaves, these children of Mary? They will be ministers of the Lord who, like a flaming fire, will enkindle everywhere the fires of divine love. [W]e know they will be true disciples of Jesus Christ, imitating His poverty, His humility, His contempt of the world and His love. They will point out the narrow way to God in pure truth according to the holy Gospel, and not according to the maxims of the world. Their hearts will not be troubled, nor will they show favour to anyone; they will not spare or heed or fear any man, however powerful he may be. **They will have the two-edged sword of the word of God in their mouths and the blood-stained standard of the Cross on their shoulders. They will carry the crucifix in their right hand and the rosary in their left, and the holy names of Jesus and Mary on their heart. The simplicity and self-sacrifice of Jesus will be reflected in their whole behavior.**

150

Mother's Day.

Four months after Mom's funeral.

I wake up to a glaring morning and sob.

It's the first heavy cry, serious cry, honest cry I've had since Mom died in January.

Mother's Day and I've driven the feminine out of my life entirely, except for Mary of course. She's all I've got where women are concerned. I suppose she should be enough, but I'm lonely and enduring a surprising rush of grief for the absence of my own earthly mother. I didn't see it coming.

I have an impulse to call Elle and wish her a Happy Mother's Day, but she's probably out with her own Mother and Nicole and I don't want to intrude on that with an unsettling reminder of my continued existence.

I call Dad instead.

We don't have much to say to each other, but we share a few tears.

Mom's gone from this world.

It's Mother's Day and she's gone.

We hang up and I'm still fairly dissatisfied, feeling profoundly alone. I go over to the bookshelf where I've placed Mom's pewter ashtray and the two books of hers I claimed: *Theology and Sanity* and *Alcoholics Anonymous*.

I bring her ashtray and the books over to the air mattress.

I thumb through *Theology and Sanity* first. I see a few college notes of Mom's. I read the book a little bit. It's by a man named F.J. Sheed. His premise here was that sanity is correspondence with reality and so, if the Catholic Faith is true, it reflects reality. And thus, if one does not know and observe the Catholic Faith, they can't even really be sane. I wonder if this made any impression on Mom when the Madames of the Sacred Heart made her read it at Lone Mountain all those many years ago.

Then I open the AA book and two handwritten documents fall out. They were written by Mom when she was trying to get sober at *Friendly House* in 1985. One is a letter to her friends and another one is a small notebook, a diary of sorts.

In her letter to her friends which was never sent, she writes:

How do others cope – normal people – that is – do they spend, gamble, be cross and hurtful, overeat, isolate? But of course the truly normal do none or some of the above yet with balance and they just COPE. Without a crutch! We all know that Celia could cope...

As I sit here at Friendly House I feel at this point a mixture of despair, emotional confusion, abandonment and some terror. At the same time I feel some peace. Does that make sense? Each day has space for reading, self-examination, long talks and of course AA. So now if I can last out the hurt of the physical and emotional separation from my husband and son and concentrate on getting well...I pray I can be a whole person again and redeem my identity and self-esteem. I want it so, but it's only obtainable through a change of attitude, spiritual enlightenment and hard work in a make-over of personal defects. I love you all – stay close to my husband and son. —C

Whoa. I'm not sure I can handle Mom's diary at this point. But I proceed. There are a number of entries that have to do with me. Mom wrote:

Feb 19: The most honest answer an alcoholic can give when asked Why did you drink?! is to say – I don't know! That's the truth. I've never known except the terrific compulsion and fear and failure. In a flash it happens— sometimes no premeditation whatsoever—you just drink. It's true, I don't know.

*Feb 20: Talked to my son. I miss him and just wanted to say Hi and hear his voice. He was **not** happy I called. I think just the sound of my voice brings out the pain inside.*

He told me we would either have a superficial conversation or a fight. I was surprised and yet even though he says he's not angry he is and I think at this period no matter what he hears about it being a disease, he doesn't accept that. He feels picked on, why me?, to have such a mother. He called the alcoholism and our separation the situation. I think part or most of him hates me. God Help me. I'll burn in hell unless I can conquer and maintain my willingness to be sober and change my life. I want for John only good and that means I'm not part of his life. My first thought this a.m. is to separate and live apart so John and his father can have peace of mind and go on with their lives. God walk me through this PLEASE. John Sr. could get an annulment because of alcoholism I'm sure.

Feb 24: I am so depressed. I'm really trying to get spiritual. I have no future. I've ruined it. What do I want? I'm no good – deserve hell. Who knows God's purpose for me?

March 3: Now it's your turn to suffer Mom. I hate you and your disease. Leave me alone. *I feel like John would use those words if he was honest with himself. I pray with all my heart for him every nite, not to forgive me for this curse but to be okay with himself.*

And finally, I read a full two page letter to me, written only in her diary, never sent, never read by another soul:

March 17, 1985

I

John, my Son, I woke up early thinking of you. I tried to be you at 15, a sophomore boy with an alcoholic mother in a treatment center. Believe it or not I can feel your pain and

354

resentment because you are part of my flesh, part of my emotions and we are bonded as mother and son.

I cannot compare my experience as a 15 year old sophomore girl to yours in exactly the same way but, my thought this morning goes back many years ago, when at your age on December 15 I said goodbye to my father as he left for his dental office and when I got home from Christmas shopping with my friends, did not expect my life to have changed so drastically in a few hours. My father had dropped dead in his dental office that morning while working on a patient. The M.D. next door who rushed in pronounced him dead on the spot. I never saw him again. My horror, my grief was explosive. At God I guess – How dare God do that to Celia and me? How could God take a husband and father away that suddenly without warning?

II

All of a sudden Celia was a widow and I was fatherless. How could life be so unfair? There was no more Dr. Richard John Cosgriff. That made me feel like half an orphan – what was my world now going to be – what was Celia going to do – I'd never known insecurity up to that point. I was terrified, my friends pitied me, everyone wanted to help and no one knew quite what to do or say. But God knew what He was doing. He had given me Celia as a mother – with all her gentleness, she was also strong and she was there for me. That is why God gave you Dad – your Dad – he's always there for you. As much as you resent his criticism, his fatherly control, he is (and this is not partiality), a great Dad who loves you completely. I've had a long life experience and have known Dads of friends, Dads among our married friends, Dads I've read about and so on. He is your Dad by no accident.

III

My predisposition to alcoholism was in me at birth no doubt and it did progress. So what I'm trying to say is that God gave you Dad and me for a reason and He is watching over all of us. In the Bible there is that passage that begins, To everything there is a season, and a time for every purpose under heaven. The more I pray, the more I look into myself, truly look into myself, the more firmly I believe that God had a divine purpose for me and alcoholism, for you, for Dad, for all of us in our own way and with our own results.

Getting back to my drastic life change at 15, my life continued to change for the next 2 years of high school and into college. I felt less than others because I had no father. Money became scarce. The lovely house I grew up in had to be sold right after I graduated from high school and Celia and I had to move to San Francisco and live in a small apartment. I know this is wrong but I thought at the time, Oh, an apartment, that's where poor people live. We're poor now.

I was making it through college though, Dad had set up a fund for me and Celia had some money from the sale of the house. All through those years God was watching over Celia and me.

Some of those Lone Mountain girls are close friends to this day. I had a wonderful college experience, became a good teacher and, of course, met and married your Dad and had you –

Oh John I'm so sorry, so sorry to be an alcoholic mother for you. God how you must hurt. God I wish I could hold you this minute and let you sob and let me sob and somehow begin again. I love you so much. I am so sorry sorry sorry sorry sorry sorry sorry sorry sorry sorry...

Part Ten: The City of God
Locale: The Interior Life
Preferred Handheld Device: Rosary
Age: 41
Occupation: Disciple
Condition of Soul: Improved, at least one would hope

151

I go to confession up at the Abbey now twice a week during holy hour at eight. It's usually a different priest every time, though Father Polycarp is always available to me by appointment.

Tonight it's a priest I've never met before. He's much older than the young angelic Father Polycarp. This man is grizzled, late seventies maybe. He looks like he's been through some wars. He has a soft European accent and bids me sit down.

I make the sign of the cross and say, *Forgive me Father for I have sinned. It's been three days since my last confession.*

I tell him I'm going to confession twice a week now at the suggestion of Father Polycarp. I say, somewhat sheepishly, that I'm coming out of a very destructive period, that I've abused alcohol and drugs and that I'm trying to get straightened out.

He says, *That's okay. I'm a friend of Bill's.*
Really?

Yeah, the old priest says, I've been sober about thirty years or more now.

Oh, I say, wishing the tables were turned and I could hear his life story.

He asks, Have you been Catholic long?

Oh yeah, I say, I'm a cradle Catholic, but it feels new to me now.

He smiles.

When'd you make your general confession?

About a month ago.

When'd you quit drinking?

About three weeks ago.

Ouch. Are you okay?

Well, yeah, it's weird. I tried to drink after the general confession and this deliverance prayer Father Polycarp said, but I threw up and then I went to a bar and everything that happened there freaked me out. So I just kind of, uh—*stopped.*

He asks, Did you go into withdrawals?

No, not like the shakes or the D.T.'s or anything like that. I smoked grass too so I didn't have to drink so much and I quit both at the same time. I feel weird though, a little sick all the time. I'm not sure I was the heaviest drinker in the world as far as quantity, but no one ever loved it more than me.

He smiles. He asks, Do you feel a sense of loss?

Yes, I say. I feel a grief. I can't hardly drive through Laguna now because I drank all over town. I drive by the places I drank and I can't believe I can't go in there again. I also feel ashamed.

Because of the people you hurt?

Yes, but also because I was so stupid. I really thought I figured out *better living through chemistry* and had this whole new way of life like nobody ever thought of before.

See, I didn't drink until I was thirty-four because of my Mom and then when I started—

It was like flipping a switch, he says.

Yeah, I say.

It's a bitter irony, he says, that we who love it so well can't have it. The others just don't appreciate it like we do, do they?

Ha, I guess not, I say.

What is your name?

John, I say.

Listen here John, I think you've received some special graces for sure that enabled you to stop drinking, but you need to make sure you can stay stopped. Have you considered some treatment for substance abuse?

Oh yeah, I've just been kind of wigged out about it, you know, making the call, going in somewhere. It's hard for me to speak English these days. I feel very sluggish.

He says, Go check it out. There are some special problems we alcoholics have that other people don't have. You can get some things in treatment you can't get anywhere else. So go, *go* be with your kind. But remember, the Church has things you can't get anywhere else either, right?

Right, I say.

He continues reflectively, slightly pained, I sit around in meetings of alcoholics and listen to people grapple with the concept of God, he says, I can't say anything dogmatic of course but I think to myself, *well ye-ah—what about experiencing God in the sacraments?*

I nod, wondering how exclusive this Christianity, this Catholic Faith, really is.

Father, do you mind if I ask something—most people these days, most Catholics even—seem to think the sacraments are just symbols. What about all those people, all those Protestants and well-meaning Buddhists, and all those *spiritual-but-not-religious* types? Do they not know God at all? Are they, uh—you know, *damned?*

Hm-mm, he chuckles, that's a little beyond the scope of what we can do in a ten minute confession, he responds. Let me say this. I believe Jesus Christ is God. I believe He founded the Catholic Church. I believe He instituted certain sacraments that He said were necessary for salvation, for the sanctification of the human soul. I believe the Church has administered those sacraments faithfully, through all kinds of weather, for two thousand years. Yet I also believe God is sovereign and can do what He wants. In theory, He can work outside His Church, outside the sacramental system He established. So maybe somebody could find a welcome in the afterlife doing something other than what Christ established. The Church has spoken on that and has allowed for a few possible exceptions. But why wouldn't someone want to honor Christ the way He left Himself with us? In the Eucharist for example? *It's so beautiful.* Isn't that what a good Father would do for his children? *Feed* them? With his very self if he could? It's not burdensome. Neither is baptism. To be received with living water—*water, how lovely*—and Spirit. His yolk is easy, but it's still a yolk. I wouldn't want to presume on God's mercy by doing something else. The only way we can know for sure we're obedient to the totality of Christ's design for us is in the Catholic Faith. I think it would be very foolish to arrive at the moment of death having never been baptized, having *never* confessed even one sin, *never* eaten of Christ's body and blood like He told us to, without which we have no life in us. You're home, John. The Catholic Church is *home* during our brief time here. *Welcome home.* But please, stay sober, he adds. If you're an alcoholic like I'm an alcoholic you might be a good Catholic but if you drink you'll be a *dead* Catholic.

152

I take Father's advice and get some formal assistance in my recovery from alcoholism and drug addiction.

As part of that process, I'm duly advised to help other alcoholics get and stay sober. This methodology is tried and true, though many claim not to understand why it is that one alcoholic helping another actually *works.*

Mother Teresa had something to say on this subject. She said, *The fruit of silence is prayer. The fruit of prayer is faith. The fruit of faith is love. The fruit of love is service. And the fruit of service is peace.*

Those who work among alcoholics find that when the alcoholic is in service, he has a greater interior peace and is less likely to return to alcohol. I don't question it. Given my newfound Catholicity that method of recovery makes perfect sense to me. In fact, it fits neatly with the corporal and spiritual works of mercy—feed the hungry, comfort the sick, visit the imprisoned, instruct the ignorant, pray for others, etcetera. Christ proclaimed the doing of those things would separate the sheep from the goats.

Maybe this idea of *one alcoholic helping another alcoholic* grants interior peace because those works of mercy lead people toward, rather than away from, their salvation, and deep down the soul knows it, even though it's not man's way.

153

About six months after my last drink, under formal guidance from other sober alcoholics, I find myself with a peculiar new assignment. A man calls me up and asks me if I would talk to a heroin addict facing some serious criminal charges and try to help him get and stay sober. I don't want to do it.

Listen, I tell the intermediary, I'm not a heroin addict. I'm not sure I'm the right guy for this.

No problem, he says.

But give the guy my number, I say suddenly. If he calls me maybe I'll give it a shot.

Two days later I get a phone call from Mike, one of the nicest most personable sounding men I've ever had the pleasure to talk to. He doesn't sound like a *heroin addict* at all.

I guess considering I was picturing a drooling spectacle out of *Trainspotting.*

Mike sounds like a salesman from the Midwest.

He reminds me a little of a younger version of Dad, with whom I've sadly not spoken since Mother's Day.

Mike, I tell him, you know this is part of our method of recovery—one alcoholic helping another—you're a drinker too, right?

Yeah man, he says. I've got the DUI's to prove it.

So I'm willing to meet you, I continue, but you have to know I never did *H.* I'm afraid of needles. I took some of my Mom's opiates when she was dying but they lobotomized me and I just sat there with my mouth open staring at flies. So I'm not an opiate guy.

That's alright, he says. Do you know anything about God? Because I've been down this road before in recovery and I feel like I never really got the spiritual part. I'd do good for a while and then when the heat was off I always screwed up again.

Maybe I do, I say. But I have a fairly specific idea of who God is and it's not very popular these days.

I'm half-Jewish, he says, but I have this feeling about Jesus, there's just too much written on Him. My wife is Catholic. She keeps saying I should become Catholic. I don't know what to do. Are you religious?

Silence.

Meet me tomorrow at the *Starbucks* at the bottom of Laguna Canyon Road, I say. Maybe I can help you out.

154

Mike is waiting for me at an outside table. He's nervous, eyes darting this way and that. Good looking guy, this Mike, five or six years older than me, not at all what I expected.

I ask him, So what's been going on?

Ahhh, well, it's a long story. I've been doing H and drinking and coke since I was in my teens. I was in the service, married a girl overseas, got busted over there, got thrown in the brig, then I got out and had a few kids with her. After that I did pretty good in business, different kinds of sales, but I always go back to the life. After a while we split up and I got involved with organized crime, did some work for them, got busted, got married again, had a daughter, went straight for a while, but eventually ended up in a shootout with the S.W.A.T. team. It was on the news. I'm not bullshitting you. They told me to come out with my hands up so I did and they had all the laser dots on my chest and they yelled, *Don't move* and I turned around and walked back inside. They didn't shoot. So then I went to jail for a while again and eventually got out. I got clean, married my current wife, had two kids, but then—

Mike turns his head sideways and tries not to cry.

Then what, bud?

I went back out. Things were so stressful, we'd started a business, all kinds of stuff happened between us. I just picked up. It calms me down. Otherwise my head races, dude, it just races.

Yeah, I say.

So eventually I felt like the cops were watching me at home and I grabbed a knife and ran outside. One of the neighbors called the cops and they rolled up after I ran back inside. My wife was freaked out. The cops came in and they found the drugs and they charged me with possession and some other stuff, the knife and all that.

I ask, So were they really after you before that?

I don't know man. My mind is playing tricks on me. Anyway I could be looking at doing some serious time especially with my record. I just can't do this anymore, John. I can't. I don't have it in me. I'll be fifty in a few years. I'm so—so *tired*.

Okay, I say. You've been using for over twenty years on and off. I have to say you look completely normal except for the twitching and shiftiness. I wouldn't think you'd look as good as you do after twenty years.

It's like, my medicine, Mike says. When I don't have something in my system I get really freaked out.

Have you ever tried other kinds of medicine? Like psychiatric medicine?

Yeah, nothing's ever really helped.

So how willing are you to do what I ask you to do?

John, I'll do anything. But I want the spiritual part of recovery this time. I don't think I ever got it.

Okay, I say. But before we get into any of that stuff I want you to see a psychiatrist. I think maybe you've got something else going on—I'm not saying you're *crazy* or anything like that—but it's just a sense I have. I believe you when you say that heroin is like your medicine, but I think there may be some alternatives.

155

A few days later Mike calls me all excited.

He says, The doctor thinks I've really got something that can be treated! He gave me one prescription. I took it last night and I feel pretty good. It totally slowed my head down.

Good, Mike!

I meet him a week later and he does seem different, a little less agitated. I'm encouraged.

John, he says, My kids are three and five. I don't want to go to prison this time.

I try to reassure him but since I've been acquainted with the local District Attorney's office I have to remain silent because I know they're a very efficient, very effective prosecuting agency that doesn't just give cases away.

What's your situation now with your wife?

We're separated, he says. I'm renting the basement of a house in Laguna. It's really scary down there. Wanna come over?

Ha, maybe, I say. Let's talk for a while.

I say, Tell me your thoughts on the spiritual life. What does it mean to you?

I believe in God, he says.

Who or what do you understand God to be?

My Mom was Jewish but my Dad didn't really let her practice. We lived in Missouri and it was just—I went to a Pentecostal revival once. But I got this Star of David tattoo later in life. I identify with my Jewish roots. My Mom and I used to watch *The Ten Commandments*—you know the old one with Charlton Heston?

Cecil B. DeMille?

Yeah!

I've never seen it, I say.

You've never seen it? You gotta come over and watch it! It calms me down. It makes me think of my Mom.

Okay, I find myself saying.

Four hours later, I've seen the whole of *The Ten Commandments* and Don Rickles' quip comes to mind when he spotted Charlton Heston sitting in an audience at a gala: *If you were Moses I'm a Mau Mau fighter pilot!*

Thanks, Mike. I don't think I ever would have watched this if I hadn't been invited.

Mike says, I was gonna join *Jews for Jesus* a few years ago but I just couldn't get it done.

So you think Jesus is the Messiah?

I'm not a theology guy, but I think there's something to it, yeah. There's just too much written on it, too much has happened to think that's all fake.

He seems so earnest, so pure in this belief, more so even than skeptical old me, even after all I've seen and experienced the past few years.

So this current wife of yours, she wants you to become Catholic?

Yeah, all three of my wives have been Catholic. One of my sons is devout. He's coming out this weekend to check up on me. Wanna meet him?

Sure, I say.

156

A few days later, Mike's son Brian flies into town from the Midwest. He's in the military, very squared away, humble, grounded. He's here to attend Mike's preliminary hearing in court the following week.

Hi Brian, I say, nice to meet you.

Nice to meet you sir, he says.

He looks a little nervous what with his Dad being in hot water again. I can tell he's looking at me wondering, *Who's this guy?*

I ask, So Mike tells me you're a practicing Catholic?

Yes sir, he says.

Me too, I say.

Perhaps you'd like to go up to holy hour tonight and pray for a while? There's a Catholic monastery up in the hills. They have confession and sing the divine office. It's very beautiful.

Sounds good, he says.

Mike says, Are you trying to trick me into going to Church, *Padre?*

You'll like it, I say, It's very calming.

We drive up to the Abbey together and Mike is immediately impressed.

He says, *It has a military feel up here, like barracks or something.*

I say, Yeah, it's a kind of a military operation. They're engaged in spiritual warfare. Saint Michael the Archangel is their patron. Just like your name.

Mikha'el, he says.

Right.

We enter the chapel and the priests are already fully into singing the Psalms. It's transcendent.

Brian knows just what to do, genuflecting as we cross in front of the Blessed Sacrament exposed on the altar and making the sign of the cross and genuflecting again as we enter the pew.

Michael is ungainly and awkward. He has a hard time sitting still. I give him some reading material. Brian takes his rosary out of his pocket and begins praying on his knees.

The holy hour, and especially the silence, is exceptionally long for Mike as he's still detoxing from everything that was so recently flooding his system.

After it's over Brian brightens considerably when he sees someone he knows up front. He relaxes his military bearing and waves. He's waving to a postulant, a young man who's considering joining the community and is in residence with them for a while. He wears a black suit and tie like the other postulants.

Brian and Mike walk up and hug the young man. I wait in the back. They step outside and have an ebullient conversation.

Afterwards they skip toward me and Mike says, That's a kid from our old neighborhood back in Missouri. He and Brian went to the Catholic grade school together back there and now he's becoming a priest!

Great, I say. Small world. *Another funny little coincidence,* I think.

As we head down the steep hill to leave the Abbey, Mike gets a phone call. It's his wife. He has her on the speaker phone. She's furious with him, hissing and spitting, saying she found some emails on his computer.

I'm gonna testify against you! I hope you die in prison. They're going to stab you to death, I'll see to it!

Honey, stop, Mike says, I'm sorry. I didn't do it. I don't know what you're talking about.

You're out with a girl now, aren't you, you bastard?

No, I'm with Brian and John—

Yeah right, who's John?

John, say hello to my wife—

Bullshit, she says, I know about you. You LIAR!

She hangs up the phone in a rage.

Mike begins to hyperventilate. He can't drive. The car starts to drift toward the soft shoulder. I grab the wheel.

Mike, stop the car!

He manages to get his foot on the brake and I throw the vehicle into park. I run around the outside and Brian escorts his father to the other side of the car. In a matter of minutes that joyous reunion in the chapel has turned to ash. Mike is shaking, almost convulsing.

I try to reassure Mike but even I'm unsettled by the venom I heard coming over the phone.

But more than her anger, the *timing* of his wife's accusations bother me.

I've seen some things now—in my life and in others—a strange interplay between moments of grace and inexplicably hateful attacks. Increasingly I realize Saint Paul's assessment is true. Our battle is not directly with flesh and blood, but against spiritual evil.

I dare not speak any of this in the presence of Brian and Mike.

It'll be okay, Mike, I say, she'll calm down.

157

The day of the preliminary hearing in Mike's court case is a dark one.

Brian and I sit in the gallery and listen to the prosecutor present evidence against his father, including Mike's prior felonies. Then they put the responding officers on the stand. Brian tells me he has to leave the room.

I'm sorry sir, he whispers to me, I can't take this.

I follow him out.

Hey Brian, I'm the son of an alcoholic too—my Mom, I say.

Yeah, well my Dad's more than an alcoholic, he says, fighting back tears. He wipes his eye with a sleeve. He's lived a pretty wild life, Brian says. You know he used to ask me if he could get me a hooker when I was on leave. I said, *Dad, Dads are not supposed to get their sons hookers!*

I can't really help myself and I burst out laughing.

Brian laughs too, but starts to cry a little. I've only been with one woman my entire life and we were married, he says.

Brian, I say, you're a Catholic man. You understand spiritual warfare?

Yes, he says. I think. I mean, who really understands it?

Your friend from Missouri up there with the priests, he's majoring in it. He'll be immersed in the study of it the next ten years before he's ordained. But your father knows little about it. He doesn't have our Faith yet. Mike made sure you got a good Catholic education, right?

Yeah, my Mom in Missouri did too.

I'm going to try and help your father straighten out, I say. Would you please pray the Rosary for your Dad and me when you get back home?

Sure, he says. He looks at me for a moment and says, I think you're the best thing to happen to him in a long time.

We go back in and, big surprise, the judge thinks there's more than enough evidence to hold Mike to answer to the crimes as charged and binds him over for trial in three months.

Mike looks back at us helplessly.

158

Brian heads for the airport the next day.

Mike isn't doing well. Whatever progress he made has evaporated, except for the fact he's still physically sober. Barely.

He calls me up and says, I want to hit that needle so bad, he whimpers, is that okay with you, *Padre?* I can taste it.

No, but I understand, I tell him. Let's go back up to the Abbey tonight. I have some spiritual warfare prayers I want us to pray.

We sit through the holy hour again and Mike is very fidgety. I leave him for a few moments and go to confession. After I come out the hour has come nearly to an end. After it's over I ask one of the priests if he'd give Mike and me a blessing, but especially Mike. He says yes, of course, but looks very deeply at Mike and asks, *Are you open to a blessing, Michael? Because it comes from God?*

Yes, Father, Mike says, looking as eager for a blessing as a nun taking the veil. He looks twice the Catholic I am. After we're alone on the grounds we find a clearing and I pull out the sheaf of deliverance prayers I brought with me.

Now Mike, I will not say these prayers over you, but we can say them together. Here goes:

Prayers against Evil, I read aloud. We recite:

Spirit of our God, Father, Son and Holy Spirit, Most Holy Trinity, descend upon us. Please purify us, mold us, fill us with yourself, and use us. Banish all the forces of evil from us; destroy them, vanquish them so that we can be healthy and do good deeds.

We command and bid all the powers who molest us—by the power of God Almighty, in the name of Jesus Christ our Savior—to leave us forever, and to be consigned into the everlasting lake of fire, that they may never touch us again.

In the name of the Lord Jesus Christ, by the power of His cross, His blood and His resurrection, we bind you Satan, the spirits, powers and forces of darkness, the nether world, and the evil forces of nature.

We ask forgiveness for and renounce all negative inner vows that we have made with the enemy, and ask that Jesus Christ release us from these vows and from any bondage they may have held in us. We claim the shed blood of Jesus Christ, the Son of the living God, over every aspect of our lives for our protection.

Dear Lord Jesus, please forgive us for all the times we have not submitted to Your will in our lives. Please forgive us for all our sinful actions, for making agreements with the enemy, and for believing the devil's lies. We now submit to you as our Lord, dear Jesus. Now we break every agreement that we have made with the enemy.

Lord Jesus, please send an assignment of angels to remove and bind to the abyss all demons and their devices that had access to us because we believed their lies. We now ask You to establish a hedge of protection around us, over us and under us, and seal it with your blood, Lord Jesus Christ.

After we finish we're silent on our walk back to the car.

As we're driving down the hill Mike gets a call from his wife.

She's fuming, even angrier than the last time, telling him she's going to see that he's ruined, that he'll never see his children again, that she's leaving and he'll never find her, that she hates him, that he's ruined their lives.

Mike is shaking. We switch places, I drive. He looks like he's about to have a stroke.

He says, John, I don't think I'm gonna make it man, this is too much.

159

A day or two later I get a call from another friend in recovery who's with Mike.

John, John, the friend says, *Mike's on the floor flopping around. I think he's having a seizure!*

Call 911, I say. Or take him to the emergency room!

He won't go. He says they'll just give him a bunch of drugs and wreck his sobriety.

I'm over my head here, I say. It sounds like he needs medical attention. Can he talk?

I don't know, the friend says, I'll put the phone near his head.

Ahh, laa, eee, *John I can't, I can't—*

Yes you can, Mike! *You can!*

I try to be affirmative but he sounds like he's going to die.

The friend says, *He was talking about killing himself with a hotshot earlier.*

Okay, I say. Just do your best. Try and get him back to the house in Laguna or the hospital if he'll go. I'll come down there.

I have this sudden instinct to *baptize* Mike.

I've never had an instinct like that before, but it comes upon me strongly because it seems that Mike really is going to die.

His death seems imminent and this possibility does not surprise me, since I nearly hung myself in the grips of my despair.

Over fifteen percent of alcoholics commit suicide.

It's common.

I can't stop it, although when I get there I will try to convince him to check himself in somewhere.

But what I *can* do is baptize him for all the good it'll do, if he wants it.

I pull a copy of the Catechism of the Catholic Church out of my desk.

I look for *emergency baptism* in the index because I don't want to overstep my bounds.

Mom told me about a couple involved in a shark attack on Stinson Beach near San Francisco and how the man baptized his girlfriend as she was bleeding out on the wet sand.

So I'd always had it stuck in my head that anybody could perform an emergency baptism in *danger of death.*

But since I'm not a hundred percent sure that Mike is really in *danger of death* because he hasn't been half eaten by a shark, I don't want to overdo it here.

But when I look it up I see that the words of the Catechism are not *in danger of death* but instead *in case of grave necessity.*

I think this qualifies.

I shut the book.

160

I drive down the hill and find Mike in near catatonia, staring at the wall in his basement. There's a foul stench down here. I've been told the previous tenants were meth addicts. I don't like the feel of the place.

Mike, buddy, how'd you like to come with me to *Saint Catherine of Siena's* up the street?

He shakes his head ambiguously.

I don't know how to tell you this, but I'd like to baptize you.

He turns his head and looks at me strangely, like a lizard.

Let's go, I say, assuredly.

What the heck am I doing?!!!

We arrive at Saint Catherine's at two in the afternoon. The small Church is totally empty, thank God. They have a large holy water font at the back of the Church in the center of the main aisle. The water is burbling and flowing.

Well, here goes nothing.

I spit it out:

Michael, please kneel down.

He kneels down next to the water.

I glance around like a cat burglar, then as quickly as I can I scoop two big handfuls of water and pour them over the front of Mike's head, dousing the edge of his hairline and pouring water along the top and sides of his cranium.

I say, I baptize you *Mikha'el* in the name of the Father, Son and the Holy Ghost. Amen.

I make the sign of the cross over his forehead for good measure, though I don't believe it's necessary to effect his baptism—just the water, the words, and my intention to do what the Church has always done since Christ declared: *Verily, verily, I say unto thee, unless one is born of water and the Spirit, he cannot enter into the kingdom of God.* (John 3:5)

I feel dizzy.

He looks up at me as if to say, *That's it?*

That's it, I say.

Let's go over to the tabernacle and say a prayer or two.

You see here, Mike, they keep the consecrated host, the Body of Christ, in the tabernacle. This has deeply Jewish roots. I'll explain later. In the meantime, welcome to Jews for Jesus. Let's say the Lord's Prayer:

Our Father—

We pray.

After we're done with that I tell Mike I have a couple prayer cards for him.

One is a prayer to Saint Michael the Archangel, I say, and here's another one called the Memorare.

Let's say it together now:

Remember, O most gracious Virgin Mary, that never was it known that anyone who fled to your protection, implored your help, or sought your intercession, was left unaided. Inspired with this confidence, I fly unto you, O Virgin of virgins, my Mother. To you do I come, before you I stand, sinful and sorrowful. O Mother of the Word Incarnate, despise not my petitions, but in your mercy, hear and answer me. Amen.

Now Mike, I want you to notice something about that prayer. It's a solemn promise that never was it known that *anyone*—not just any *Catholic*, but *any person*—was *left unaided when they called upon our Blessed Mother.* She's a Jewish mother, just like your Mom was. Jesus gave her to us at the time of His crucifixion. She's a gift to the entire Church and according to this prayer, to *anyone* that calls upon her. It has been my experience that she will lead you to her Divine Son. She's not a goddess or a deity or anything like that. But she's a saint, and in God's economy the angels and saints can help us, just like we're helping each other right now. God wants His creatures to minister to each other. The communion of saints is real. They're there for God and they're there for us. It's my advice to you that you say these three prayers every night: The Lord's Prayer, the Prayer to Saint Michael and the Memorare. I will be praying for you too.

Really, I can scarcely believe the things that come out of my mouth these days. I said all that to Mike with *conviction.*

Hey John, Mike says, thanks. You wanna watch *The Ten Commandments* again?

Sure, I say, and we camp out in the basement for the night watching Charlton Heston show Yule Brenner what's what.

Moses' God is God, old Yule has to finally concede.

I fall asleep on Mike's floor, hoping to avoid the cockroaches.

161

A few days later Mike appears in court for a pretrial conference. Since the baptism he's been fully functional, very little fear. I wonder why the change. It couldn't just be the baptism, could it? Maybe it's the prayers. But still, he's facing a trial in a couple months and every trip to court is potentially triggering. I can't make it that day, but I'm stunned to gasping when Mike calls me up and says the prosecutor dropped all the charges. They don't do that in Orange County very easily. I mean, they found Mike with the drugs, they found Mike with the paraphernalia. They have a confession. That part of the case was solid. And it's gone with a wave of a pen?

Mike's in disbelief.

Also, his wife's much improved, much calmer, much more willing to give it a try so long as he stays sober. I don't fully understand this shockingly positive turn of events.

Mike says, I know why, John. It was from God. I'm getting a real chance here. A lot of people had it in for me but they turned cooperative. God knows I'm sincere. You gave me the baptism, and the monks have been praying for me. Eric called and said his friend told him I'm still on the priests' prayer list. And the Memorare. Whenever I say it, a great peace comes over me. *It's all real,* John. Don't doubt it, padre. You're really good at this. You need to help a lot of people get sober.

It's not me, Mike. I think truly I'm just—I don't know what I'm doing. We've been very fortunate. This was all extremely haphazard. I mean I can't go around baptizing alcoholics and casting out demons.

He pauses for a second and then says, *Why not?*

162

A few weeks later Mike and I attend a deliverance seminar put on by a visiting African priest who's garnered quite a following. People come from all over North America to see him.

He begins his presentation by asking us in a regal accent fit for an African prince, *What was the most important day of your life?*

377

People look around, one person says something from the second row.

That's right, the priest bellows, *the day of your baptism!* That's the most important thing you have, is your baptism! Especially for the purpose of spiritual warfare. I tell you now, don't ever try these deliverance prayers or any of these things with someone who's not baptized! It will only make them worse. Leave them as they are; they're better off that way! Because the one who is baptized in the name of the Father, Son and the Holy Spirit has a pledge from Christ: *I have to defend you!* He places his hand palm forward, chest high, to indicate I suppose, Christ having *pledged* as it were, His spiritual protection to all those who are baptized in His name and follow Him in the manner He established.

I turn and look at Mike who's looking back at me. We're both thinking the same thing—he was *not yet baptized* when he received the strangely vicious attacks after we said those deliverance prayers. We recall the way he was beaten down by his wife and others after his first night up at the Abbey in the presence of the Blessed Sacrament. I was praying the *Anima Christi* that night for Mike's intentions.

During that whole period Mike was unbaptized—and the deliverance prayers made him worse.

This floors me. It's not unlike the shocking experience after my general confession where I went and found the passage in the Gospel according to Saint John which describes Christ's grant of authority to forgive and retain sin. *Of course confession is a channel of supernatural grace and so is baptism.*

So must be *all* the sacraments. Yes, *it's all real.*

An old friend of mine from high school gives me a call.

He says, Didja hear? Father Alex died.

Father Alex died?

Yeah, he says. I thought you'd want to know.

Father Alex was a newly minted Franciscan when I met him, assigned to Bishop Montgomery High School straight out of the seminary. He caused a huge sensation because he looked so young and had a luminous smile. He was part Asian and reminded me strangely of the character Linda Hunt won an Academy Award for in *The Year of Living Dangerously*. But most sensational of all he rode a skateboard around town and was known as *the skateboarding priest* in the local newspaper.

When he walked into a room on campus, everyone lit up. He counseled everyone, was available to everyone and, when Mom was flat on her back and away in treatment, he became the very light of Christ to me, though I didn't recognize it for what it was at the time. We walked down to the Redondo Beach Pier from school one day, talking the whole way about life and how to make it through. When we got to the pier we both looked down over the railing like everyone always does, watching the waves surge toward the shore.

He said, When I was your age John, I used to feel like I was *drowning.*

I remember thinking what a gifted counselor Father Alex was, taking a visual cue from the ocean and bringing it into our conversation, establishing his own vulnerability and reassuring me that if he made it through, I would too. I never forgot it.

And now he's dead.

Father Alex was about ten years older than me, so he experienced a very early death.

How?

I dunno, the friend says, it was sudden. But the funeral is this Saturday out in the Valley. I don't think I can go. Maybe you can represent for us?

That's an odd request, I think. This friend is really more of an acquaintance, somebody I reconnected with vaguely at the class reunion. But after the phone call I can't get the funeral out of my head. News travels fast and I expect there to be a huge contingent of high school people there.

164

The morning of Father Alex's funeral brings a blinding cloudburst, raining like a scene out of *The Ten Commandments.* Even though the church is packed, there's only a small contingent of my high school peers there. It's mostly people from other parishes where Father Alex had served. The Archbishop gives the homily and says what a terrible blow it is to lose a priest. *Look at the need,* he says, *look at the need.*

I have this strange stirring in my gut.

Should I become a *priest?*

What a ridiculous notion.

Five years ago I was afraid of priests, thinking the worst of them and conveniently forgetting about priests like Father Alex and some others who were always there for me growing up.

The funeral was attended by nearly every priest in the Diocese and many of the women religious too. I think of the priestly community up in the hills and their astonishing witness.

Why aren't there more like them?

Why aren't there more like Father Alex?

They seem so beleaguered now, so diminished.

380

Nearly everyone looks at them sideways, as if to say *are you one of those weirdos too?*

I never see a priest around town in clerical dress.

Are they all too ashamed? It wouldn't be without reason.

And yet I've discovered something startling—the sacraments appear to have the power of supernatural grace. I don't know how anyone who claims the name of Christ would leave the sacraments on the table.

It seems tragic to me, rather incomprehensible, that one could claim Christ but deny His Church, or redefine *church* to include everyone who ever *accepted Christ* but rejected His sacraments, everyone who failed to honor Him the way He left Himself with us.

It's as though the sacraments and the full complement of Church power is hidden in plain sight—it's technically available to people but the apprehension they'd have to overcome to access it these days keeps them away.

If confession is real, and baptism is real, and the Eucharist is real, that must mean that the sacrament of holy orders—the priesthood—is *real.* And how could it not be? Father Polycarp isn't superhuman. He's not a magician. He knocked the stuffing out of me with that absolution *in persona Christi* and deliverance prayer.

How?

Because he has Christ's *authority.*

After all my years in the presence of priests and an ever-dwindling number of women religious I came to view them as weak, not worth listening to, antiquated curiosities or worse, control freaks clinging to a dead mythology but trying to wring the last bit of privilege out of it.

But now, sitting here at Father Alex's funeral, I feel ashamed of my historic attitude toward priests, ashamed of my attitude toward the Church as just some old manmade club no better or worse than the *National Fuchsia Society,* just bigger and more severe, full of hypocrites and perverts.

If the Catholic Faith is *true,* then the Church must be something more than a human institution. I'm steadily reading the things that have been written of Her, that She is the Mystical Body of Christ, the Bride of Christ, the New Jerusalem, the Church Militant on Earth, the Church Suffering in Purgatory, the Church Triumphant in Heaven. I'm increasingly moved by the possibility of these truths. History shows She is continually misunderstood, maligned, attacked, infiltrated, diminished and reborn.

It seems to me somehow that the Catholic people are on the other end of a spiritual genocide of sorts. It's fitting that I would be sitting at the funeral of a dead priest, the one who meant the most to me growing up, taken out in his late forties or early fifties. He was, indeed, too beautiful for this world.

A casualty perhaps of intense unrelenting spiritual warfare? Alone in the post-modern priesthood?

Am I supposed to—*replace him?* I could never be like him. He was warm and wonderful and incredibly nice.

I am not so nice.

But maybe—circumstances, such as they are—call for something other than *nice.*

I dunno, I dunno.

But I can't forget the Archbishop's mention of the *great need for priests.* I look around at the mourner-stuffed church and have to agree.

There is a great need, but only if the Catholic Faith is true in its entirety, in its astonishing supernatural claims, otherwise we should shut the whole thing down immediately.

I'm downtown for a court appearance in the *Star Trek* merchandising case for Captain Pike. I feel ethereal, unattached to the hallway floors. I pass preening lawyers counseling their distraught or tight-lipped clients, and I pass mothers holding crying babies and clerks pushing wire baskets full of files. The hallways are dreadfully long in the Stanley Mosk courthouse, like one of those nightmares where the hallway actually lengthens as you walk it.

I carry my briefcase. I dress in a dark suit. Yet I'm no longer the single-minded litigator I once was.

I look upon all these hundreds of people now and think of their souls.

How presumptuous of me, how absurd, how self-important!

But I do.

I once thought I could achieve redemption, even glorification, in a courtroom, scuttling after a priesthood of sorts in this secular church, with its rituals and trappings. Yet I see here today in these overlong hallways a chronic, perpetual brokenness, with only one apparent means of true restoration.

The hallway hums with tension.

I remember prancing through this place like some of the young high-rise law firm associates I'm looking at now, all wingtips and pomade and high heels and red lipstick.

It's a veneer.

The exaggerated woundedness in this building, the brokenness—is that why I was supposed to pass through the oppressive tunnel of my legal career, to be immersed in broken relationships, in conflict, in recriminations, in ugliness, in the ice cold breakdown of *the world?*

So that I could see so clearly the difference between man's way and God's way? So that I could so clearly see my own brokenness that would not be healed by anything in the world?

Those sonorous lines from *Imitation of Christ* come back to me:

To carry the cross, to love the cross, to chastise the body and bring it to subjection, to flee honors, to endure contempt gladly, to despise self and wish to be despised, to suffer any adversity and loss, to desire no prosperous days on Earth— **this is not man's way.**

Indeed. I know man's way. It was as natural to me as breathing. It's been placed upon me now to do the opposite, to take a contrary path, the narrow path of which Christ spoke so challengingly, the path that Chesterton referred to when he said the Christian way of life has not *been tried and found wanting, but found difficult and left untried.*

Of course I feel strange. And of course, before my conversion, the goings-on in this hallway looked perfectly normal to me.

I see things differently now, it's true. But that's not enough. I can't do things God's way unless I'm animated by the Spirit of God:

If you rely upon yourself, you can do none of these things, but if you trust in the Lord, strength will be given you from Heaven and the world and the flesh will be made subject to your word.

How crucial *trust* seems to be. That's not my strong suit.

I fight the urge to kneel down right here in this hallway with these people and take their hands and pray with them, and tell them there is a higher reality, that this temporal prison is not our final destination. We're standing on a train platform. Let's catch the right one. Let's be *saints.*

Ha! Yeah, right. They'll call security so quick I'll be back on Hill Street faster than a celebrity defendant.

I don't think this is what people are looking for in a lawyer.

My days in this line of work might be coming to an end.

166

After the hearing I head back to my car. I notice the new Catholic Cathedral is equidistant between the state and federal courthouses, probably a sneaky trick by the Archdiocese to get lawyers to go back to church.

Instead of continuing down Hill Street toward my parking space, I take an impulsive left turn and enter the Cathedral campus on foot. I go into the administrative offices and tell the receptionist I think I might have a vocation to the priesthood. She looks at me strangely and calls someone from the backrooms.

A nice woman comes out and hands me a phone number of one of the priests in charge of new vocations. I put the number in my pocket and walk to my car.

167

Father Joe, the Vocation Director, meets me a few days later at a parish in Manhattan Beach. I tell him my wending tale of worldliness, diabolical disorientation, and conversion. He listens quietly.

He says, I think your vocation might be genuine, John. You have an Augustinian story. It's not bad, full of consolations and desolations. It might be right for the times. There's no extreme rush. You have at least a couple years to think about it, at least in this Diocese. We need many priests. We take older vocations. You need to discern. I want you to have a spiritual director who's a priest in this Diocese and I want you to be in contact with me every few months. We have meetings periodically for the men who are discerning. You're encouraged to come to those as well.

168

I get a call from a parishioner at Saint Lawrence Martyr concerning my father. I'm alarmed, thinking something has happened.

The man says, Oh no everything's fine. I just wanted to tell you that your Dad is going on a men's retreat and we're asking the family members and friends to write a note of encouragement to the men on retreat. And there's a Mass at the end that we'd like you to show up to as a surprise. He gives me his email address and the time of the Mass.

I struggle writing the requested letter to Dad.

I know I need to try and make peace with Dad but he still seems so angry so much of the time. If I apologize he'll just say something like Damn right you should apologize. I just can't go through it. And plus I meant what I said. He needs to go to confession! I know how much it would help him.

But I write the letter anyway. The tone is rather grim, I realize, but I can't bring myself to warm it up for the sake of making nice:

Dear Dad,
I hope the retreat is going well.
The family members and friends of the retreat participants were asked to write letters that would provide some affirmation for you all.
Obviously this is a difficult period for us.

It's also a difficult time in the world, and circumstances seem primed to cause dissension.

I do love you and ask your forgiveness for any disrespect or anger I've shown you.

I made a general confession recently and it required a detailed and searching examination of conscience.

One of the things you used to tell me was that Humility is truth.

What I've noticed of late is the way in which the opposites of humility—the ego, the appetite and pride—are at a fever pitch. I suppose it's always been this way, but it comes through the culture in every possible medium now. The chest beating and glorification of self is normal and encouraged it would appear.

These qualities are precisely the ones associated most closely with Satan. Too prideful to remain a faithful part of God's plan, the evil one splintered off and formed a cult of glorification of self. We are called to reject that attitude and behavior, even in our response to it.

The truth is most people are living in a state of mortal sin which, I am coming to believe, leads to damnation, to an old fashioned real hell. Christ said it would be few who would be saved. I think about that a lot, how few is few? The Church has taught on that in the past although She has no official teaching on numbers. There is a famous sermon by Saint Leonard of Port-Maurice, a Franciscan. He tells us to strive to be among the fewest of the few, not being afraid to overshoot the mark. Why not aim for sainthood? What else is there? I have a certain holy fear now, a true fear of God. It's also said one who has fear is not yet perfected in love. I plead guilty. I expect judgment and pray for mercy. I hope I have enough time to do some service for God after living like He didn't exist for so long. I want more than to jam my foot in the door of salvation, I want what the saints had—the life of the soul growing in grace.

We should ascertain the higher law, the natural law, the moral law, God's revealed law, and follow it.

The twenty centuries of Church experience, observation, revelation and teaching provide enough sustenance and example to follow. You had more training in these matters than I had, but I'm attempting to make up for lost time, and to pay special attention to the wisdom and practice that has been suppressed. Even many people with the older formation have been debauched and compromised by what has gone on in this most recent stretch of the world system and in the Church Herself.

I believe Mom may be in purgatory. I base this on my observations of her the day and night of her death, on the nature of the single dream I had of her since her death, on my sense of where her spirit and soul were in the years leading up to her death, her voracious attachment to the world, and my limited understanding of the doctrine of purgatory. Before this, the idea of praying for the dead or offering Masses for the dead seemed like an antiquated custom.

Now, it seems entirely reasonable to me.

We should both pray for Mom, at least one Ave Maria and Lord's Prayer per day, and ensure that Masses are offered for the repose of her soul. We must also pray for Christopher and offer Masses for him as well.

When I looked through your photo albums after her death, I couldn't help but notice that half the people in the photos are dead now. Whatever they did on this planet, the places they lived, the businesses they engaged in, the families they raised, seemed rather dwarfed by the enormity of Creation and the length of time before and after their own lives. Our time in this realm is a blip, a wisp compared to the time before and after we are gone from this place.

The most important thing is to cooperate with God in the sanctification of our souls.

What I've found over the last seven years is that although I first desired pleasures and my idea of freedom, and then mystical experience, the religious experience led me through mystical experience into a desire for total uniformity with the will of God.

This experience of dying to self in order to live for God is well covered in the writings of our saints. However, it is considered so bizarre in contemporary Southern California at least that there is very little support or understanding of what it means or how it works. Like many other concepts and practices that were formerly well understood, the death of the self—a true form of humility—has been lost or suppressed.

In this effort, there are certain basic practices that I'm now aware of and engaging in that I highly recommend for you: (1) A general confession, followed by routine confession every four to six weeks, including a daily examination of conscience; (2) The Lenten practices of prayer (especially the Rosary), almsgiving (giving or mercy or charity) and fasting, done TOGETHER, produce a tremendous spiritual power and grace in the individual and in the world; (3) Reading and learning about the well-established doctrine of Spiritual Warfare (which is largely ignored or suppressed today); (4) Reading the writings of the Saints, and the Doctors of the Church in particular; (5) Reading and studying the Bible in light of the timeless teachings of Holy Mother Church on the meaning and interpretation of it. After all, the New Testament especially is the holy text of the Catholic Faith regardless of what anyone else may claim.

As Father Alex once wisely told us, the Church in this century would be very small, comprised mostly of mystics— those who receive some special grace like Saint Paul to see through the thick smoke of Satan. I had no idea what he was talking about at the time. We have all the examples we need to live through a period such as this—involving a profound collapse of the authentic Faith—in Saint Athanasius, Saint Francis, Saint Catherine of Siena, and many others—which does not necessarily mean it will be easy or pleasant.

This is what little I think I know about the Catholic spiritual life at present. I am a neophyte at best. I do not mean to preach. Thank you for introducing me to the Catholic Faith and for making sure I was baptized and received the sacraments.

The Catholic Faith truly must be the Pearl of Great Price, because it cost me everything I had to get it. Good luck to you going forward.

—John

169

The night of the Mass which ends the retreat, all the friends and family gather in church to surprise the retreaters.

Then they march the men in who've been sleeping on cots in the church hall for a day or two. They look like hammered jerky, hair askew, bags under their eyes, wrinkled clothes. Some of them look like they've been crying.

What did they do to them?

The men are surprised to see all their friends and family in the pews. Dad comes down the center aisle of the church to take his place for Mass. He has tears in his eyes.

After Mass he comes up to me and gives me a bear hug.

He says, *John,* guess what? They made us go to confession!

I'm in disbelief. Wow, who could arrange it? I wasn't sure he'd ever be able to walk into the confessional under his own power after all these years. But confession found *him.* Why am I surprised anymore by these odd turnings? This seems to be the new normal, the way things are, not easy by any stretch, particularly because my relationship to the world seems ever more remote, tenuous, strained. But truly, the paranormal is now normal. *If it's odd, it's God,* or so some people say. I believe them.

170

I head back to Laguna after the Mass, relieved to have found a measure of peace and normalcy with dear old Dad. I have much to discern it appears. Am I to live in the world? If so, I'll probably need to seek that annulment and consider remarrying for real this time, in and through the Church with a sacramental marriage, openness to life, the whole bit, no monkeying around.

Or maybe I'm to remain single and chaste until my dying day like a Catholic Carson Drew, just practicing law or engaging in some other sort of enterprise and spending the rest of my time in devotion and service to others.

What sounds very peculiar to me is the priesthood.

The Church is so badly compromised.

What would I be walking into?

Just who do I think I am?

I guess that's what discernment is all about.

In the meantime, I'll keep doing what I've been doing and do more of it.

171

Wendell and Louise and I settle into a nice rhythm. I do a lot of activities in recovery, helping other alcoholics and addicts get and stay sober, and accepting that same help myself. I feel comfortably sober but my work ethic was destroyed. I have a miserable time trying to pay off debt and get steady work. I'm not the same person. I don't relate that well to commerce anymore, to the give and take of the marketplace. It's not that I think I'm above it, it's just, well, there's such a thing as a *state of life* in Catholic practice. You're supposed to live up to it, whatever it is. If you're in the world you're supposed to be a good lay Catholic and fulfill your duties of that state. But I have to wonder whether I'm supposed to leave the world altogether. That's how it feels at the moment.

I go up to the Abbey to see Father Polycarp and tell him about my visit to the vocation director in the Diocese of Los Angeles. He's cautiously supportive.

It's not wrong of you, John, to look into it. I told you I foresaw great holiness for you.

Yeah, Father, but the *priesthood?* I didn't see that coming when I walked into your confessional.

You've experienced the power of the sacraments. You see they're ignored by so many. You see the beauty and truth of Catholic theology, the *rightness* of it. And so it's your charity, it's the love you're beginning to feel for others in God that's driving you in that direction. If that's truly what's in your heart, *generosity*, then that's a right motivation. But still, you have to be called to it and you have to be fit with no canonical impediments. You'll have to work through all of that. Take your time. I'd suggest you read some of the major texts on Catholic spiritual direction. And if they told you that you needed to have a spiritual director in the Diocese you should probably obey that if you're really discerning a vocation there.

Okay, I say. What *are* some of the major texts on Catholic spiritual direction?

There's one that I'd recommend you read first, and then we can talk about the others. It's a little heady, but the first volume I think you can handle. It's called *Three Ages of the Interior Life* by Father Reginald Marie Garrigou-

Lagrange. He was a Domincan with a strong grasp of Thomistic theology. He examined the mystical theology of figures like Saint John of the Cross and Saint Teresa of Avila in light of the systematic theology of Saint Thomas Aquinas and showed how they lined up, and how this way of holiness is available to every disciple of Christ in the Catholic Faith, not just a few great saints. It's a foundational text.

Thanks, Father.

Also, you know, we have a Third Order. It's for laypeople. It takes about two years of formation but then you share in our charism. We can talk about it more later.

What is your charism?

Well, I wouldn't want to be under-inclusive, but basically one could say our charism is the pursuit of Christian perfection. Remember Christ said he wanted us to be perfect as our Father in heaven is perfect. He wouldn't have called us to perfection if He didn't not leave us the means to make it possible. We have those means in the Catholic Faith, John.

172

I finally get my hands on a copy of *Three Ages of the Interior Life,* written in 1938 and 1939. It's a summary of a course in ascetical and mystical theology that had at that time been given for over twenty years at the Angelicum in Rome.

Just as *The Imitation of Christ* shook me and the first chapter of the Gospel according to Saint John captivated me, the first few pages of *Three Ages* nearly knocks me out. It's like this: these major texts of the Catholic Faith are describing phenomena that I've actually experienced here in Southern California in the twenty-first century. It's like they were written just for me.

Perhaps it's a strange blessing that I didn't have any real formation or much Catholic theology when I went through my conversion.

I lived it all experientially.

Now, in reading these basic texts, this one written not even seventy years ago, I'm seeing in high contrast everything I suffered along with the reasons why, and everything I yearn for, along with a sharp description of how to get there. I don't know that I'll ever get over the shock and comfort of reading the following introductory words from Father Garrigou-Lagrange on the interior life:

By way of introduction, he wrote, *we shall briefly recall what constitutes the one thing necessary for every Christian, and we shall also recall how urgently this question is being raised at the present time.*

I. THE ONE THING NECESSARY

As everyone can easily understand, **the interior life is an elevated form of intimate conversation which everyone has with himself as soon as he is alone, even in the tumult of a great city. From the moment he ceases to converse with his fellow men, man converses interiorly with himself about what preoccupies him most.** *This conversation varies greatly according to the different ages of life; that of an old man is not that of a youth. It also varies greatly according as a man is good or bad.*

As soon as a man seriously seeks truth and goodness, this intimate conversation with himself tends to become conversation with God. *Little by little, instead of seeking himself in everything, instead of tending more or less consciously to make himself a center,* **man tends to seek God in everything, and to substitute for egoism love of God and of souls in**

Him. This constitutes the interior life. No sincere man will have any difficulty in recognizing it. The one thing necessary which Jesus spoke of to Martha and Mary consists in hearing the word of God and living by it.

The interior life thus conceived is something far more profound and more necessary in us than intellectual life or the cultivation of the sciences, than artistic or literary life, than social or political life. Unfortunately, some great scholars, mathematicians, physicists, and astronomers have no interior life, so to speak, but devote themselves to the study of their science as if God did not exist. In their moments of solitude they have no intimate conversation with Him. Their life appears to be in certain respects the search for the true and the good in a more or less definite and restricted domain, but it is so tainted with self-love and intellectual pride that we may legitimately question whether it will bear fruit for eternity. Many artists, literary men, and statesmen never rise above this level of purely human activity which is, in short, quite exterior. Do the depths of their souls live by God? It would seem not.

This shows that the interior life, or the life of the soul with God, well deserves to be called the one thing necessary, since by it we tend to our last end and assure our salvation. This last must not be too widely separated from progressive sanctification, for it is the very way of salvation.

There are those who seem to think that it is sufficient to be saved and that it is not necessary to be a saint. It is clearly not necessary to be a saint who performs miracles and whose sanctity is officially recognized by the Church. To be saved, we must take the way of salvation, which is identical with that of sanctity. *There will be only saints in heaven, whether they enter there immediately after death or after purification in purgatory. No one enters heaven unless he has that sanctity which consists in perfect purity of soul. Every sin though it should be venial, must be effaced, and the punishment due to sin must be borne or remitted, in order that a soul may enjoy forever the vision of God, see Him as He sees Himself, and love Him as He loves Himself. Should a soul enter heaven before the total remission of its sins, it could not remain there and it would cast itself into purgatory to be purified.*

The interior life of a just man who tends toward God and who already lives by Him is indeed the one thing necessary. **To be a saint, neither intellectual culture nor great exterior activity is a requisite; it suffices that we live profoundly by God.** *This truth is evident in the saints of the early Church; several of those saints were poor people, even slaves. It is evident also in St. Francis, St. Benedict Joseph Labre, in the Cure of Ars, and many others. They all had a deep understanding of these words of our Savior:* For what doth it profit a man, if he gain the whole world, and suffer the loss of his own soul? *If people sacrifice so many things to save the life of the body, which must ultimately die, what should we not sacrifice to save the life of our soul, which is to last forever? Ought not man to love his soul more than his body?* Or what exchange shall a man give for his soul? *our Lord adds.* One thing is necessary, *He tells us.* To save our soul, one thing alone is necessary: to hear the word of God and to live by it. *Therein lies the best part, which will not be taken away from a faithful soul even though it should lose everything else.*

173

I spend a little time at Dad's office in Gardena. He needs help in the business and I don't have much of a law practice anymore. We work on some projects together. Both of us having received the sacrament of confession, well, we can handle each other's company a little bit better.

We sit in his office one day and he pulls out a picture of himself, Mom and me on some vacation up in the mountains.

He asks, Do you remember this trip?

Yeah, I say. That was a good time.

Your mother really did a lot of things for me I didn't appreciate enough.

She admired you, I say. One day we were sitting outside the office before we went to the hospital and she said, It just amazes me that your Father's efforts have paid for every pencil, every scrap of notebook paper in that office. He created it all from nothing, she said.

Hm, he says. What seems commonplace to me seemed amazing to her.

She also said, I tell him, that in all the years she knew you she never heard you once utter anything unethical. That's high praise.

174

I start to split my time between Laguna Beach and Gardena, trying to come into the office a few days a week. It's hard to move the dogs around place to place, disrupting their routine. I like to get them settled when I can. They're happy so long as they're with me.

I get the urge to pray in a Catholic Church so I look some up and see that there's one around the corner from Dad's office. It's a poor parish, nothing of the grandeur and history of the Mission, but I like its simplicity, its humility. They never had the money to make many of the modernizing changes like taking the tabernacle from behind the center of the altar and putting it in a side room.

There it sits, gleaming right beneath the crucifix behind the altar.

Two African women, not African American, but African, pray very fervently in the front pew. A Vietnamese gentleman sits way in the back. I take my place among them in the afternoon sunlight and pray the Rosary. The universal Church, I think wistfully.

175

On Saturday I come to Dad's office to take care of a few things and decide to go to confession at the little parish church around the corner from the office. I enter the confessional and kneel down. At the abbey I tend to go face to face but here I am behind the screen.

I tell the priest that it's been a week since my last confession. I tell him of my sloth and my difficulty getting started. I tell him I'm not entirely sure what I'm supposed to do with myself after my conversion and feel that I'm sinfully slow to figure it out. I tell him there's a problem with my diligence and then I'm not snapping back from my seven year bout with drink—

He stops me and says in a beautiful dusky Irish brogue, *John, did it ever occur to you that you might not be ready to work at full tilt yet? I'm Irish and I have a lot of truck with alcoholics. That's quite a thing to recover from. You're lucky to be alive. Perhaps what's needed now is a little patience. And perhaps a little humility? You're confessing sloth, but I think I hear pride.*

Wow. What a confessor. Who is that man behind the screen?

I think about his counsel for days. It was so effortless, so concise, so gentle.

I knock on the rectory door and meet Monsignor Aburn. He's a true Irish gentleman, unassuming, semi-

398

retired, living in the rectory, still administering the sacraments, playing a round of golf on Tuesday. He's happy to meet with me. I tell him that I'm discerning a vocation to the priesthood in the Diocese of Los Angeles. He's delighted. I tell him that the vocation director said I need a spiritual director in the Diocese.

I say, I was very taken with the advice you gave me in the confessional. I was wondering if you'd be my spiritual director?

Of course, he says. I'd love to. It's a very personal thing, you know, choosing a spiritual director or a confessor. You should be advised I'm not very rigorous. I see human weakness as almost the constant state of things. I'm more into mercy than penance. But I would like you to make a general confession with me so I know what's gone on.

That would be my second one, I say.

That's okay, he says, you may have missed a few things and plus, you can consider it a devotional. The other thing I'd like to show you is my devotion to the stations of the cross. I do it year round, not just during Lent, and I do my own version of it, from Scripture. It's a very grounding devotion.

I'm honored you would spend some time with me, Monsignor. Thank you.

176

Confession with the Irish Monsignor is a gentle experience, not as fraught with the unknown as my first general confession with Father Polycarp. I'm a little better organized. This senior Irish priest has seen it all, heard it all, forgiven it all *in persona Christi*.

He says very little as I reach deeply as I can.

I tell him I didn't know to confess something in my first general confession. I didn't know how *angry* I was at Mom and Dad. I was angry with Mom for her insane drunkenness and everything that went with it. But I'm sober now, and I look back and I see that I went insane on brown liquor. It was horrible. I was horrible. I really didn't have compassion for Mom's affliction before. And it's true, Father, it's true, I *hated* her for it. I confess it to God now. It was a sin. And I denied God when I was so very young. I confess it now. I'm sorry for that. It was a mistake. I didn't understand my Dad's rage properly. I understand it now. I confess the sin of anger toward my father. I see now why anger is one of the seven deadly sins. It drove me to all sorts of strange behaviors, other sins. I didn't understand the wounded nature we all bear. I just didn't understand, or the offer of Christ to sanctify us and grant us peace.

Yes, well, John, that's a very deep and good confession, Monsignor says. But even with the peace Christ gives us here, you know that you'll always have a spiritual longing that cannot be entirely satisfied so long as we're in this skin. You will struggle with sin, with yourself, until your last breath, even if you advance in the spiritual life greatly.

He pinches a part of the skin around his wrist for emphasis.

I know, Monsignor, I know.

He asks, Have you ever read *The Hound of Heaven?*

I gasp a little. *The Hound of Heaven?* You know it?

Oh yes, he says. *I fled Him down the nights and down the days,* he intones. It's one of my favorites. Francis Thompson. I think it would be a good one for you. You pushed the Faith away so young, and for some understandable reasons, but that led to a lot of moral failings and eventually a need to kill the pain. But the Hound of Heaven ran you down, didn't He?

Yes.

You can you stop running now, he says.

177

I find myself in various Catholic churches alone late at night more often. Sometimes I lay prostrate in the center aisle if I'm sure nobody's looking.

These days, if I'm among others, I'm usually with drunks or monks.

The sober drunks recover lost pieces of themselves through service to others and attempt to practice at least natural virtue through their understanding of God.

The monks discover reaches unknown to those of us so helplessly tethered to ourselves. They wage an all-out war against the world, the flesh and the devil by submission to God's grace as transmitted by Christ in the constitution of His Church and institution of the sacraments, as well as strict obedience to His commandments.

I find I need both the former drunks and present monks, while I make this fearful and final exchange of *Stella Artois* for Stella Maris.

178

While I bitterly regret hurting other people, I can't entirely regret my painful bout with drink. In my case, the whisky did its job.

The whisky burned.

It burned down everything I thought I owned.

It burned up my obsession with created things so that I was left with nothing but spirit and ash.

Were it not for the purifying fire fed by the brown liquor, I doubt I would've ever knelt at the foot of the cross with all the others astride time and space. I realize now that the Catholic Faith is not merely a theory or a good idea. It's either a theological reality or it's a tissue of lies. I contemplate the mysteries of the Church, the miracles of the Church, and the diversity of Her saints—young, old, men, women, European, African, Asian, American, across centuries and cultures, in wartime and peacetime. The spiritual world opens now like a secret vista.

Perhaps only as a consequence of having been infantilized and humiliated by drink would I have cried out of the depths to God.

With warm pleasure do I now consider the confounding artifacts of Christian history—like the Shroud of Turin, the image of Our Lady of Guadalupe on Juan Diego's tilma in Mexico City, the Eucharistic Miracle at Lanciano, and all the extraordinary Eucharistic miracles.

Apart from the actual grace of God it is only the coherent witness and stewardship of the Catholic Church breathing through the centuries that makes it possible for me to entertain the truth of the Incarnation of Christ. There seems to be so much in the world that wants to tear that witness to rags from day to day.

I wonder why the extraordinary evidence for the truth of the Catholic Faith is not more widely proclaimed by the prelates and priests of my time.

I think sadly of my peers; not one in fifty emerged from the seventies and eighties with the Catholic Faith. Not one in a hundred could defend the luminous dogmas and doctrines proclaimed by Holy Mother Church. Yet I've found those dogmas and doctrines not the stultifying millstones they were made out to be, but white hot phantasms of truth and freedom.

My generation didn't lose the Faith.

They never had it to begin with.

The reasons for this are various and becoming more apparent.

I feel especially isolated from my peers.

It seems those Catholic school graduates from my era would be the very last to understand my conversion, and perhaps the first to ridicule it. However, I have them in mind most days. If I could give them a sliver of what I found in the garden that was (or should have been) entrusted to us, if they knew what was buried beneath the surface, if I could only share with them the fullness of the truth in all its glorious dimension, I would.

For now, and, as I'm told by people like Thomas a Kempis, so long as I breathe earthly air, I'm going to labor under the burden of my own rebellion. I've got a long way to go. I've made a strong start by grace, and by grace I hope to continue. The graces I received should be more than sufficient for my salvation, provided I persevere until the end and continue to work out my salvation in fear and trembling.

179

I used to express bewilderment as to why they named a grade school after a saint who met such a grisly end. But after all is said and done, I think old Saint Lawrence the Martyr had it just right when they ordered him to bring the treasures of the Church around and he presented his persecutors with a bunch of poor, holy souls. Saint Lawrence had a mouth on him. I respect that. And he knew they were going to kill him for it. It's funny how one can look upon such a fate with a kind of sweetness.

The *halo of hatred* that surrounds Christ and His one, holy, catholic and apostolic Church is a constant, a fixed reality. It takes various forms and slithers in even to the inner life of the Church from time to time. There's always a Judas, aided and abetted by the mystery of iniquity. I've seen that up close and personal. I've seen real supernatural evil in the world and I've seen it in me.

If I have anything to say in summary let me say it in the spirit of the good thief crucified next to Jesus, who was not the greatest theologian, but who knew what he saw and knew it couldn't be of this world.

Oh there are balms for what ails us, indeed there are, physical and psychological remedies. But as Saint Augustine learned so well, the spirit longs to rest in God and will find no true and lasting peace without.

I can't tie this up with a pretty ribbon. Mine is not that kind of story. Perhaps it's best for me to close now with the words Saint Lawrence the Martyr spoke while they burned him alive, words I understand a little better now:

Turn me over, I'm done on this side.

AFTERWORD

A scholar may study Catholic doctrine, not reject it bitterly, and may even say repeatedly: *You are blessed to have faith; I should like to have it, but I cannot believe.* And he tells the truth: he wishes and he cannot (as yet), for study and good faith do not always conquer the truth, so that it may be clear that rational certitude is not the *first* certitude on which Catholic doctrine rests. This scholar therefore *knows* Catholic doctrine; he *admits* its facts; he *feels* its power; he agrees that there existed a man named Jesus Christ, who lived and died in a prodigious manner. He is touched by the blood of the martyrs, by the constitution of the Church; *he will willingly say that it is the greatest phenomenon that has passed over the world.* He will *almost* say that it is true. And yet he does not conclude; he feels himself oppressed by truth, as one is in a dream where one sees without seeing. The day comes, however, when this scholar drops on his knees; feeling the wretchedness of man, he lifts his hands to heaven and exclaims: *Out of the depths I have cried to Thee, o Lord!* At this moment something takes place in him, scales drop from his eyes, a mystery is accomplished, and he is changed. He is a man, meek and humble of heart; he can die, he has conquered the truth.

—Father Henri-Dominique Lacordaire, O.P. (1850)

Endnotes and Attributions

Page 1: *The Law, my boy, puts us into everything. It's the ultimate backstage pass! It's the new priesthood, baby!*

Dialogue from Devil's Advocate, a motion picture produced by Warner Bros. Pictures (© 1997), based on the novel by Andrew Neiderman.

Page 5: [Did I really just see] *that-shrink-from-Beverly-Hills-you-know-the-one-Dr.-Everything's-Gonna-Be-Alright?*

A song lyric from Let's Go Crazy!, a single recording by *Prince and the Revolution*, from the album Purple Rain (© 1984).

Page 7: *Traumnovelle*, a reference to *Rhapsody: A Dream Novel,* also known as *Dream Story* (German: *Traumnovelle*), a 1926 novella by the Austrian writer Arthur Schnitzler. *Traumnovelle* formed the basis for the feature film *Eyes Wide Shut*, directed by Stanley Kubrick.

Page 7: *[T]here's a dark alley for every perversion in your sickening city.*

A line from Night and Fog (San Francisco), a poem by David Trinidad, contained in The Outlaw Bible of American Poetry (© 1999), collection compiled by Alan Kaufman, published by Thunder's Mouth Press, an Imprint of Avalon Publishing Group, Inc.

Page 9:
I want to hold you close like a lute and cry out with our loving.
You would rather throw stones at a mirror?
I am your mirror, here are the stones.

I believe this is a Coleman Barks translation of a Rumi verse. I no longer have the original source in my possession, but highly recommend all of Coleman Barks' translations of Rumi.

Page 16: *Of all the many ways a man will lose his home*
there ain't none better than the girl who's moving on.

A song lyric from Valentine, a single recording from the *Old 97's* album, Fight Songs (© 1997).

Page 16: *I find myself regarding existence as though from beyond the tomb, from another world; all is strange to me; I am, as it were, outside my own body...I am depersonalized, detached, cut adrift. Is this madness?*

A passage from <u>The Journal Intime</u> by Henri Frederic Amiel, a Swiss poet and philosopher, Professor of Aesthetics and French Literature and then Professor of Moral Philosophy at the Academy of Geneva, describing what would come to be known as the phenomenon of depersonalization. (© 1880, approx.)

Page 18: *pink rising off the Pacific.*

A song lyric from <u>Standing Still</u>, a single recording by recording artist Jill Cohn, from her album, <u>Window to the Wise</u> (© 2002).

Page 26: *I wake to black flack and the nightmare of fighters.*

A line from <u>The Death of the Ball Turret Gunner</u>, a poem by Randall Jarrell (© 1945).

Page 37: *In this life, you're on your own.*

A song lyric from <u>Let's Go Crazy!</u>, a single recording by *Prince and the Revolution*, from the album <u>Purple Rain</u> (© 1984).

Page 53: *She don't remember 'Retha Franklin, Queen of Soul—*

A song lyric from <u>Hey Nineteen</u>, a single recording by *Steely Dan* from the album <u>Gaucho</u> (© 1980).

Page 56: *I am a very simple man, Sayuri. I do not like things put before me that I cannot have.*

A line from <u>Memoirs of a Geisha</u>, a novel by Arthur Goldan, published by Alfred A. Knopf (© 1997).

Page 57: *How strange to think of giving up all ambition!*
Suddenly I see with such clear eyes
The white flake of snow
That has just fallen in the horse's mane!

A poem called <u>Watering the Horse</u>, from <u>Silence in the Snowy Fields</u>, a collection of poems by Robert Bly, published by Wesleyan University Press (© 1962).

Page 59: *For the first time, in that night alive with signs and stars, I opened myself to the gentle indifference of the world. Finding it so much like myself—so like a brother, really—I felt that I had been happy and that I was happy again. For everything to be consummated, for me to feel less alone, I had only to wish that there be a large crowd of spectators the day of my execution.*

A passage from <u>The Stranger</u>, a novel by Albert Camus, initially published in France in 1942 by Editions Gallimard, first United States publication by Alfred A. Knopf, (© 1946).

Page 74: *Confessing all the secret things in a warm velvet box; he's the priest, he's the doctor, he can handle those shocks—*

A song lyric from <u>Mercy Street</u>, a single recording by Peter Gabriel, from his album <u>So</u> (© 1986).

Page 92: *[G]irls come and kiss me, say that you'll miss me, get me to the church on time.*

A song lyric from the musical <u>My Fair Lady</u>, composed by Frederick Loewe, with lyrics written by Alan Jay Lerner (© 1956).

Page 95: *Traveling with me, you find what never tires,*
The earth never tires;
The earth is rude, silent, incomprehensible at first—Nature is rude and incomprehensible at first;
Be not discouraged—keep on—there are divine things, well envelop'd;
I swear to you there are divine things more beautiful than words can tell.

A passage from *Song of the Open Road*, a poem by Walt Whitman from his poetry collection *Leaves of Grass*. (© 1855 to 1891).

Page 99: *Lit-tle Bun-ny Foo Foo*
    Hoppin' through the forest
    Scoopin' up the field mice

And boppin 'em on the head!
...

Little Bunny Foo Foo is a children's poem by an unknown author, involving a rabbit harassing a population of field mice. The rabbit is scolded and eventually punished by a fairy. Like many traditional folk songs, there are multiple versions with differing variations. The poem is sung to the tune of Down by the Station (1948), and melodically similar to the popular French Canadian children's song Alouette (1879). The rhyme is usually sung by an older person to a younger child, using a repetitive tune that reinforces the meter, accompanied by hand gestures. In this mode of transmission, it is a form of tickle play that teaches and reinforces motor skills, often passed as childlore.

Page 101: [It's as though something sinister is following me, formidable and billowing,] *wearing the Linconish coats of night—*
...wearing the Linconish coats of night is a line I heard Robert Bly perform from a then in-progress collection of poems he was working on. It was around the time he published The Night Abraham Called to the Stars. It may have found its way into Eating the Honey of Words. In any event, I don't know of a written source for it.

Page 130, *passim*: *The Hound of Heaven*
All references herein to the poem The Hound of Heaven by Francis Thompson, as well as the commentary thereon by G.K. Chesterton, are from The Hound of Heaven and Other Poems, published by Brandon Books (© 2000).

Page 134: *So drink up all you people*
Order anything you see
Have fun you happy people
The laughs and the joke's on me
Pardon me but I got to run
The fact's uncommonly clear
Got to find who's now her number one
And why my angel eyes ain't here
Excuse me while I disappear

Song lyrics from <u>Angel Eyes</u>, music composed by Matt Dennis, with lyrics by Earl Brent (© 1946). Memorably performed by Frank Sinatra on his classic record <u>Only the Lonely</u>, as referred to herein.

Page 141: *The Sign of the Twisted Candles*
I quoted some passages from <u>The Sign of the Twisted Candles</u>, the ninth volume in the <u>Nancy Drew Mystery Stories</u> series. It was published by Grosset & Dunlap, under the pseudonym Carolyn Keene. Walter Karig later claimed authorship. (© 1933.)

Page 167: *the temple bell stops*
but the sound keeps coming
out of the flowers
A poem by Matsuo Basho, Japanese poet, 1644-1694, source of this translation unknown (at least to me). It's just one I remember.

Page 168: *I was at this time of living, like so many Atheists or Anti-theists, in a whirl of contradictions. I maintained that God did not exist. I was also very angry with God for not existing. I was equally angry with God for creating a world.*
A passage from <u>Surprised by Joy, The Shape of My Early Life</u>, a work of non-fiction by C.S. Lewis, published by Harcourt Brace (in the United States) (© 1955).

Page 174: *He sees angels in the architecture,*
spinning in infinity.
He says, Hey! Hallelujah!
A song lyric from <u>You Can Call Me Al</u>, a single recording by Paul Simon, from his album <u>Graceland</u> (© 1986).

Page 183: I find an essay by Dale Ahlquist, President of the American Chesteron Society on the subject of Chesterton's analysis of conversion to the Catholic Faith, wherein he describes three stages.
The piece by Dale Ahlquist to which I refer is one I found online at <u>http://www.chesterton.org/lecture-49/</u>. It appears to

be entitled "Lecture 49: The Catholic Church and Conversion" by Dale Ahlquist. He is referring in his lecture or essay to a book by G.K. Chesterton entitled The Catholic Church and Conversion.

Page 188: *These spiritual window-shoppers*
who idly ask:
'How much is that?'
'Oh, I'm just looking.'
They handle a hundred items and put them down,
shadows with no capital.
Even if you don't know what you want,
buy something!
Be part of the exchanging flow.

Passage from a Coleman Barks translation of Rumi, version perhaps from Poems of Rumi, wherein Barks and Robert Bly read/perform poems of Jalāl ad-Dīn Muhammad Rūmī, a 13th Century Sufi poet, in an audiobook published by Audio Literature (© 1989).

Page 193: Thank you for this, Basho:
Inside this pitiful body which has one hundred bones and nine holes, there is something called Spirit, which is like a flowing curtain easily blown around by wind. It was Spirit that got me to writing poetry, at first for amusement, later as a way of life. At times, my Spirit has been brought down so low that I almost quit writing, and at other times the Spirit became proud and powerful.

From the journals of Matsuo Basho, Japanese poet, 1644-1694, source of this translation unknown (at least to me).

Thank you for this, Mirabai:
The colors of the Dark One have penetrated Mira's body; all the other colors washed out.

Making love with the Dark One and eating little, those are my pearls and my carnelians.

Meditation beads and the forehead streak, those are my scarves and my rings.

That's enough feminine wiles for me. My teacher taught me this.

Approve me or disapprove me: I praise the Mountain Energy night and day.

I take the path that ecstatic human beings have taken for centuries.

I don't steal money, I don't hit anyone. What will you charge me with?

I have felt the swaying of the elephant's shoulders;

And now you want me to climb on a jackass? Try to be serious.

The Energy that holds up mountains is the Energy Mirabai bows down to.

He lives century after century, and the test I set for him he has passed.

A passage from <u>Mirabai: Ecstatic Poems</u> by Mirabai, or Meera or Mira Bai, 16th Century Hindu poet, as translated by Robert Bly and Jane Hirshfield, published by Beacon Press (© 2004).

Thank you for this, Kabir:

We sense that there is some sort of Spirit that loves birds and animals

and the ants—

perhaps the same one who gave a radiance to you in your mother's womb.

Is it logical you would be walking around entirely orphaned now?

The truth is you turned away yourself,

and decided to go into the darkness alone.

Now you are tangled up in others, and have forgotten what you once knew, and that's why everything you do has some weird failure in it.

Friend, hope for the Guest while you are alive.

Jump into experience while you are alive!

Think...and think...while you are alive.

What you call salvation belongs to the time before death.

If you don't break your ropes while you're alive,

do you think

ghosts will do it after?

The idea that the soul will join with the ecstatic

just because the body's rotten—
that is all fantasy.
What is found now is found then.
If you find nothing now,
you will simply end up with an apartment
in the City of Death.
If you make love with the Divine now, in the next life you will
have the face of satisfied desire.
So plunge into the truth, find out who the Teacher is, believe in
the Great Sound!
Kabir says this: When the Guest is being searched for, it is the
intensity of the longing for the Guest that does all the work.
Look at me, and you will see a slave of that intensity.
Who is it we spend our entire life loving?
A passage from The Kabir Book. Forty-four of the Ecstatic Poems of Kabir, Versions and/or Translations of Kabir, a 15th Century Indian poet, by Robert Bly. Published by Beacon Press (© 1977).

Thank you for this, Rumi:
Ecstatic love is an ocean, and the Milky Way is a flake of foam
floating on that ocean.
The stars wheel around the North Pole, and ecstatic love,
turning in a wheel, turns the stars.
If there were no ecstatic love, the whole world would stop.
Do you think that a piece of flint would change into a plant
otherwise?
Grass agrees to die so that it can rise up and receive a little of
the animal's enthusiasm.
And the animal soul, in turn, sacrifices itself. For what?
To help that wind, through one light waft of which Mary
became with child. Without that wind, all creatures on Earth would
be stiff as a glacier, instead of being as they are, locustlike,
searching night and day for green things, flying.
Every bit of dust climbs toward the Secret One like a sapling.
It climbs and says nothing; and that silence is a wild praise of
the Secret One.

For the life of me, I can't find the precise source for this particular translation of a famous passage by Rumi, but I am quite certain it is from a Coleman Barks and/or Robert Bly translation.

Page 197: [Dwarfed, doling out their little apothecary-ground] *pills and powders to get us through this passion play.*

A song lyric from <u>Coyote</u>, a single recording by Joni Mitchell, from her album <u>Hejira</u> (© 1976).

Page 201: *Warning to the Reader*

Sometimes farm granaries become especially beautiful when all the oats or wheat are gone, and wind has swept the rough floor clean. ...

The poem <u>Warning to the Reader</u>, from <u>Selected Poems</u> by Robert Bly, published by Harper Collins (© 1991). Also to be found in other, earlier poetry collections by Robert Bly.

Page 206: *The mark of Descent, whether undertaken consciously or unconsciously, is a newly arrived-at lowliness, associated with water and soul. The lowliness happens particularly to men who are initially high, lucky, elevated. When a man enters this stage he regards Descent as a holy thing, he increases his tolerance for ashes, eats dust as snakes do, increases his stomach for terrifying insights, deepens his ability to accept the evil facts of history, accepts the job of working seven years under the ground, leaves the granary at will through the rat's hole, bites on cinders, learns to shudder, and follows the voice of the old mole below the ground.*

A passage from the book **Iron John: A Book About Men** by Robert Bly, published by Addison-Wesley (© 1990).

Page 215: References herein to *The 54 Day Novena* are to a publication called <u>Rosary Novenas to Our Lady</u>, by Charles Lacy and John Brokhoff, published by ACTA Publications, Booklet edition (© 1995), containing a setting of the historic "The 54 Day Novena" as described therein.

Page 218: I pack up my stuff and leave.

    Don't look back you can never look back
    I blow a tire on the way to my parents' house.
    Thought I knew what love was

I unpack the trunk to reach the spare.
What did I know?
I kneel in the dark on the shoulder of the Seal Beach offramp.
Those days are gone forever; I should just let 'em go but—

Italicized quotes from <u>The Boys of Summer</u>, a single recording by Don Henley from his album, <u>Building the Perfect Beast</u> (© 1984).

Page 269: *All good dreamers pass this way some day.*
Hiding behind bottles in dark cafés.
Dark cafés.
Only a dark cocoon before I get my gorgeous wings and fly away.
Only a phase, these dark café days—

A song lyric from <u>The Last Time I Saw Richard</u>, a single recording by Joni Mitchell, from her album <u>Blue</u> (© 1971).

Page 307: Saint Alphonsus Liguori, in his famously stark exhortation, *Preparation for Death,* put it like this:

Imagine that you behold a person who has just expired. Look at that body still laid on the bed, the head fallen on the chest, the hair in disorder and still bathed in the sweat of death, the eyes sunk, the cheeks hollow, the face the color of ashes, the lips and tongue like iron, the body cold and heavy. The beholders grow pale and tremble. How many, at the sight of a deceased relative of friend, have changed their life and retired from the world?

There are many translations of <u>Preparation for Death</u> by Saint Alphonsus de Liguori. I am not sure from which one this quote is drawn. I highly recommend this work and all the works by this great Saint.

Page 342, passim: References to <u>The Imitation of Christ</u> by Thomas a Kempis, of the 15th Century, are to a translation no longer in my possession. There are many translations of this important work, thought to be the best selling devotional work of the Christian Faith.

Page 344: References to <u>True Devotion to Mary</u> by Saint Louis de Montfort, of the 17th and 18th Century, are to a translation no longer in my possession. There are many translations of this important work.

Page 352: Reference to <u>Theology and Sanity</u> by F.J. Sheed is to the 1953 Sheed & Ward edition. There have been many editions since by other publishers.

Page 392: References to <u>Three Ages of the Interior Life</u> by Father Réginald Marie Garrigou-Lagrange, O.P. (1877–1964) are to a 1947 edition published by B. Herder Book Company. There are many more recent editions by various publishers.

Page 403: The *halo of hatred* that surrounds Christ and His one, holy, catholic and apostolic Church is a constant, a fixed reality.

The reference to the "halo of hatred" is from the G.K. Chesterton work, <u>The Everlasting Man</u>, published in 1925 by Hodder & Stoughton. In context, Chesterton wrote the following of the early Christians: "And there shone on them in that dark hour a light that has never been darkened; a white fire clinging to that group like an unearthly phosphorescence, blazing its track through the twilights of history and confounding every effort to confound it with the mists of mythology and theory; that shaft of light or lightning by which the world itself has struck and isolated and crowned it; by which its own enemies have made it more illustrious and its own critics have made it more inexplicable; the *halo of hatred* around the Church of God."

Page 405: The "Afterword" herein is a quote by Father Henri-Dominique Lacordaire, O.P. (1850) which can be found, among other places, in the first chapter of <u>Three Ages of the Interior Life</u> by Father Réginald Marie Garrigou-Lagrange, O.P., cited above.

Made in the USA
Monee, IL
01 December 2022

18958613R00246